DISNEYLAND ON THE MOUNTAIN

DISNEYLAND ON THE MOUNTAIN

Walt, the Environmentalists, and the Ski Resort That Never Was

Greg Glasgow
Kathryn Mayer

ROWMAN & LITTLEFIELD
Lanham • Boulder • New York • London

Published by Rowman & Littlefield
An imprint of The Rowman & Littlefield Publishing Group, Inc.
4501 Forbes Boulevard, Suite 200, Lanham, Maryland 20706
www.rowman.com

86-90 Paul Street, London EC2A 4NE, United Kingdom

British Library Cataloguing in Publication Information Available

Library of Congress Cataloging-in-Publication Data

Names: Glasgow, Greg, 1971– author. | Mayer, Kathryn, 1984– author.
Title: Disneyland on the mountain : Walt, the environmentalists, and the
  ski resort that never was / Greg Glasgow, Kathryn Mayer.
Description: Lanham : Rowman & Littlefield, [2023] | Includes
  bibliographical references and index. | Summary: "An in-depth look at
  Walt Disney's last, unfinished project-Mineral King, a Disneyland-like
  resort at the top of a mountain-and the controversy that surrounded it,
  including the budding environmental movement that made sure the resort
  never saw the light of day"—Provided by publisher.
Identifiers: LCCN 2022057021 (print) | LCCN 2022057022 (ebook) | ISBN
  9781538173671 (cloth) | ISBN 9781538173688 (epub)
Subjects: LCSH: Mineral King Valley (Calif.)—History. | Environmental
  Protection—California--Mineral King Valley—History. | Nature
  Conservation—California—Mineral King Valley—History. | Disney, Walt,
  1901–1966. | Resort development—California—Mineral King
  Valley—History.
Classification: LCC F868.T8 G53 2023 (print) | LCC F868.T8 (ebook) | DDC
  979.4/86—dc23/eng/20230329
LC record available at https://lccn.loc.gov/2022057021
LC ebook record available at https://lccn.loc.gov/2022057022

To our parents—
Charlie and Leora; Jack and Jody—
with love and gratitude

CONTENTS

AUTHORS' NOTE

This is a work of nonfiction, as sourced through books, press clippings, archival documents, archival footage, archival interviews, meeting notes, and numerous author interviews with people who were there at the time, as well as interviews with the descendants of people involved in the Mineral King story. In some instances, we have re-created narrative scenes using all of these sources, which are as accurate as possible. Direct dialogue is used only when backed up by sources and accounts of those who were there. Full notes on sources are available at the end of the book.

1

A MAGIC KINGDOM

September 19, 1966

Walt Disney's heart began to beat heavier as he started up the hill. The slope wasn't steep, but even the slightest incline seemed to be a challenge for him these days. Surrounded by towering trees and accompanied by the sounds of birdsong, Walt took slow steps as he made his way to the top of the rise. It was September 19, 1966, and Walt had gathered members of the press in California's Mineral King valley to tell them about his latest venture—the passion project he had been quietly working on for the past six years. Convinced the Disney company should add a ski resort to its growing experiential entertainment empire, Walt had chosen Mineral King as the perfect spot for a year-round outdoor tourism mecca that would capture the magic of the mountains in true Disney fashion.

Clad in a sweater vest, heavy camping jacket, and woolen trousers, Walt—now sixty-four—was prepared for the cold September day. A fedora cap shielded his eyes from the heavy rain droplets that were falling intermittently, but the warm outfit appeared to be doing little to make him feel better as he walked toward the clearing.

Finally taking a seat at a white folding table placed between two large trees in a flat part of the valley, Walt looked around to see the reporters eagerly waiting to hear about his vision for the natural wonderland that surrounded them. He was never more in his element than when he was in front of a crowd, sharing his latest dream. And this dream was one he was determined to turn into a reality, despite his failing health and despite the

Walt Disney, left, with California governor Pat Brown, center, and Willy Schaeffler, right, at their September 19, 1966, media briefing in Mineral King, talking about their plans for the resort. Herald Examiner Collection/Los Angeles Public Library.

fact that the project was attracting the ire of a growing environmentalist movement that was hell-bent on ensuring his vision would be as unlikely to happen as a real-life flying elephant or magical fairy godmother.

Seated between his friend Willy Schaeffler, a German ski champion who was Walt's collaborator on the project, and California governor Edmund "Pat" Brown, Walt explained his vision for a bustling vacation destination where, after a long day of skiing, guests could go ice skating, dogsledding, or tobogganing, watch the latest Disney film, or unwind in one of several restaurants. In the summer, visitors could fish, camp, hike, study wildlife, go on a picnic, or take a sightseeing tour on a ski lift.

When Walt had started planning Disneyland some fifteen years earlier, he was excited to create entertainment that wasn't bound by a movie screen. To build three-dimensional, real-world attractions that would transport kids and adults alike into an all-encompassing realm of fun and magic. Mineral King would do the same thing, but with the natural world as its backdrop.

"We hope that we can develop it in such a way that the families can come up here and have access to this great, wonderful wilderness area,"[1] Walt told the reporters. The snow conditions in the area were so promising, he said, that he envisioned Olympic skiers training at Mineral King even before the resort was fully open to the public.[2]

Skiing was one of Walt's favorite pastimes, though he was the first to admit, with a laugh, that he wasn't that good at it. Goofy didn't fare much better in Disney's 1941 animated short *The Art of Skiing*—Walt's famous accident-prone, floppy-eared canine character skied backward, tumbled down mountains, lost his skis on the slopes, and went headfirst into the snow in the eight-minute film—even if the cartoon did demonstrate Walt's affection for the sport. A skier since the 1930s, when he had turned to more family-friendly recreation after suffering a neck injury playing polo, Walt had been one of the first stockholders in the Sugar Bowl ski area near Lake Tahoe. While taking ski lessons with his wife, Lillian, Walt met Austrian skiing champion Hannes Schroll at the Badger Pass Ski Area in Yosemite National Park, where Schroll was head of the ski school. The two men became friends, and in 1938, when Schroll and his business partners wanted to build a new resort in the eastern part of the Sierra Nevada, he asked Walt for assistance. Walt was so strapped for cash at the time that he had to make his $2,500 investment in four installments,[3] but in honor of his contribution, Schroll—an avid yodeler who supplied the first instance of Goofy's trademark yell in *The Art of Skiing*—changed the name of one of the Sugar Bowl peaks from Hemlock Peak to Mount Disney.[4]

Walt's interest in the ski business had grown even more in 1960, when he had served as chairman of pageantry at the Winter Olympics in nearby Squaw Valley, overseeing everything from the opening and closing ceremonies to ticketing and parking. It was important to him to build a resort that serious skiers would appreciate, and he knew they would love Mineral King's huge natural bowls, five-mile runs, and five-thousand-foot drop.

Those runs would start high above the valley floor, near the tops of Lookout Point, Sawtooth Peak, and Miners Ridge, skiers gliding through fresh powder as they took in some of the most scenic vistas in the Sierra Nevada.

"When I first saw Mineral King five years ago, I thought it was one of the most beautiful spots I had ever seen, and we want to keep it that way,"[5] Walt said when announcing the project back in December 1965. That's why his plan called for as little human footprint as possible. No cars would be allowed. Ski lifts would be camouflaged, the village would be situated so it would not be seen from the valley entrance, and service areas would be hidden underground.

Just as he had completely transformed the amusement park experience from seedy, dirty tourist trap to family-friendly oasis with Disneyland, Walt also knew ski resorts were ripe for change. Skiing was fun, sure, but the experience left a lot to be desired. The ski resorts of the day offered an athletic challenge, but they were mostly rudimentary, with minimal parking, dining, or lodging. They were tailored to adults, not families. Besides skiing, followed by a drink or two at the resort bar, there was nothing else to do. It was a day's activity, at best.

Walt would change that.

✿ ✿ ✿

Walt seemed invigorated as he spoke that September afternoon, as he usually was when he shared his plans or talked about the dreams he was trying to get others to buy into. When he had pitched the idea of *Snow White and the Seven Dwarfs* to a soundstage full of studio employees back in 1934, Walt didn't just describe the Evil Queen—he *became* the Evil Queen, transformed into an old woman with a crackly voice, hunched over with arthritic hands offering a poison apple to the docile, pale, and childlike Snow White. Now, years later, his enthusiasm was palpable as he talked about the recreation wonderland he was to build. Walt didn't have to act out the scene; Mineral King *was* the scene, with its dramatic sky, low-hanging clouds, sharp cliffs, and stands of trees so green they looked like they had been painted. It was both the hero and the villain. And just like the studio employees who had been enthralled watching Walt act out the plot of *Snow White*, the press members could not take their eyes off Walt as he described what would be once his development was underway in one of California's great unspoiled wildernesses.

✿ ✿ ✿

Mineral King—nestled in the Sierra Nevada mountains, equidistant from Los Angeles and San Francisco—was the perfect spot for the ski resort Walt had in mind, but all was not perfect in the valley. Like any beautiful mountain area, it had dangers lurking behind its scenic peaks and fields of colorful wildflowers. Avalanche danger was high. Rusty old equipment, left over from the valley's brief moment as a gold- and silver-mining mecca in the late 1800s, littered the landscape. Worst of all was the road into the

The Mineral King area was seen by many as one of the great untapped winter sports destinations in the country. National Park Service.

place, which could be described as primitive at best. Walt had endured it several times now, and it seemed to get worse—and feel longer—with each journey. Twisting, winding, filled with ruts, only partially paved, and washed out in places, the road also was impassable for most of the winter due to snow. It was one of the biggest impediments to Walt's development, forcing visitors to drive more than two hours to go the fifty-eight miles from Visalia, site of the nearest airport, to Mineral King.

But Walt had always been stubborn, and nothing would stop him once he had his mind set on a goal. He had turned acres of orange and walnut trees in Anaheim into Disneyland, and his new Florida theme park—which Walt and the Disney company were in the beginning stages of building—was to be located on what was originally miles of swampland.

Walt had been leaning on the state government to do something about the road for a while now, and one big reason for today's press conference was so Governor Brown could deliver the news that the state was soon to receive a $3 million grant from the federal government to improve the road into Mineral King.[6] The plan was to replace the "goat path" with a sleek, modern, all-weather highway—at a total cost of $25 million—that would bring visitors to a parking structure at the edge of the valley. They would take a scenic cog railway ride the rest of the way into the resort, transitioning from the hectic modern world to the peaceful snow-covered village the same way walking through the front gate of Disneyland marked the transition from reality to a world filled with magic.

When Walt had finished speaking, Governor Brown took the microphone, sharing more information about the new highway and calling attention both to Walt's "staggering imagination" and the similarly staggering impact the Mineral King resort was to have on California's economy—$1 billion over the next fifteen years. Looking businesslike in his blue suit, red tie, and horn-rimmed glasses, Brown, sixty-one, told the onlookers that, "I hope that ten years from today, I can stand here with Walt Disney again and look around at the wonderland that will have been created. For what greater achievement can man attain, what greater legacy leave his children, than to treat the natural resources that God has given with respect, to use them with prudence, to give man a place to find pleasure after the day's work is done? Together we will have done that."[7]

❄ ❄ ❄

Walt couldn't have said it better himself. After decades of making movies, television shows, and more, Mineral King was another part of the legacy he wanted to leave, along with the California Institute of the Arts, a new Disney-funded art school that was still in the planning stages; the second theme park he was building in Florida; and, of course, Disneyland, which had opened just over a decade earlier, in 1955.

Walt's amusement mecca in Anaheim—some 250 miles south of Mineral King—was born from his idea that family members of all ages needed a place they could have fun together. Walt had borrowed against his life insurance to raise some of the money to build Disneyland,[8] and though some in the company had begged him not to waste his money on the grimy, flailing amusement park business—in the early 1950s, Walt had described New York's famous Coney Island as "so run-down and ugly" that it was "almost enough to destroy your faith in human nature"[9]—Walt's hunch was right. Disneyland had been thriving over the past decade.

It wasn't that long ago that Walt had sat on a green bench in L.A.'s Griffith Park, watching as his two daughters spent hours playing on a merry-go-round. It was an outing he hosted most Sunday afternoons, after he picked the girls up from Sunday school. He would look around and see bored parents watching their kids go up and down repeatedly on the colorful mounted horses. Walt would say, "There's nothing for the parents to do. You've got to have a place where the whole family can have fun."[10]

When Disneyland first opened, Walt often sat on a bench on Main Street, watching guests as they entered or left the park. He studied their faces, overheard their complaints or praise, and always took their comments to heart, making sure he had his ear to what the public wanted. Disneyland was a place for families to come together, but it was also Walt's answer to the nationwide feelings of restlessness and worries about the future that were beginning to define the post–World War II era. The war had left many young servicemen disillusioned with typical American life; women who had taken on new roles while their husbands were fighting overseas were now struggling with a return to normalcy; and the nuclear bombs that had exploded over Japan in August 1945 had instantly created a new global reality in which nations could be wiped out at a moment's notice. Disneyland was a safe haven, and with its old-fashioned town square, fire station, ice cream parlor, and steam-powered railroad, it was a place Walt hoped would remind people of the simpler times he remembered fondly from his childhood.[11]

Disneyland was Walt's darling, but with its man-made lakes, carefully manicured lawns, and paved roads, it lacked one of his great passions: wilderness and natural beauty. The Mineral King project was his way of sharing that passion with more people. Like at Disneyland, families could have fun and be entertained there, but their trip would have a backdrop of towering peaks, pastoral meadows, regal evergreens, and clear mountain streams. Instead of taking pictures with Disney cast members dressed up like giant ducks and mice, guests could observe the slew of animals that called the Mineral King area home, including black bears, mule deer, and yellow-bellied marmots. It would be a real-life Adventureland.

Walt had nearly lost his breath when he first saw Mineral King several years earlier—a pristine valley like something out of *Bambi*, with streams and little lakes and miles and miles of evergreen trees. With its endless vistas and snowy peaks, it was a world away from the crowded streets of Hollywood and the hectic, demanding pace of a movie studio. To Walt, doing all he could to preserve the wilderness there was about much more than good business, appealing to conservationists, or even creating a great visitor experience. A love and respect for nature and wildlife was a theme that ran not just through his movies, but through his life.

✿ ✿ ✿

Born in Chicago in 1901, Walter Elias Disney moved with his family to a farm in Marceline, Missouri, when he was four years old. He later described those years as among the happiest of his life, remembering helping his parents grow corn, wheat, and sorghum; raise chickens, pigs, and cows; and churn butter to sell at the local market.[12]

The farm experience made a big impression on Walt, so it's no wonder early Disney cartoons were filled with animals like cows, horses, goats, and chickens. In *Mickey's Follies* (1929), for instance, Mickey puts on a show in the barnyard with a cast featuring dancing ducks, dancing chickens, and a singing pig, while the 1931 Silly Symphonies title *Birds of a Feather* features everything from swans and peacocks to woodpeckers and owls.

"I think that everything you do has some effect on you, and that old farm certainly made an impression on me," Walt said. "I don't know a lot about farming, but when I see a drawing of a pig or a duck or a rooster I know immediately if it has the right feeling. And I know it because of what I learned during those days on the farm."[13]

Walt understood the power of animals to evoke emotion and provoke a response from audiences. That's why his early animated features—*Snow White and the Seven Dwarfs* and *Fantasia*—had included a wealth of animal characters, from the realistic forest creatures in *Snow White* to the anthropomorphized hippos and alligators in *Fantasia*. But in 1937, when he purchased the rights to Felix Salten's novel *Bambi: A Life in the Woods*, Walt demanded a whole new level of natural realism. Always looking to push the art of animation forward—and always looking to be taken more seriously as an artist—he insisted that the studio's first film with an animal protagonist (*Dumbo* would end up being released earlier, though its production would start later) would be based on the movements of real forest creatures.

Disney animators already knew how demanding Walt could be, and they became nervous when he told them that he wanted the deer, including Bambi and his love interest, Faline; the rabbit, Thumper; and the skunk, Flower, to practically leap off the screen in the story of how Bambi becomes the Great Prince of the Forest. Luckily for the animators, Walt began searching for an artist who knew how to draw animals to give them some fundamentals. He eventually found Italian painter and sculptor Rico Lebrun, who was then teaching animal art and anatomy at L.A.'s Chouinard Art Institute. In addition to coming to the studio to train the animators, Lebrun put together a forty-page book of sketches of deer skeletons in various poses, in order to "familiarize the men working on Bambi, Faline, and other deer characters with possibilities for unusual yet organically possible actions, stances, and expressive poses."[14]

In addition to receiving Lebrun's guidance, Disney animators made regular visits to the Griffith Park Zoo, just a short walk from the merry-go-round that later inspired Walt to build Disneyland, to study animals and their behavior. Walt even set up a small zoo at the studio where animators could study in detail the movement of rabbits, owls, skunks, and a pair of fawns named, of course, Bambi and Faline.

"We had an awe and respect for this project," Walt said upon the film's release in August 1942. "I respect nature very much, and by watching and observing the habits of creatures of nature, man can learn a lot."[15]

The film's realistic animal movement, paired with beautiful impressionistic backgrounds created by Chinese-born artist Tyrus Wong—who took inspiration from classical Chinese paintings of the Song dynasty—drew praise from movie critics. Bambi was "an appealing, wonderfully articulated little deer, whose progressive discoveries of rain, snow, ice, the seasons, man, love, death, etc. make a neatly antlered allegory," wrote the reviewer for *Time* magazine. "Bambi's rubber-jointed, slack-limbed, coltish first steps in the art of walking are, even for Disney, inspired animation."[16]

The critics liked it, but the film divided audiences. The shocking scene in which Bambi's mother is shot, off-screen, by hunters, terrified many children, as did the scene at the end of the film where hunters accidentally set the forest ablaze, orange and yellow flames flickering over dry trees and sparks showering down like fading fireworks as animals flee to safety. In a world being torn apart by World War II—the attack on Pearl Harbor happened eight months before the film's release—the image of a peaceful forest paradise destroyed by "Man" and his guns was a powerful one. The burgeoning environmental movement seized on *Bambi* as an educational tool, with the National Audubon Society comparing its consciousness-raising power for conservation issues to that of *Uncle Tom's Cabin* prior to the abolition of slavery.[17]

Bambi lost money at the box office, but Walt's experience making the movie and working with live animals moved him profoundly. It also inspired him to create a series of films that, by giving children a new appreciation for nature and wildlife, helped to create a generation of environmentalists.[18]

✳ ✳ ✳

Whether it was taking to the skies with flamingos and pelicans in 1952's *Water Birds* or stalking prey with alligators in 1953's *Prowlers of the Everglades*, Disney's True-Life Adventures series allowed movie-theater-bound audiences to travel the world to spend time with a huge variety of animal species. Produced between 1948 and 1960, the collection numbered six full-length features and seven shorts; together they earned eight Academy Awards.

Camera crews—a surprisingly large number of them married couples—often spent two or three years gathering footage for a single film. Most of the titles were shot in North America, though some ventured to more far-flung locales, including Africa (*The African Lion*), South America (*Jungle Cat*), and the Arctic (*White Wilderness*).

The series was born in the years just after World War II, when Walt began to consider adding educational films to the Disney roster as an additional source of profit. When he read about American servicemen who were returning to Alaska after having been stationed there during the war, he told Disney staffer Ben Sharpsteen, "That's our last frontier, the last undeveloped place in the United States. We should have some photographers up there."[19]

After seeing some of their work—he was particularly amused by footage they'd shot of bears scratching themselves[20]—Walt hired Alaskan husband-and-wife filmmaking team Alfred and Elma Milotte, who owned a photography studio in Ketchikan, to travel the state to document as much of daily life as they could. When they finished, the footage Walt found most intriguing was not of gold mining or native peoples, but that of seals in their natural habitat. He asked the couple to put together a short film with the mischievous animals as its stars.

Seal Island, a twenty-seven-minute film assembled from the Milottes' footage, won the 1949 Oscar for best live-action short subject, two-reel, and kicked off Disney's True-Life Adventures series, which over the years included movies featuring beavers, elk, lions, tigers, and many other animals.

"Our films have provided thrilling entertainment of educational quality and have played a major part in the worldwide increase in appreciation and understanding of nature," Walt said of the True-Life Adventures series. "These films have demonstrated that facts can be as fascinating as fiction, truth as beguiling as myth, and have opened the eyes of young and old to the beauties of the outdoor world and aroused their desire to conserve priceless natural assets."[21]

The series also gave birth to Disney's Buena Vista film distribution company, which Walt and his brother and business partner, Roy Disney, created when RKO, the distributor they worked with, showed little interest in the company's new line of wildlife movies.[22] When RKO passed on *Seal Island*, Walt asked Pasadena's Crown Theatre to screen the film for one week, qualifying it for an Academy Award nomination. The day after *Seal Island* won the Oscar for best live-action two-reel short subject, Walt took the award to Roy's office and said: "Here, Roy. Take this over to RKO and bang them over the head with it."[23]

As usual, Walt's instincts were right on. Audiences loved the True-Life Adventures movies—not just because they revealed a world beyond their front doors, but because Walt, a born storyteller, gave the animals human characteristics. Two ducks in *In Beaver Valley* are described as "a pair of honeymooners, up from the south," and in *Jungle Cat*, what starts as "an all-out argument" between two jaguars turns into "a romantic love spat."

Elsewhere, lively music helps bring scenes to life, whether it's bighorn sheep butting heads to the rhythm of Verdi's "Anvil Chorus" or footage of two scorpions set to a customized square dance tune dubbed "The Stingaree."

"Our aim in these pictures is to present animal nature honestly, in all its phases of comedy and sometimes tragedy," Walt said. The films, he added, focused on the creatures' "family life, training of the young, heroic defense of the helpless, and the elemental emotions which govern their existence as our fellow creatures on this earth. So presented, they tug at our sympathies and understanding, and therefore more humane regard. I am sure that children all over the world—and their parents as well—have a kindlier attitude toward wild creatures after having seen them in our True-Life Adventures."[24]

The success of the 1950 Oscar-winning True-Life Adventures short *In Beaver Valley* prompted Walt to write, in the company's 1950 annual report, that, "In my years in the motion picture business, I never had more enjoyment than I am getting out of the production of our True-Life Adventures series. They have completely fascinated me."[25]

But the films were not without controversy. *The Vanishing Prairie* (1954) was banned in New York because of a scene that showed a buffalo giving birth.[26] Former farm boy Walt was incensed. "Aren't we getting prudish when we say natural processes are objectionable? I want my children to know about these things, and to learn them from nature; they are part of existence, as natural and unashamed as breathing,"[27] he said at the time. "It would be a shame if New York children had to believe the stork brings buffaloes too."[28]

Another of the films later became even more controversial: 1958's *White Wilderness*, shot in the Arctic and featuring footage of polar bears, walruses, and caribou, as well as stunning shots of glaciers breaking apart, contained a scene allegedly showing a group of lemmings committing mass suicide by throwing themselves off a cliff. The footage was later found to have been faked: without Walt's knowledge, the filmmakers had placed a number of lemmings onto a snow-covered turntable, then driven them off a precipice to the sea below. The myth of lemming mass suicide continues to this day.

* * *

The True-Life Adventures series also played a large role in the planning for Disneyland. True-Life Adventureland was what Walt originally wanted to call the section of the park themed after the remote African, Asian, South American, and Caribbean jungles seen in True-Life Adventures titles like *The African Lion* and *Jungle Cat*. To give the land an exotic feel, Imagineers planted orange trees upside down so their wide roots were exposed. Disney horticulturist Bill Evans had traveled to many tropical regions around the world, and he knew real jungles could be monotonous. So he decided to create a "Hollywood" jungle more akin to what visitors would have seen in movies like *Tarzan the Ape Man* or *The African Queen*.[29]

Walt had hoped the area's flagship Jungle Cruise ride could include real animals, but the plan was nixed when it was explained to him that real animals sleep for a large part of the day.[30] So it was mechanical elephants and hippos that guests encountered when Disneyland opened in 1955, the same year Walt received the National Audubon Society's Audubon Medal for having "played a major part in the world-wide increase in appreciating and understanding of nature."[31]

Mickey Mouse was in every sense a movie star by the 1950s, adorning clocks, piggy banks, phonographs, and more, but Walt became a star in his own right among environmental groups—a conservation hero and a poster boy for their causes. Several organizations lauded him with praise and awards: In 1952, the National Association for Conservation Education and Publicity called out True-Life Adventures title *Nature's Half Acre* as "a film that promoted conservation of natural resources,"[32] and in 1956, Walt received a Department of the Interior Conservation Service Award for his "contribution to the understanding and appreciation of conservation principles."[33] And in 1966, the American Society for the Prevention of Cruelty to Animals had presented him with a first-of-its-kind gold medallion for his work on behalf of animals. Another proud moment for Walt came in 1955, when the Sierra Club—one of the largest environmental organizations in the country—presented him with an honorary lifetime membership in thanks for the True-Life Adventures series and the education it provided.[34]

Walt Disney in 1956 after he was awarded the Department of the Interior's Conservation Service Award for his "contribution to the understanding and appreciation of conservation principles." Walt received multiple accolades for his environmental efforts in the 1950s and 1960s. Valley Times Collection/Los Angeles Public Library.

Aware of Walt's strong feelings on conservation, the National Wildlife Federation approached him to become spokesman and honorary chairman for its National Wildlife Week in 1956. It was a role Walt relished so much he reprised it for the next ten years. He recorded a series of public-service announcements to educate American audiences about environmental concerns, in 1956 saying, "Over a period of years, we've come to appreciate more and more the wonder and wisdom of nature's infinite plan for the survival of her creatures. But sometimes nature's design is changed by civilization. When this happens, we must help nature preserve her vanishing creatures."[35]

* * *

Protecting the wildlife in Mineral King was important to Walt as well, and as he sat at the makeshift conference table under the tall trees in Mineral King, he talked about how his plan for the resort would prioritize keeping the animals' habitat intact.

Members of the press looked on, struggling to scribble notes as their hands shook from the mountain cold. Most were shivering, wearing only their business suits as the day's weather report had called for sunshine. But by the time the press conference started, the sky was blotted out by heavy dark clouds that had rolled in over the tall peaks surrounding the valley. Mineral King veterans in attendance shook their heads, knowing that anyone who had spent time in the mountains had enough foresight to bring a jacket—even with an optimistic forecast.

After Walt brought the press conference to a close, thanking Governor Brown for the state's help with the road, he stood up from the table and chatted briefly with some of the journalists present. Although Walt showed his usual enthusiasm—he was jovial and affable with the reporters—they couldn't help but notice he looked different. He looked gaunt, weaker, older.

"Is he okay?" a pair of press members whispered to Robert Jackson, a Disney executive who was handling public relations for the Mineral King project and overseeing the event.

Jackson shooed away their concerns. "It's the high altitude, and the cold," he explained.[36]

After a few minutes, Walt stood up, excused himself, and walked into the nearby general store operated by two longtime residents of Mineral King. After several minutes, the press began looking for him, requesting to take a photo of Walt with Governor Brown. Jackson went inside the store and found Walt sitting, hands extended, warming himself in front of a wood-burning stove.

Jackson was struck by Walt's ashen complexion. For the first time, he was worried about his boss's well-being. He knew that Walt was scheduled to enter the hospital in November for a "checkup and therapeutic measures"[37] due to his increased coughing, chest pain, and shortness of breath. Suddenly Jackson feared Walt wouldn't be around for Mineral King's opening day, scheduled for 1971. Staffers like him had seen their boss reinvigorated during the planning for Mineral King, seen his eyes shining the way they did when he was building a vision in his mind. And Walt's enthusiasm was contagious—when he talked about the project, people could almost see the skiers zipping down the hill and feel the fine snowy mist that flew up as they carved their turns. They could see them in the village, talking boisterously in the restaurants and bars as they relived their day on the slopes.

After giving him a few more moments by the fire, Jackson approached Walt. "They want a photo of you," he said. Walt barely looked up. "Can you delay a few minutes until I catch my breath and can rest a while?"[38] he asked. His voice was so soft it was almost a whisper.

"Sure," Jackson said, before returning to the journalists outside to assist with photo setups. Walt emerged a few minutes later and posed for pictures with Governor Brown.

After the photo session in the natural splendor of Mineral King, the entire group sat down to eat lunch—chicken and hot baked beans, with plenty of coffee to combat the cold. As the journalists began to depart, Walt looked up at the wide sky over Mineral King. The sun was still hidden by clouds, casting a faint glow on the tree-covered slopes.

Shortly after, around 2 p.m., Brown departed by helicopter while Walt and the other Disney people left by motorcade, crossing the stately arched Oak Grove Bridge over the Kaweah River before taking the winding, bumpy road to the Visalia airport for the flight back to company headquarters in Burbank. Sitting in the backseat of the car, Walt watched in the rearview mirror as the Mineral King valley slowly grew smaller and more distant, before it finally disappeared.

2

FINDING THE PERFECT SPOT

1961

A helicopter dipped down through the blue California sky, casting a shimmering shadow on the snowy mountainside as it approached. The chopper found a flat spot to land near the top of the tall slope, and Willy Schaeffler clambered out, ready to explore. The forty-five-year-old German downhiller strapped his skis on before pushing off with a yell, careening to the bottom of the hill over ungroomed slopes and through a maze of trees and shrubs. It was 1961, and Schaeffler was on the hunt for the best location for his new ski-resort venture with Walt Disney.

Everything he had heard about Mineral King was true, Schaeffler thought, as he glided to a stop at the bottom of the slope. The snow quality was excellent, the views breathtaking, and the valley floor perfectly suited for a welcoming collection of hotels, restaurants, and shops. It was the closest thing the German skier had seen in America to the famous European peaks that drew winter sports enthusiasts from all over the world.

Schaeffler lived for these kinds of adventures—the more extreme the better. He had climbed up and skied down mountains all over the world, daredeviling his way to the bottom, where he'd stand with his ski goggles pushed up on his forehead, his signature look, to give his expert opinion on the hill's ski-area potential. For the past few months, Schaeffler had been exploring mountains all over Southern California—and even some in Colorado—for his project with Walt Disney. He had been especially

excited about the visit to Mineral King, which had taken on an almost leg-
endary status in the ski community as a great untapped location. Schaeffler
also had heard about the valley's remarkable features and giant bowls from
Walt, whom he had met when the two worked together on the 1960 Winter Olympics in California's Squaw Valley. Walt had taken a few summer
vacations in the Mineral King area at the invitation of local landowner Ray
Buckman,[1] and he told Schaeffler—who was overseeing the skiing events
at the Games—he thought it might be the perfect location for the ski area
he wanted to build. When Walt sent Schaeffler and economist Harrison
"Buzz" Price, Walt's advisor on new developments, on a helicopter journey
around the undeveloped peaks of Southern California, he made sure Mineral King was at the top of the list.

   Though Walt and Schaeffler had met by chance at the 1960 Olympics,
they soon became fast friends, forming a dynamic duo of spectacle and
sport. Impressed by Schaeffler's skiing prowess and his knowledge of how
ski runs should be constructed, Walt took Schaeffler aside several times
during the Winter Games to talk about his vision for a family-friendly ski
resort unlike any that existed at the time. Schaeffler was equally impressed
by Walt for his attention to detail, his creative vision, and his ability to get
others to buy into his plans. He signed on as Walt's partner, and the two
became a formidable team sharing qualities of stubbornness, determination, and a no-nonsense approach. Schaeffler was strong-willed, yet highly
passionate—maybe even more so than Walt. It was a personality born from
a life of struggle.

❊ ❊ ❊

Described by one writer as "dictatorial, outspoken, stubborn, wild, honest, sensitive, dynamic, egocentric, virile, unpunctual, reserved, generous,
moody, dogmatic, fiercely intelligent, unpredictable, physically rugged,
skeptical, cultured, disciplined, critical, and persevering,"[2] Wilhelm Josef
"Willy" Schaeffler had become an undeniable presence in the skiing world
since arriving in the United States in 1948 as a self-described "political
persecutee of the Nazi government." Born in 1915 in the Bavarian town of
Kaufbeuren, Schaeffler was skiing on barrel staves at age three and com-
petitively by age eight. He won the Bavarian Junior Alpine Championships
in 1932 and was named to the 1936 German Olympic team, but he broke
both of his legs just before the Games—"Willy came whooshing off the
end of a ski jump squarely into a loose toboggan,"[3] as Sports Illustrated put
it—and was unable to compete.

German ski champion Willy Schaeffler, who worked on Disney's Mineral King project from 1960 to its demise in 1978. Courtesy of the U.S. Ski and Snowboard Hall of Fame.

When the Nazis rose to power in the early 1930s, Schaeffler's family were among the Germans who were outspoken in their opposition to the party. When Schaeffler was drafted into Hitler's army in the early years of World War II, he was immediately labeled a "political unsafe." Placed in a battalion with other German political dissidents, Schaeffler was sent to the Russian front, where he was captured and tortured by the Soviets. He escaped by disguising himself in the uniform of a dead Russian guard, then returned to the front lines, where he was wounded again in a firefight. He survived, but the ordeal left Schaeffler with pieces of shrapnel in his heart, a shrunken lung, and a permanent distrust of authority.[4]

After World War II ended in 1945, Schaeffler began teaching U.S. Army forces in Germany—including a young George Patton—how to ski and rock climb. It was at that time Schaeffler met American Army officer Betty

Durnford, who would become his wife of fourteen years. With Betty's assistance, Schaeffler immigrated to the United States in 1948, at the age of thirty-two. He had no money, but he did have four pairs of skis.

One of his first orders of business upon arriving in America was to reach out to Larry Jump, cofounder of Colorado's Arapahoe Basin ski area, to inquire about working at the resort as a ski instructor. "Six weeks ago I arrived in the United States as a political persecutee of the Nazi government," Schaeffler wrote. "I am writing to you at this time to tell you of my qualifications as a ski school leader and organizer of new ski territories."[5]

Jump did Schaeffler one better, inviting him to Colorado to help construct the growing resort's ski hills. Given the title of trail supervisor, Schaeffler was in charge of cutting, sawing, and pulling logs off of trails as they were constructed.

Around the same time, Schaeffler was hired as ski coach at the University of Denver, where his demand for perfection and his unforgiving training regimen—which included forcing skiers to run up and down the stairs of the school's football stadium with another skier on their shoulders—led his team to sweep the NCAA championships year after year.[6] Thanks to his success with the DU ski team, Schaeffler became a fixture on the pages of *Sports Illustrated*. In 1957, he convinced the magazine to publish his series of illustrations introducing U.S. skiers to the Austrian "shortswing" skiing technique, "the revolutionary reverse-shoulder technique that has swept Europe," according to the text that accompanied the illustrations of Schaeffler demonstrating the method.[7]

Schaeffler's reputation took another leap forward in the late 1950s, when he was recruited to oversee the skiing portion of the Squaw Valley Olympics. With his sharp Germanic features, heavy accent, intense blue eyes, and perpetual squint, Schaeffler was a presence both feared and revered during Olympic preparations in Squaw Valley, where he ran the ski events and created the alpine courses. He walked the mountain for four days before declaring Squaw Valley worthy of competition, and he even brought the University of Denver ski team to California to test the runs as he designed them.

Organizers of the Squaw Valley Olympics had a knack for finding leaders whose attention to detail and demand for perfection would keep the planning for the Games moving forward. The skiing events had Schaeffler at their helm, while the athletes' village, opening and closing ceremonies, and other elements of showmanship at the Games were overseen by none other than Walt Disney, who was brought on to make sure a long-shot Winter Olympics would be a success.

✿✿✿

The sports world was taken by surprise in 1955, when the International Olympic Committee awarded the 1960 Winter Games to the tiny Squaw Valley ski area in Northern California. The move was the result of a publicity stunt by Squaw Valley owner Alexander Cushing, who submitted his bid for the Games after reading that the nearby Reno ski area was submitting a bid of its own.[8] Squaw Valley was a struggling resort with just one chairlift, two tow ropes, and a fifty-room hotel; Cushing was its only permanent resident. But Cushing was wealthy and well-connected, and he soon got California congressman Harold "Bizz" Johnson and California

Willy Schaeffler, left, with Walt Disney, center, in 1960 at the Winter Olympics in Squaw Valley, California. It was there the two started planning their own recreation destination. © Bill Briner All Rights Reserved.

governor Goodwin Knight on his side. What started as a lark—Cushing later admitted to *Time* magazine that he "had no more interest in getting the Games than the man in the moon"[9]—turned into a crusade. Cushing eventually gained the support of President Dwight D. Eisenhower, who signed a resolution in support of the Squaw Valley bid. When the IOC met in Paris to make its final site selection, Cushing argued that the Games belonged to the world, and that the Winter Olympics shouldn't automatically be awarded to a European country. He said Squaw Valley, spartan by European standards, would return the Olympics to its roots and would offer athletes "a natural meeting place of privacy and dignity."[10] He submitted his bid in English, French, and Spanish, and he commissioned a three-thousand-pound model of Squaw Valley to help make his case. It sat in the lobby of the American embassy in Paris, and Cushing personally escorted delegates to view it.

Convinced by Cushing—along with Squaw Valley's eminently skiable terrain and 450 inches of yearly snowfall—the IOC awarded the 1960 Winter Games to Squaw Valley, which edged out odds-on favorite Innsbruck, Austria, by two votes. They would be the first Winter Olympics in America since 1932—and only the eighth Winter Games overall.

Organizers moved quickly to ensure that the California Olympics would be successful. And for world-class entertainment that would be rivaled by no Games before them, there was just one man they trusted with the job.

* * *

When Prentis Hale showed up at the Disney studios for his lunch date with Walt in 1958, he had only an hour to convince Walt to become part of the 1960 Winter Olympics. The California businessman and chairman of Broadway-Hale Stores Inc.—a popular chain of department stores on the West Coast—had been named organizing committee president of the 1960 Winter Games, and he was desperate to make them not only a major success, but a spectacular one. Among other things, he wanted to bring a new level of visual spectacle to the opening and closing ceremonies. He wanted Hollywood flash and legitimacy. He wanted something that had never been done before. He wanted viewers to sit in front of their television sets to watch the Olympics opening ceremony or a hockey game as excitedly as they did popular programs such as *Gunsmoke* or *I've Got a Secret*. And Walt—whose successful Disneyland project proved he could pull off live entertainment just as well as the magic he made on the movie screen—was the man who could help him do it.

Walt listened as Hale laid out the proposition: He wanted Walt to be responsible for the opening and closing ceremonies, the victory ceremonies held after each event, and the Olympic torch relay,[11] as well as the Olympic Village, where the athletes would live during the competition. Walt was immediately intrigued, especially since he was a fan of skiing and other winter sports. The Olympics were a premier event, of course, but they were mostly a sporting event. They had little fanfare or other entertainment value, an area in which Walt thrived. But Hale proposed that could change. Walt, always full of ideas, immediately had thoughts about how to make the Olympics more flashy, more fun, more futuristic.

After agreeing to be involved as chairman of the Games' pageantry committee, Walt started recruiting from within the Disney ranks to ensure the event would be a success. He appointed his son-in-law Ron Miller, assistant director at the Disney studios, pageantry coordinator; Tommy Walker, director of customer relations at Disneyland, was assigned the role of pageantry director; and Card Walker (no relation to Tommy), vice president of Walt Disney Productions, was named director of publicity.[12]

The Olympic Village, where the athletes were housed, was where Walt focused much of his attention. Athletes had stayed at hotels and local homes during previous Games, but Squaw Valley's remote location required the construction of new lodging facilities.[13] Four dormitories were built in close proximity to one another and to the competition venues—a deliberately intimate arrangement that fostered sportsmanship and socializing among athletes from different nations during a time of tension and lingering animosities after World War II.[14] By putting all of the athletes in a central place, the village created an opportunity for Walt to do what he did best: entertain them. "Nothing is more important than creating lasting goodwill among our visitors," Walt told his team, "and we shall do everything we can to make their stay a happy one."[15]

He called on a few famous friends in order to achieve the task. TV and radio star Art Linkletter, who had co-hosted Disneyland's live opening special in 1955, became vice president in charge of entertainment, and he and Walt worked together to bring stars up from Hollywood to entertain the Olympic competitors. Evening extravaganzas, hosted by Linkletter, started at 8:30 every night[16] in the Olympic Village dining hall. Audiences of up to 1,500—composed of athletes, officials, and journalists—gathered for performances by the likes of jazz pianist George Shearing; actress and swimmer Esther Williams; Hollywood costume designer Edith Head, who hosted a fashion show; Western stars Roy Rogers and Dale Evans; musician and comedian Jerry Colonna; entertainers Red Skelton, Bing Crosby, and Jack Benny; and singing group the Sons of the Pioneers.[17]

Redheaded entertainer Danny Kaye, fresh from films like *The Court Jester* and *The Five Pennies*, performed on opening night. Kaye, who spoke twelve different languages and could sing songs from all over the world, was a favorite among the international athletes. The troupe from Disneyland's Golden Horseshoe Revue—a Western-themed musical stage show that ran from 1955 to 1986 at the park's Golden Horseshoe Saloon—came to Squaw Valley for a night to stage a mock gunfight and bar brawl. The show was so convincing that a security guard at one point called for help.[18] Disney also arranged for twenty-five feature and twenty-five short films to be screened in two theaters constructed especially for the occasion. The films, all from 1957 and 1958, included *Separate Tables, Inn of the Sixth Happiness, Auntie Mame, Peyton Place, Funny Face, The Defiant Ones, Gigi, Teacher's Pet*, and Disney's own *Perri*, a "True-Life Fantasy"—a spin-off of the True-Life Adventures series that allowed for more fictionalized storytelling—about a female forest squirrel.[19] The athletes loved the nighttime entertainment, and Walt took notes all the while, working out how shows and live entertainment could enhance the ski resort he and Schaeffler were starting to plan.

For some of the Games' larger design challenges, Walt enlisted the talents of Imagineering legend John Hench, who had worked at the Disney studios for years, starting in the story department. In the 1950s, Hench worked on such live-action films as *20,000 Leagues Under the Sea* and *The Living Desert*; he then went to the Disneyland team, where he helped design Tomorrowland and Adventureland. As the Games' official décor director, Hench oversaw the construction of thirty "snow" sculptures (made of wire mesh and papier-mâché) depicting athletes competing in various winter sports. The idea came from Walt, who took inspiration from the ancient Greek custom of building marble sculptures for Olympic champions. The snow sculptures—depicting a skier, hockey player, figure skater, and more—lined the "Avenue of the Athletes" that separated the village area from the competition area. Walt wanted a similar feel to Disneyland's Main Street, U.S.A., which for visitors marked the transition from the "real world" to the park's fantasy lands beyond. Two twenty-four-foot statues—a female skier and a male speed skater—flanked the Tower of Nations. Also designed by Hench, the huge metal structure featuring the crests of the thirty participating countries was topped by the five Olympic rings. Hench also came up with a new design for the Olympic torch that was smaller in height and easier for runners to hand off to one another.[20]

Designed by Disney Imagineer John Hench, the Tower of Nations at the 1960 Winter Olympics featured the crests of the thirty participating countries and was topped by the five Olympic rings. © Bill Briner All Rights Reserved.

Among Hench's other responsibilities was helping to plan the opening ceremony, which Walt wanted to be reminiscent of the Main Street parade at Disneyland.[21] There would be athletes in place of costumed characters, but the lively marching-band music and spectacular fireworks would remain the same, stirring in spectators a similar feeling of hope and camaraderie. Always a believer in the power of music to move a crowd, Walt paid special attention to the musical aspects of the ceremonies. His team recruited musicians and singers from high schools in Nevada and California to perform at the opening ceremony, and Charles Hirt, from the music school at the University of Southern California, was named choral director. Hirt had helped to create Disneyland's Candlelight Processional—a Christmastime event featuring a narrator reading the Christmas story and local youth choirs performing traditional holiday songs—and was used to conducting large groups of young singers.

But when opening day finally arrived, a blinding snowstorm threatened Walt's vision of a grand outdoor ceremony. Vice President Richard Nixon, scheduled to arrive by helicopter, had to drive in instead. Bumper-to-bumper traffic on snowy roads had cars backed up for twelve miles, preventing journalists and other guests from getting to the ceremony on time. Hoping for a miracle, Walt decided to wait out the storm—motivated in large part by the high school musicians who had paid their own way to the Games in the hopes of appearing on television. During a musical rehearsal that morning, remembered Hirt, "I stood up there [at the podium] facing what I thought was the choir. I hoped and prayed it was, because I couldn't see them, the snow was falling so hard. [Band director] Clarence Sawhill relayed my beat to the band because he couldn't see the choir either."

Walt asked the chorus director what he proposed they do. The only alternative was to move the ceremony to an indoor ice-skating arena that would accommodate just a fraction of the young musicians. "I told him that I couldn't stand the thought of saying to these people who had worked so hard for so many months that only some of them could be among the bands and choruses in the skating rink," Hirt recalled. And though the TV crews wanted to play it safe and take the ceremony indoors, Walt listened to Hirt, who said, "Let's dare to have everybody in this."

"That's all Walt needed to hear," Hirt remembered. "Over the loudspeaker, we told everyone to go into formation. The clock ticked down to showtime, and at that moment, the sky parted and the sun shone. It was a miracle. My choir was in front of me. I could see them. Clarence could see his band, and he could see me. And the program went off without a hitch."[22]

The ceremony involved the release of two thousand pigeons, a barrage of eight cannon shots, one for each Winter Olympics held so far, and the eruption of fireworks in the daytime sky—the first recorded daytime use of the celebratory explosives.[23] The festivities began with a drum roll as the flag of each participating nation was raised. Fanfare came courtesy of the United States Marine Band, which—along with fifty-two high school bands and a 2,645-voice choir—launched into "The Parade of the Olympians."

After Nixon made a declaration to open the Games, the Olympic flame arrived. First lit in Norway, in the hearth of the house where modern skiing legend Sondre Norheim was born, it was flown across the sea to Los Angeles, where a relay of more than five hundred high school students ran the torch more than six hundred miles to Squaw Valley. Actor Karl Malden—who would soon appear in Disney's live-action *Pollyanna*, starring Hayley Mills as the ultra-positive teen—delivered the Olympic prayer, something that had not always been done in previous Olympic ceremonies. It was an addition that some found controversial. ("Walt felt that prayer represents one of the freedoms of America and that we should definitely have it," Tommy Walker said.[24]) U.S. figure skater Carol Heiss, who days later would win a gold medal, recited the Olympic oath. More than thirty thousand balloons of all colors were released as 665 athletes departed the stadium. "It is my conviction that you'll never see anything of that kind so well done in your lifetime," a reporter for the *Los Angeles Times* wrote of the ceremony, while a *Variety* columnist called the event "the greatest show on Earth."[25]

It was a fitting start to the 1960 Winter Games, which would go on for ten more days and host athletes from thirty nations. Besides being the first Games to be televised in the United States (CBS paid $50,000 for the rights),[26] they were the first to utilize video instant replay, and the first to use computers as part of the scoring process. They also were the first to use artificial ice (heat from the refrigeration units was used to warm spectators and melt snow from the rooftops).[27]

Walt was there for all eleven exhausting days, even hustling across the property to help out with tickets, parking, and security when he wasn't managing entertainment in the athletes' village. Schaeffler was equally busy farther up the mountain, overseeing the downhill ski races and making sure the courses he had constructed stayed well-maintained.

After the Games ended, Walt went back to Burbank and got to work on projects including *One Hundred and One Dalmatians*, a new True-Life Adventures title, and his weekly television show. But his mind was still on the mountain, and he wasted no time in contacting Schaeffler to put the ski-resort project in motion. He connected Schaeffler with Price, the economist who had already served as an important resource for Walt in the early 1950s, conducting studies to determine the best location for Disneyland. Then part of the Stanford Research Institute associated with Stanford University, Price had looked at everything from land prices and freeway accessibility to average temperatures and pollution levels before recommending a 160-acre span of orange groves and walnut trees in Anaheim as the statistically perfect spot for Walt's first theme park. Impressed with Price's work, Walt encouraged him to form his own consulting firm, and in 1958 Price—with funding from Walt—opened Economics Research Associates, setting the firm up as a one-man operation before adding other experts to join his team.

With Walt's encouragement, Schaeffler and Price looked at locations in Colorado and California for the ski-resort project, but it soon became clear that Walt was most interested in sites in Southern California. Price and Schaeffler went first to Mount San Gorgonio outside of Palm Springs, where, Price later remembered, "The mountain was great. The market was immense. We hiked to the top and Willy astounded me by skiing down the 2,000-foot face, without skis, on his boots, an early example of the advantage of 'short skis.' I hiked down to a waiting Willy."[28]

Walt soon learned, however, that the Sierra Club was opposed to development on San Gorgonio, and he told Schaeffler he had no intention of crossing the organization that had made him an honorary lifetime member several years earlier. So he sent the pair next to California's Mammoth Mountain, to inquire about buying the resort lock, stock, and barrel. No deal. So it was off to other mountains in the area, including the ones surrounding Mineral King. "Mineral King was by far the best available site for the project Walt had in mind," Price wrote. "It had maximum market exposure, summer and winter, and it had the physical attributes he was seeking: three huge bowls, five-mile runs, and a 5,000-foot drop. It had the required scale and scope for the creation of a resort with a draw strong enough to generate positive economic feasibility."[29]

The area also had the advantage of some amount of existing infrastructure. Mineral King was initially developed during the California Gold Rush of the 1850s, given a kick-start in 1873, when local resident James Crabtree claimed to have a vision of an Indian ghost who led him to a mine site that Crabtree named White Chief. After Crabtree staked his claim, others followed, and the district saw an influx of miners hoping to strike it rich.[30] The infamous winding road into the valley was completed in 1879, and Mineral King was soon a bustling boomtown complete with a post office, barbershop, butcher shop, two-story hotel, dairy, brewery, saloon, and general store. The area never yielded much in the way of precious metals, however, and after an 1880 avalanche destroyed a bunkhouse and the tramway used to transport ore from the mine to the valley floor, most of the miners moved on to more promising claims.

Over the following years, though, many of the miners and their families began returning to Mineral King in the summers, drawn by its cool climate and natural beauty. By 1905, the area was home to a five-acre resort that included a hotel, general store, dance hall, post office, and six private cabins. Though most of the resort was destroyed by the San Francisco earthquake of 1906, some of the cabins remained, and in the following years more cabins and summer homes were constructed, including some thirty cabins in an area called Faculty Flat—so named because its original inhabitants were schoolteachers from Los Angeles. With the rebuilding of the resort and the addition of a pack station, Mineral King continued to draw tourists as well, including campers, hikers, and fishermen, many of whom used Mineral King as their gateway to the adjacent Sequoia National Park.

Left out of Sequoia due to active mining claims when the park's boundaries were first drawn in the late 1800s, the Mineral King area was a narrow protrusion of land surrounded by the park on three sides. When Sequoia was enlarged in 1926, Mineral King was still excluded, but the area was upgraded to a federal game refuge to protect its well-known deer herd and other wildlife. By 1960 the area was home to some sixty-five family cabins, several campgrounds, and a small resort consisting of a general store, dining hall, post office, and several rental cabins.

The land wasn't approved for development, but Walt and Schaeffler had conducted a few informal conversations with members of the U.S. Forest Service—an agency overseen by the Department of Agriculture—who indicated the bureau was interested in partnering with a developer to build a year-round recreational resort in the area. Walt had a good feeling it was just a matter of time before the land became available, and he wanted to make some preemptive strikes in an effort to keep from repeating one of the biggest mistakes of his life.

❋ ❋ ❋

Walt loved Disneyland, but he felt sharp pangs of regret every time he drove through Anaheim. No sooner were plans for Disneyland announced in 1954 than savvy developers began buying up the land surrounding the park, envisioning swarms of tourists eating at their burger joints, sleeping in their discount motels, and shopping for souvenirs in their gaudy gift boutiques. By 1960, the "neon jungle" of businesses surrounding Disneyland was taking in five times more money than the park itself.[31] Walt never forgave himself for his shortsightedness. He vowed that with any new project he undertook, he would endeavor to control as much of the surrounding land as he could, so that those hotels, restaurants, and gift shops would all be Disney-run.

In Mineral King, the land surrounding the valley was in the form of two old mining claims split up into plots owned by eighteen different families. Not wanting anyone to get wind of their plans, Walt and Price brought in Robert "Bob" Hicks, a researcher at Price's Economics Research Associates who had helped Price conduct aerial surveys for Disneyland locations in the early 1950s, to start making land deals. Price and Hicks had been classmates at the Stanford Graduate School of Business, where Price became acquainted with the Stanford Research Institute, and once he had narrowed potential Disneyland locations down to four, Price asked Hicks— a former pilot for Pan American Airways—to fly the researchers over the four sites. Hicks had conducted a feasibility study for Walt Disney Productions' purchase of a private plane, and he also had experience helping prominent politicians and executives buy land anonymously.

Hicks, who had lived in nearby Visalia in the late 1930s and early 1940s (he worked in Sequoia National Park for two summers during high school and college),[32] was tasked by Walt with buying up acres of land in the Mineral King area so there would be no competition when the resort plans were eventually unveiled. Hicks spoke the language of the locals and was able to get the deals done; it helped that he wasn't making them for an outfit with "Disney" in its name, but for another company Walt had started called Retlaw Enterprises. Originally set up in 1953 to manage Walt's personal business operations and holdings for his family, Retlaw ("Walter" spelled backward) had grown to include the rights to the "Walt Disney" name and brand, which Walt Disney Productions did not control, as well as the railroad and monorail in Disneyland.

By 1962, with Hicks making land deals in the valley and Walt and Schaeffler talking with authorities behind the scenes, the stage was set for a Disney-owned ski area in Southern California—whenever the Forest Service decided to pull the trigger on opening the land for development. Walt and Schaeffler were closer than ever to the world-class ski resort they had started discussing two years earlier.

And the word was getting out.

3

RUMOR HAS IT

1961

It was only John Harper's second time navigating the winding road into Mineral King, but already he was learning its twists and turns. How, as the road gradually rose in elevation, the scenery transformed from a patchwork of privately owned ranches and farms dotted with grazing cattle to a thick forest of towering cedars and pines. Harper had not yet memorized the locations of the two groves of giant sequoias on the route, and as he drove he craned his neck, scanning the roadside for the trees' massive beauty. The windows of his Volkswagen van rolled down to let in the fragrance of the trees and the dirt, Harper patiently steered through the road's sharp curves. He knew the path would level out when he reached the small town of Silver City, home to a general store and a handful of small cabins. From there he would enter an even thicker forest, the sky blotted out by leaves and dark green needles, as he climbed the last five miles to Mineral King proper. As the road approached its end near the banks of the Kaweah River, the ground would thicken with sagebrush, rabbitbrush, mountain mahogany, and other shrubs that had grown up on deforested spots left over from the short-lived mining boom of the 1870s. Along the river were stands of cottonwood and willow, interspersed with spates of pine and aspen.

It was Fourth of July weekend 1961, right in the middle of Harper's first summer as a Californian. A twenty-six-year-old, bespectacled petroleum geologist who had recently moved to Bakersfield—roughly 120 miles south of Mineral King—to start working for Standard Oil, Harper

spent his weekends and vacation days exploring Sequoia National Forest and other nearby wilderness areas. He fell in love with Mineral King
the first time he set eyes on it: "At once it is excitement, color, vertical
dimension, elegance marred only slightly by the hand of man," he wrote
of the place. "There is classic High Sierra scenery visible from the valley,
a pleasing blend of sharply serrate summits, ragged ridges, bold escarp-
ments, steep tongues of dark-green forest alternating with jumbled talus
and open slope."[1]

Born in Lincoln, Nebraska, in 1934, Harper had developed his love of
the outdoors as a child, when he spent summers with his family in the
Rocky Mountains of nearby Colorado. He received bachelor's and master's
degrees at the University of Nebraska, then served as an aviator in the
Navy. He joined the Sierra Club in 1961 to find fellow outdoors enthusiasts,
and he was a member of the club's Kern-Kaweah Chapter, which encompassed Bakersfield and the Mineral King area and was named for the two
rivers that flowed through the region.

On this sunny summer day, once his drive up the winding road was complete, Harper stepped out of his car and stretched his arms high, gently
twisting from side to side to awaken his spine after the three-hour drive.
After thirty minutes of exploring, he began a short climb, slowly working
his way up a series of stairstep ledges to the top of a small crag to take in
the view. As he looked out over Empire Mountain and Sawtooth Peak,
with the rugged Kaweah Peaks towering over the skyline above, it occurred
to him that Mineral King was "truly an extraordinary place. Where else in
the Sierra Nevada could one penetrate so easily into the depths of genuine
alpine country, and feel so totally removed from the demands of daily rou-
tine? . . . I felt inwardly confident that I had found the refuge to which one
could escape quite readily to recover peace of mind."[2]

Harper visited his refuge many times over the following twelve months,
journeying to the Mineral King valley with friends from the Sierra Club to
camp, fish, or rock climb. His day job was often a monotony of flat, dusty
oilfields and endless equations he worked in his small office, and Mineral
King was the antidote, with its sparkling vistas, sheer canyon walls, colorful
summits, and cascading streams. In summer 1962, however, Harper heard
troubling news about possible development in the valley. A fellow geologist
who also spent much of his time in Mineral King had it on good authority that Walt Disney was looking to build a ski resort right on top of the
unspoiled paradise. For Harper, the revelation "represented a knot in my
stomach, the realization that there were covetous eyes on my own 'personal'
Shangri-La."[3]

The famous Mineral King road—a primitive, winding path that was going to be improved to deliver guests to the Disney resort in Mineral King. National Park Service.

Bursting with the desire to share the news, Harper fired off an inspired memo to the Kern-Kaweah Chapter's advanced planning subcommittee: "Standby for a fairly fantastic 'rumor'! One of my geologist associates here has just returned from an extended Labor Day weekend at Mineral King. He reports that a conversation with the resident Forest Service ranger at the Mineral King Guard Station divulged a 'secret' literally straight out of Walt Disney."

More than one ski resort developer had looked into Mineral King over the years, Harper wrote, but the primitive access road had always been enough of a deterrent to keep any plans from moving forward. The latest scuttlebutt around the area, however, was that Walt Disney—he of Disneyland and its famous monorail—was considering using the futuristic transportation system as part of a Disney-run ski resort at Mineral King. The elevated tracks would start in the lower part of the Kaweah River canyon, below the snow belt, rising over the pines and sequoias until they reached the scenic valley area.

"One wonders if this pleasant, rather out-of-the-way retreat, the keystone to some superb high country, may become a winterized, alpine version of Disneyland," Harper wrote.[4]

Harper, who served on a Sierra Club subcommittee that dealt with nascent environmental issues in the Kern-Kaweah region, began looking into the rumor, reaching out to a monorail "operations man" at Disneyland for some intel. The Disney employee told Harper that not only had he never heard anything about building a monorail into Mineral King; he also doubted it was even possible, given the area's heavy tree cover and mountainous terrain.

Harper still wasn't satisfied. On October 13, 1962, just before winter snow closed the access road to the valley for the season, he led members of the Kern-Kaweah Chapter into Mineral King for an overnight outing and fact-finding mission. Looking out over a series of jagged peaks, at acres of dark green pines dotted with the reds and golds of deciduous trees, Harper thought once again about how a place so beautiful deserved to remain unspoiled by human development. With visions in his head of giant ski lifts overshadowing the pristine landscape, he approached the guard station to ask the forest ranger on duty what he knew about Walt Disney's interest in Mineral King. Confirming Harper's worst fears, the ranger said the Disney company had indeed conducted a survey of the area in the past year, testing the feasibility of building a transportation line into the valley.

Harper was disheartened by the Disney rumor—but he also wasn't entirely surprised by it. That Mineral King would someday be developed for skiing made sense, as the Sierra Club itself had recommended the area as a prime location for the sport back in the late 1940s—though the recommendation was more of a compromise than a ringing endorsement.

✧ ✧ ✧

The move came in 1947, soon after the Sierra Club convinced the Forest Service to abandon its plans to construct a ski area on California's Mount San Gorgonio. Located roughly fifty-five miles northwest of Palm Springs, San Gorgonio is the highest mountain in Southern California and was considered by developers as the ideal spot for a resort that would lure skiers from the Los Angeles area. But the proposed site was on national forest land, and the Sierra Club didn't want the area marred by lift towers and ski lodges. After convincing the Forest Service not to build on San Gorgonio, however, David Brower, a longtime Sierra Club member who would soon be named the organization's first executive director, didn't feel right about leaving Southern California skiers—many of whom were Sierra Club members—out in the cold. He and another Sierra Club skier, Richard Felter, rented a plane and took to the skies to conduct an aerial survey of other mountains that might serve as possible sites for new ski areas. They knew it would help their case against the San Gorgonio plan "to point out that there was in California much ski terrain not in wilderness and not yet developed for skiing,"[5] they wrote in the *Sierra Club Bulletin*.

Brower and Felter examined several locations, but the most promising, they felt, was the old mining district of Mineral King. High in the sky, they could see its snowy peaks, its evergreen groves, and its massive slopes, perfect for skiing. It was "probably the most spectacular site for commercial development on the west side of the Sierra," they wrote.[6]

With that recommendation in hand, the organization soon drafted a motion as a sort of compromise to the San Gorgonio issue: "Although the Sierra Club does not advocate the development of any particular area for skiing, the Club cannot, as a matter of principle, oppose the development of Mineral King or any other non-wilderness area."[7]

Opposing the San Gorgonio ski area wasn't an easy decision for Brower, then thirty-four, as those looking to build the resort were buddies of his, former fellow members of the 10th Mountain Division he had fought alongside in the mountains of Europe during World War II. Brower, who served as a lieutenant during the war, had earned a Bronze Star Medal and a Combat Infantryman Badge for his service fighting the German army in Italy.[8]

Born in 1912 in Berkeley, California, Brower was an avid hiker and climber who loved nature and the high country. A friend of photographer Ansel Adams, he joined the Sierra Club in the early 1930s to learn more about rock climbing. A key member of the club's climbing corps by 1937, he started contributing to the *Sierra Club Bulletin* and became associate editor of the publication in 1940, around the time he became a key staffer on the club's "High Trips" outings into the Sierra backcountry. After his combat experience in Italy as part of the 10th Mountain Division, Brower returned to the United States in 1946 and resumed his Sierra Club activities. He became editor of the *Bulletin* and pushed the club to expand its conservation efforts. When the San Gorgonio controversy arose in 1947, he was ready for the fight.

Skiing had begun to grow in popularity since Brower and his fellow soldiers returned from abroad, boosted by a mix of postwar affluence, the baby boom, and the increase in leisure time afforded by new technology—not to mention the return of mountain troops. But for skiers in the Los Angeles area, resorts were few and far between. Big Bear, near San Bernardino, was too small to accommodate large crowds, and Mammoth Mountain, some 265 miles east of San Francisco, was seven hours away, almost as far as Yosemite. Sugar Bowl was even farther. In terms of location, San Gorgonio was perfect, but it also was on national forest land in a so-called primitive area—a de facto wilderness area that had no formal legal protection.[9] Brower was an enthusiastic skier, but he was worried about the roads, buildings, and lifts that would need to be constructed on San Gorgonio, spoiling its scenic beauty.

"Can a conservation organization place the construction of ski facilities, or any development, above wilderness?" Brower wrote in the *Sierra Club Bulletin*. He reminded the "enthusiastic and sometimes even evangelical skiers" who championed the San Gorgonio ski area that "the sole value of a mountain is not just that it tips a snow slope downhill."

The proposal split the Sierra Club. Brower, going against his former combat buddies (and lots of skiing Sierra Club members in Southern California), wrote passionately against the proposed resort in the *Bulletin*: "The San Gorgonio Wild Area, unique in Southern California, is up for sacrifice. It is important—it is urgent—that all persons interested in conservation study this threat carefully, and act as soon as possible," he wrote. A public hearing was scheduled in San Bernardino, and Brower urged those who were against the project to attend. "The wilderness concept is on trial, is up for sacrifice under the guise of compromise," he concluded. "Where wilderness is concerned, there can be no compromise. Wilderness, like life itself, is absolute. A man cannot literally be half dead or half alive. He is dead or he is alive. A developed area cannot be wild."[10]

The hearing drew passionate appeals on both sides of the issue, but Brower and the Sierra Club prevailed, and the Forest Service abandoned the plan, concluding that "the San Gorgonio primitive area has higher public value as a wilderness and a watershed than as a downhill skiing area."[11]

That's when Brower started his airborne search for another nearby area suitable for skiing. The blessing the Sierra Club gave to Mineral King led to a 1949 Forest Service prospectus requesting bids to develop the area as a ski resort, prompting the club to issue an even stronger endorsement: "The Sierra Club finds no objection from the standpoint of its policies to the winter sports development in Mineral King as proposed by the U.S. Forest Service."[12] Due to the considerable expense of improving the road into the area, however, just one bid was submitted—and it fell far short of the Forest Service's requirements.[13]

* * *

Fighting on behalf of the environment was nothing new for the Sierra Club, which strove to balance the recreational pursuits of its members with zealous defense of natural areas. One of the first conservation organizations in the United States, the club was founded in 1892 by John Muir, a famous naturalist who had moved to America from Scotland with his family in 1849, at age eleven. Aware of the stresses the Industrial Revolution had brought, Muir in 1901 wrote that "thousands of tired, nerve-shaken, over-civilised people are beginning to find out that going to the mountains is going home."[14] It was a sentiment that only grew truer as the twentieth century got more complicated. The growing boom in manufacturing in the early 1900s drew workers away from rural communities and into over-crowded cities. Thousands took jobs at dangerous factories, where working conditions were harsh, hours were long, and tasks were repetitive and monotonous. Workplaces could be dangerous as well—in the latter part of the nineteenth century, more industrial accidents took place in the United States than in any other modernized country.[15]

Those dire conditions became a call to arms for conservationists like Muir, who advocated for the importance of fresh air and the peace of the outdoors as a way to counterbalance noisy city life. One of the first Americans to actively champion a back-to-nature lifestyle, Muir settled in California in 1868 and fell in love with Yosemite and the Sierra Nevada. It was there his environmental journey truly began as he roamed throughout the area, hiking, foraging, and climbing mountains. In 1890 Muir spear-headed efforts to turn Yosemite into a national park, and in 1892, Muir and Henry Senger, a professor at the University of California, Berkeley, started an "alpine club" to protect the Sierra Nevada and other wilderness areas. With Muir as its president, the group set out to safeguard Mount Rainier in

Sierra Club founder John Muir. National Park Service.

Washington and the glacier area of Montana, helping to establish national parks in both.

The club sponsored recreational excursions into the Sierra and other wilderness areas and in 1901 started a tradition of summer "High Trips," but its recreational activities stood side by side with educational and conservation efforts. The first true test of the Sierra Club's environmental clout came in 1906, when the Hetch Hetchy dam controversy began.

In April of that year, a devastating earthquake near San Francisco led to fires that killed more than three thousand people, destroyed 80 percent of the city, and demonstrated the limitations of the area's water system. City leaders began looking to the high country for water sources, and they soon landed on the Hetch Hetchy valley—located in Yosemite National Park—as the answer to their problems. If dammed properly, the millions of gallons of water from the Tuolumne River that flowed through the area daily could satisfy the city's water needs for at least the next one hundred years. The dam also would be part of a planned hydroelectric system that would generate power for the San Francisco area.

Muir and the Sierra Club, staunch defenders of environmental integrity, especially in Yosemite, protested. It wasn't just that Hetch Hetchy was part of Yosemite; it was that the valley—marked by cascading waterfalls and sheer granite cliffs—was seen by its supporters as a sacred, spiritual place that would only be desecrated by a dam.[16] Hetch Hetchy, Muir worried, could be but the first domino to fall when it came to government interference on national parks land, which is why the anti-dam movement could not waver. Environmentalists circulated petitions, wrote letters to government officials, and even testified before the Senate Committee on Public Lands. But proponents of the dam held fast, arguing not only that the valley was nothing special as far as Yosemite went, but also that the area would actually look better with the lake the dam would create. The battle dragged on for seven years until, in 1913, Congress passed the Raker Act, which permitted the construction of a dam to flood the valley. The first phase of construction was completed in 1923, when the valley was deluged with 117 billion gallons of water. It was a loss the Sierra Club vowed never to repeat.

Muir didn't live to see the Hetch Hetchy transformation—he died of pneumonia in 1914, at age seventy-six—but the passionate fight he led against the damming project did have a silver lining, as Muir predicted when he wrote of Hetch Hetchy: "The conscience of the whole country has been aroused from sleep; and from outrageous evil compensating good in some form must surely come."[17]

That compensating good came with the arrival of the Organic Act of 1916, passed just three years after Congress approved the Hetch Hetchy dam. Passed on August 25, 1916—in part due to the Sierra Club's request for federal action to safeguard the parks from future development—the act established the National Park Service. Sierra Club member Stephen Mather was appointed director of the new agency, whose mission was to conserve the parks' scenery, wildlife, and natural and historic objects.

With that victory won, the Sierra Club stepped up its activism efforts in the decades to come—including fighting proposals to build hydroelectric dams on Kings River in the Sierra Nevada, opposing a plan to construct a tunnel under Rocky Mountain National Park to divert water, and protesting the damming of lakes in Yellowstone and Echo Canyon. The organization had successfully stopped development on San Gorgonio in the 1940s, but by the early 1960s, the issue was back on the table. A new group of developers had begun putting pressure on the Forest Service about constructing a resort on a section of the San Gorgonio Wild Area before environmental legislation that was pending in Congress would make it impossible to build on the prime piece of land. Among the supporters of a deluxe skiing area so close to Palm Springs were crooner Bing Crosby and actor Bob Hope.[18]

Mineral King, however, was still fair game for skiing, and Harper and others in the Kern-Kaweah Chapter of the Sierra Club continued to hear Walt's name in conversations about development in the valley. But the man synonymous with castles and cartoons? They couldn't wrap their head around his involvement, imagining the gaudy Disneyfication that could plague the area if he were to build there. Mickey Mouse and Mineral King were akin to oil and water: they simply were two different consistencies that weren't meant to mix; instead they formed different layers, different ideas that would never blend.

On the pocket map of Kings Canyon and Sequoia national parks—the foldable kind one could pick up in any decent outdoors outfitters—the Mineral King area stood out like the thumb of a hitchhiking camper. It was a peninsula of progress in the otherwise undisturbed sea of Sequoia National Park—the Little Kern River flowing through it, passing by Florence Peak and Shotgun Pass. John Muir had helped establish the park boundaries when Sequoia National Park was established in 1890, leaving Mineral King out because of the mineral claims that were still active in much of the area, as well as the cabins and other buildings left over from the mining boom of the 1860s and 1870s. With mining operations long gone from the valley, Harper wondered—could Mineral King be annexed into the park now, or was it too late to save it from the Disney machine? The Sierra Club would soon crack Disney's "Retlaw" code and realize Bob Hicks's land purchases in and around Mineral King were on behalf of Disney, making the fight to save the area all the more urgent.

Determined to spur the club into action, Harper argued for the annexation of Mineral King into Sequoia National Park in the fourteen-page report he submitted to the southern section of the Sierra Club's conservation committee in February 1964. He also proposed that Mineral King be given the new designation of national forest "geological area" to protect it from commercial intrusion. For Harper it was a crusade, but for the Sierra Club at large, Mineral King was part of a larger chess game.

"Mineral King is a sensitive subject at this moment," southern section conservation committee chairman Bob Marshall wrote in response to Harper's report. The California-based Far West Ski Association, Marshall said, had felt let down by the Sierra Club's intrusion into development on San Gorgonio, and "there is some sentiment that we should not object to ski development at Mineral King because it is suitable, now has developments, and would relieve pressures on other areas not now developed."[19]

It seemed to Harper that it was just a matter of time until the Forest Service opened up the area to development. But to his surprise, it wasn't Walt or anyone else at Disney who finally convinced the agency to take that step—it was Robert Brandt, a well-connected Beverly Hills stockbroker who was interested in getting into the skiing business. An avid skier who had visited Mineral King dozens of times since he was a student at the University of California, Berkeley,[20] Brandt had spent $100,000 on his Mineral King study, which found the area ideal for year-round recreation and a prime candidate for a successful all-season resort.

One day Harper, who had continued to press Sierra Club leadership on the need to protect Mineral King from commercial interests, got a call from Edgar Wayburn, a Sierra Club director who would soon become president of the organization. Wayburn said he had been approached by a contact in the Forest Service, as well as by Brandt, about the possibility of the Sierra Club opposing development at Mineral King. Brandt was beginning to "get jittery," Wayburn told him, over rumors he had heard about the club challenging any plans for a ski area. Wayburn asked Harper to send him a list of reasons he thought Mineral King should not be developed as a winter resort.

The primary argument against the project, Harper replied, was that a ski area in Mineral King would have to be massive to make money: "It would be folly to assume that skiing facilities of the sort necessary to make profits for Mineral King promoters would be anything but the most modern, most automated, and most extensive."[21]

Despite the pleas of Harper and other Southern California residents who didn't want Mickey Mouse in their mountains, the Forest Service was ready to move ahead. The agency issued a prospectus for development at Mineral King on February 27, 1965, earlier than either the Sierra Club or the Disney company expected.

The prospectus called for ski lifts with a minimum capacity of two thousand people per hour; parking for 1,200 cars; a resort with overnight accommodations for at least one hundred people; and a plan for improving or rebuilding the access road to all-weather standards—at an estimated cost of at least $5 million. Bids were due on August 31, 1965; the winner would receive a three-year preliminary permit for planning purposes. Once the Forest Service had approved final plans, construction could begin.

Harper's recent missives to Sierra Club leadership on the Mineral King saga had gone largely unanswered, but once the Forest Service had issued the prospectus, he knew the club had no choice but to address the issue. He and Marshall were summoned to an emergency meeting of the executive committee of the club's board of directors on March 5 at Sierra Club president Will Siri's house near San Francisco. Siri and his wife, Jean, a fellow environmentalist, lived in the Oakland suburb of Richmond, California, fifteen minutes north of the University of California, Berkeley, where Siri worked as a biophysics researcher. Harper and Marshall met at Siri's house with executive committee members including Siri, Wayburn, Richard Leonard, and Lewis Clark, as well as club outings chairman Bob Golden and Michael McCloskey, a former Sierra Club field organizer in Oregon who recently had moved to California to become Siri's assistant.

The mood was glum. The club had been caught off guard by the Forest Service prospectus, and no one quite knew where to go from there. Wayburn brought with him a heavy photo album thick with pictures of Mineral King under a white blanket of snow. As members of the group idly flipped through the book's pages, they discussed the potential development. Everyone knew Harper was adamantly against it. To Harper's dismay, though, the leaders—after much discussion—agreed that for the time being, they needed to abide by the approval the club had given to development at Mineral King back in the late 1940s, after Brower's airplane survey of Southern California mountains. Harper, blindsided by their willingness to roll over for the Forest Service, walked out of Siri's house feeling disoriented and confused. Harper later recalled of the meeting: "I went away in a daze. A definite move to sell out the club's best interests had just been ordered."[22]

Harper knew the club would take a more permanent position on the matter at its upcoming board of directors meeting in May, but in the interim he was caught in the middle of the controversy. Still, he felt like he needed to keep fighting to save Mineral King. Later in March, Harper and his wife, Joan, joined two other Sierra Club members to meet with Sequoia National Forest supervisor Larry Whitfield and talk about the Sierra Club's concerns. Developers had been bugging him for years about development in Mineral King, Whitfield told the group, and he thought the time was right to get something going. It might be possible that the club could act as an "interested observer" once a preliminary permit was issued to the winning bidder, Whitfield said, serving as an environmental advisor of sorts as the development was planned.[23]

Weeks later, Harper watched helplessly as members of the Kern-Kaweah Chapter—of which he had become chairman in January—officially stated their support for skiing in Mineral King. The Southern Section Conservation Committee followed suit in early April. Mineral King, Harper thought, was being surrendered. Its days as his peaceful wilderness retreat were numbered.

But luckily for Harper and other Sierra Club members like him, the fight to protect Mineral King wasn't over. In fact, it was just beginning.

4

SPLIT DECISION

1965

The Empire Room at the elegant Sir Francis Drake Hotel in downtown San Francisco didn't often see this kind of drama. The thirty-seven-year-old hotel adjacent to Union Square was known for its European-style elegance, and the Empire Room—adorned with three crystal chandeliers and a series of hand-painted murals—was a popular venue for weddings and sedate corporate events.

But on this early May day in 1965, at the annual meeting of the Sierra Club's board of directors, the arguments were loud and boisterous—almost enough to rattle the vintage light fixtures.

The drama started late in the day, after the seventy-eight club members present—among them famed nature photographer Ansel Adams, sixty-three, who was then living on the Monterey peninsula near Carmel, and author Wallace Stegner, fifty-six, who would soon publish his Pulitzer Prize–winning novel *Angle of Repose*—already had discussed election of officers, the signatures required to deposit checks into the Sierra Club bank account, and the organization's position on pest control (the club, not surprisingly, was opposed to the use of any poisons that could harm plants or other animals).[1]

The next matter on the agenda was Mineral King, an area with which the club was already familiar thanks to now-executive director David Brower, who had viewed the Mineral King area by air back in 1947 and declared it fit for skiing. Now the Forest Service was taking the club at its word: it had issued a call for bids in February to companies interested in building a ski resort in the valley. The deadline for submissions was August 31.

An emergency meeting at Sierra Club president Will Siri's house two months prior had resulted in an interim decision to endorse the Mineral King development while attempting to have some amount of input on the plans, but now it was time for the Sierra Club to take an official position on the matter.

The room erupted. Sides were chosen. Many of the directors were opposed to the idea of a ski resort in one of the club's favorite hiking and camping spots, but some longtime Sierra Club members were worried about what it would look like for the organization to go back on its word. If they did so, would they ever be trusted again? The Forest Service, they argued, had issued its prospectus in large part because it was relying on the Sierra Club's blessing. Not to mention that many club members were skiers themselves and excited about the prospect of having such choice slopes so close to home. Development at Mineral King was inevitable, they said, so it would be wisest for the club to suggest limitations on the plan so it would do as little damage as possible.

But others were incensed. Why should the club be bound by a decision made nearly two decades ago? Yes, the club had given its blessing to the development of Mineral King, but that was for what members envisioned as a basic rope-tow system into one bowl and a simple overnight lodge—not the deluxe resort envisioned in the Forest Service prospectus, which would bring thousands of people into the valley each day.

The Sierra Club now contained a number of young activists in its ranks, and they were absolutely against a commercial ski area in the Mineral King valley, which they described as "an informal place in the midst of mountains and a jumping-off place for the wilderness about it."[2] Why had the Forest Service conducted no public hearings prior to issuing its prospectus? Something smelled fishy.

These young Sierra Club members had grown up with the horrific man vs. nature scenes of *Bambi*, had witnessed cars and factories spewing noxious fumes into the air, the pollution of the Great Lakes, and the devastation of nuclear bomb detonations. They found their rallying cries in the writings of Sierra Club founder John Muir and in Rachel Carson's *Silent Spring*, a hugely influential 1962 book about the adverse environmental effects of pesticides, DDT in particular. Carson, a marine biologist-turned-full-time nature writer, wrote about ocean life in the 1950s, but by the end of the decade had turned her attention to conservation. She began looking into pesticides in the late 1950s, when the U.S. Department of Agriculture started spraying DDT and other chemicals from airplanes in an effort to eradicate a nationwide fire ant infestation. She researched the effects of DDT on plants and animals—particularly birds—as well as what she said was the deliberate spread of misinformation by chemical companies.[3] *Silent Spring* helped lead to the creation of the Environmental Defense Fund and the Environmental Protection Agency and ultimately resulted, in 1972, in a ban on the use of DDT.[4]

The din in the Empire Room grew louder as members opposed to the Mineral King development pointed out—emphatically—that the road that would need to be constructed to accommodate the kind of traffic the Forest Service was talking about would seriously damage some eleven miles of Sequoia National Park, not to mention a number of giant sequoias that lined the current primitive road into the area.

Brower tried to keep the discussion on track and quiet the angry debate. All things considered, he was in favor of the development the Forest Service wanted to build in Mineral King. The club had offered the site as one of the best potential ski areas in Southern California, after all, and maybe it could count on the Forest Service to keep things modest.

Director Edgar Wayburn, fifty-eight—who had joined the Sierra Club in the 1930s, in part to ski at the organization's Clair Tappaan Lodge in Northern California[5]—introduced a motion: The Sierra Club would uphold its earlier decision that it supported development of a ski area in Mineral King, but it would "urge that every effort be taken by the Forest Service and the winter sports developer to assure close compliance" with a number of points, among them forbidding vehicular traffic on all trails; keeping subsidiary development, such as servicing and overnight accommodations, below eight thousand feet; forbidding commercial development not directly related to winter sports; and keeping all development as inconspicuous as possible, with no facilities visible from the ground outside the basin.[6]

The room erupted again. The Sierra Club needed to oppose the development completely, many members felt, as well as the road that would cut through Sequoia National Park to deliver visitors to the resort.

"I didn't know it was going to be in the national park," Adams said of the road to the proposed ski area.

Longtime club member and director Martin Litton could hold his tongue no longer. "Look at the map, dumbhead!" he shouted. He held up a map of the area and began to speak in righteous outrage at the "terrible thing" that was about to happen. Sequoia National Park was about to be ruined because the Sierra Club was too scared and stuck in its ways to reverse an outdated decision.[7]

"Do you realize that everything you're talking about, all the access to Mineral King, is going to cut Sequoia National Park right in two?" Litton demanded, pointing again at the map. "The access road will go right up that east fork of the Kaweah River, and nobody proposes anything different. If anything were proposed different, it would come from the south and cut the Golden Trout Wilderness right in two!"

Brower thought back to the 1947 plane ride and his first view of Mineral King from the air. The club had offered up Mineral King in large part to stop skiing on San Gorgonio, but it looked as if a resort on that mountain was now back on the table as well. He had thought skiing would work well at Mineral King, but he was envisioning a small area like the one he was used to at Badger Pass, not the large commercial development the Forest Service seemed to have in mind. He had heard that Walt Disney was in serious consideration for the development, and who knew what sort of gaudy monstrosity he was planning.

That's when Brower stunned everyone. "I want to take back everything I said. I agree with Martin."[8] Litton's words had persuaded him that though it was tempting to appear reasonable and find a middle ground, the Sierra Club could not compromise something that wasn't theirs to compromise.[9]

Inspired by Litton's passionate argument, as well as the opinions voiced by younger members of the club, some of the other directors who had voted for the earlier proposal changed their minds as well. The discussion took up the rest of the day Saturday and extended into a jam-packed Sunday agenda that was set to address everything from the Wilderness Conference of 1965 to the club's position on the underground detonation of nuclear weapons on the Amchitka island in Alaska.

When the dust finally settled, those opposed to a ski area in Mineral King had won the day. A final resolution was passed: "The Sierra Club opposes any recreational development in the Mineral King area as contemplated in the Forest Service 'Prospectus for a Proposed Recreational Development at Mineral King in Sequoia National Forest' dated February, 1965." The club would also ask the Forest Service again for a public hearing.

◦◦◦

In early June, with the Sierra Club's position on Mineral King firm at last, Siri instructed his new assistant, Michael McCloskey, to issue a press release outlining the resolution. Siri himself brought the word to Charles Connaughton, regional forester for the Forest Service, at the same time making the club's first formal request for a public hearing on the Mineral

King development. Connaughton's reply came a few weeks later: The Forest Service, he wrote, "cannot accede to your request for a hearing."[10] The agency had been working on Mineral King development since 1949, the forester said, and it had held a hearing in 1953, more than ten years earlier. McCloskey began work to appeal Connaughton's decision, but as far as the Forest Service was concerned, it was full speed ahead on Mineral King development plans, with bids due in less than two months.

Several weeks later, inspired by the May board of directors meeting that led to the Mineral King resolution, Sierra Club director Fred Eissler decided to reacquaint himself with the area, taking a nine-day family outing into Mineral King to remind himself what it was the Sierra Club loved so much about the area and to gather what information he could about the proposed resort. He spoke with Forest Service employees, cabin owners, packers, and others who had heard rumors about the development and its potential impacts. During his stay in Mineral King, Eissler was reminded of what a special place it was: "Where else in the Sierra does a primitive road reach to the headwaters of a major river?" he wrote in his report on the outing. "Where else does a road provide such direct access to so many alpine passes?"[11]

Though he determined that a ski resort would destroy the unique character of Mineral King and the area around it, calling the issue "one of the highest priority conservation problems faced by the club,"[12] Eissler also returned with encouraging news: while camping at Mineral King's Cold Springs Campground, he had met Bill Bergren, a Pasadena resident who spent much of his free time in the wilderness in and around Mineral King. Bergren was not a Sierra Club member, but his family had camped in the Mineral King area for many years. He had read the Forest Service prospectus for the ski resort, and like John Harper, he was adamantly opposed to the commercialization of an area he held dear as a scenic escape from hectic everyday life.

Bergren had spent the past few months writing more than twenty letters to public officials in Tulare County, Sacramento, and Washington, pressing for public hearings on development and requesting more information on proposed improvements to the access road. A well-known presence in the Mineral King campgrounds and in its general store and café, Bergren began talking to cabin owners about the Forest Service's plans. With the help of property owner Kenneth Savage Jr., Bergren organized the longtime cabin owners in Mineral King—some of whom lived or summered in cabins that had been in their families for decades—into the Mineral King District Association, an organization that shared the Sierra Club's goal of preventing further development in the valley. The cabin owners came from around California, and in some cases even farther, to Mineral King every summer to greet old friends, to go fishing, hiking, or picnicking in familiar surroundings during the day, playing kick-the-can or dressing up for evening dances in nearby Silver City after the sun went down. For these residents, Mineral King was a magical place they would do almost anything to save.

* * *

In Burbank, meanwhile, Walt and the Disney team spent the summer of 1965 reviewing the Forest Service prospectus carefully as they started to put their Mineral King bid together. Economist Buzz Price had been working the numbers for Walt, and his sixty-nine-page report included data on population and tourism growth, national forest and national park use, winter sports trends, required facilities, and more. Walt had creativity to spare, but he also was a businessman, and he liked to supplement his intuition with hard numbers. Price was his man when it came to data.

Price himself was a skier who, as a young boy obsessed with numbers, had tracked how many runs he had made at California's Mammoth Mountain (465) and kept track of how many times he played each of his treasured LPs.[13] Price graduated from the California Institute of Technology soon after the end of the Great Depression, then worked as a mechanical engineer for tools and equipment manufacturer Ingersoll Rand in New York before joining the Army. After his military service, Price moved with his wife to South America to work as a sales engineer, returning to the States after three years to attend the Stanford Graduate School of Business. Price then went to work at the Stanford Research Institute, where he enthusiastically entered the new field of economic consulting, and in 1953, he drew the assignment that would change his life—conducting site studies and economic planning for Walt Disney's new project that aimed to reinvent the amusement park.

"Walt, as he insisted on being called by all who worked for him, was about to create a park based on an unnamed new approach," Price remembered. "It would eventually be called a theme park, and it would feature a host of new, revolutionary ideas all at once."[14]

After conducting his successful location study for Disneyland, Price went into business for himself but stayed connected to Disney, putting together additional studies on the park's attractions, ticketing, and transportation. Price had overseen two researchers—including Bob Hicks—and investigated ski areas in California, Colorado, and Idaho to put together the

Mineral King report, which found that skiing was on the rise and ripe for disruption.

"The two decades since 1945 have seen a sharp increase in all forms of recreation activity in California,"[15] Price wrote in the report. That demand would only increase as the population grew. Household incomes were growing as well, and a much-hyped 1965 Senate subcommittee report predicted Americans would be working just fourteen hours a week by the year 2000, with an estimated seven weeks of vacation time per year. That added up to lots of leisure time that resorts like Mineral King could help to fill—and lots of money to be spent.

Although California residents would be the primary users of Mineral King, Price also noted the large number of out-of-state tourists who visited northern and southern California in the same trip, often passing the Mineral King site on their way from one region to the other. Couple that with the growing number of visits to national forests and the increasing amount of winter sports facilities being constructed on national forest land, and Walt's preferred site was primed for success—though Price predicted more visitors during the summers than in the winters. They would camp, hike, fish, play tennis, and swim, and the ski lifts could carry them to higher elevations for more exploration.

The sport of skiing had been growing steadily since the end of World War II, but so far no ski areas in California—including Mammoth Mountain and June Mountain—had achieved the popularity of destinations like the venerable Sun Valley in Idaho, or Colorado favorites Aspen, which had opened in 1946, or Vail, which opened in 1962. That was partly due to poor snow conditions, as well as a lack of summer activities, Price wrote. Mineral King could be the first California ski area to be considered among the country's best.

From the beginning, Walt's concept for Mineral King included lots of family-friendly activities beyond skiing, including ice skating, tobogganing, and sleigh and dogsled rides. Those activities, referred to as "snow play" by Price, were rare in the ski industry and would give the Disney resort an advantage when it came to attracting families and nonskiers. "Few areas in existence today consider the non-skiing family in their facilities design, advertising and promotion," Price wrote, estimating that snow play would account for nearly 50 percent of the visitor volume at Mineral King by 1976.

When Walt built Disneyland, he didn't have enough money left over to build a hotel as well. The only hotel on the property—the Disneyland Hotel, which opened about three months after Disneyland itself—was owned and managed by Jack Wrather, one of Walt's friends and business associates. The hotel had Disney in its name, but not its operations. Things would be different at Mineral King, however—the project would mark Disney's first foray into building and managing its own hotels. For Walt and the company, it would be yet another opportunity to ensure magic and immersion in the entire vacation experience.

Price's report detailed the year-round facilities he recommended at Mineral King, ranging from a "high-priced luxury hotel" with two hundred rooms to temporary units for summertime use—some of which would allow occupants to cook their own meals. In between were a modest hotel and a two-hundred-room dormitory where beds could be had for four dollars per person per night.

Since Mineral King would attract visitors from different income levels, it was important for the resort to offer a variety of food service facilities, from gourmet restaurants to cafeterias and more moderately priced eateries. For higher-income skiers, Price recommended a gourmet restaurant, accessible only by ski lift, on one of Mineral King's peaks, which would add to a total count of 2,600 restaurant and cafeteria seats by 1976. Average ticket price was estimated at $2.

Using Price's thorough report as their guide, Walt and his team worked on the Mineral King bid in secret throughout the summer of 1965, as speculation grew throughout Southern California about why a man named Robert B. Hicks was buying up acres of land in the valley, why a twenty-five-mile stretch of the twisting, torturous road into Mineral King was suddenly part of the state highway system, and which companies would be responding to the Forest Service prospectus when the deadline arrived on August 31.

If skiers in Southern California had high hopes for what a resort in Mineral King might look like, those hopes were boosted infinitely higher in August, when the news broke: Walt Disney Productions, the company behind the fantastic and wildly popular Disneyland in Anaheim, was going to apply to create a recreation destination in Mineral King. On August 18, the company's board of directors, at its regular quarterly meeting, had voted its full approval for moving forward with a development bid for the area. The company wanted Mineral King to be "a year-round recreational facility for everyone, regardless of age, income, leisure-time interests or athletic abilities," Walt said when announcing Disney's intention to throw its hat in the ring. The other priority for the Mineral King project, he said, "is the necessity to preserve the great natural beauty of the site. That is a must."[16]

The stage was set. Walt had not only conquered the worlds of animation, film, television, and amusement parks, but also redefined each venture, each industry as he went. Now he was ready for his next challenge—trying to get Walt Disney Productions into the ski business. And it would be one of the toughest mountains the company would ever climb.

5

A HOLLYWOOD BIDDING WAR

1965

The normally quiet town of Porterville, California—a mountainside village located some fifty miles north of Bakersfield—looked more like a movie set than a sleepy little town on this late August day in 1965. Porterville was known for its small-town charm, annual rodeo, and close proximity to Sequoia National Park. Save for one Hollywood moment in its history—Walt Disney Productions had filmed some of the family drama *So Dear to My Heart*, starring Burl Ives and Harry Carey, in Porterville in 1946, and the train depot the studio had built for the production inspired the Frontierland stop on the Disneyland Railroad—the town didn't experience a lot of glamour. And it certainly wasn't accustomed to celebrities arriving by private plane at the tiny Porterville Municipal Airport.

Today was different, though. Cameramen, reporters, and photographers jostled for position outside the airport while locals gathered in a crowd, holding signs and streamers and flags to welcome Walt Disney and his entourage to town. Porterville residents were used to seeing Walt on their television sets every Sunday night, introducing that week's movie, cartoon, documentary, or nature special on his weekly *Walt Disney's Wonderful World of Color* program, but to see Walt in person, stepping off the airplane, with his fatherly smile and trademark mustache, was like catching a glimpse of a movie star.

It was August 31, 1965, and Walt was among the bidders who had come to Porterville—site of Sequoia National Forest headquarters—to deliver their Mineral King proposals. When his Gulfstream private plane landed at the Porterville airport after its short flight from Burbank, Walt, clad in a suit and tie, walked down the airstair and was met by his friend Ray Buckman, a longtime Mineral King resident who had sold several acres of land in the area to Disney one year earlier and was advising the company on its Mineral King bid. Others from Disney's Mineral King team had accompanied Walt to Porterville, including Willy Schaeffler, public relations assistant Frank Allnutt, economist Buzz Price, and Bob Hicks, who had become project manager on the Mineral King endeavor after lobbying Walt for the role. As the men made their way to the Sequoia National Forest building, some clutching large artists' cases containing the maps and drawings of the Disney proposal, Walt stopped to meet the locals, shake their hands, and talk to them about his plans.

It was the first time the company had shared its ideas for Mineral King outside of the studio walls. Disney was so worried that its competitors would catch wind of its proposed plans that when Allnutt and Disney executive Robert Jackson had checked into a local motel on a previous visit to Sequoia National Forest headquarters in Porterville, they looked for telephone wiretaps and other hidden microphones that might be used to bug their room.[1]

Arriving in Porterville by another route was Robert Brandt, the stockbroker who had prevailed on the Forest Service earlier in 1965 to put the Mineral King area up for development bids. Brandt's entrance was, quite literally, even bigger than Walt's: he pulled into town towing a fifty-five-foot house trailer he had set up as a viewing area for his proposal. It included a large-format, three-dimensional model of the entire Mineral King valley as he envisioned it, complete with scale-model hotels and ski lifts. The trailer, however, wasn't the most attention-grabbing element of Brandt's entrance. That was the woman riding along with him: Brandt's wife, Hollywood starlet Janet Leigh. The *Psycho* actress, a native of the nearby California town of Merced, had become a household name in 1960 after her iconic shower scene in the Alfred Hitchcock flick horrified viewers and nabbed her an Academy Award nomination and a Golden Globe. She had found further fame in other films since, including the 1963 movie musical *Bye Bye Birdie* with Dick Van Dyke, who the next year sang and danced again, this time atop London's chimneys, in Walt Disney's megahit *Mary Poppins*. Ironically, Leigh had been discovered in 1946 at the Walt-funded Sugar Bowl ski resort, where her parents worked. A staff photographer had added a picture of Leigh to a photo album that was placed in the lobby for guests to peruse,

Stockbroker Robert Brandt with Hollywood starlet Janet Leigh on their wedding day in 1962 in Las Vegas. The couple bid against Walt Disney to develop Mineral King—and nearly won. Sands Hotel Photograph Collection, Special Collections and Archives, University Libraries, University of Nevada, Las Vegas.

and it was seen by actress Norma Shearer. Shearer took the photo with her back to Hollywood, and MGM soon contacted Leigh to sign a contract.

Leigh and the thirty-eight-year-old Brandt had made headlines three years earlier, when they wed the day after Leigh had divorced actor Tony

Curtis in an expedited proceeding in Juarez, Mexico. Brandt and Leigh had met at a tennis party hosted by crooner Dean Martin and his wife, Jeanne, where Brandt impressed the actress with his wavy, thick, black hair and movie-star good looks. Their wedding ceremony took place on the patio of the presidential suite at the Sands Hotel in Las Vegas, where the Martins were staying while Dean performed nightly shows in the theater downstairs. That evening, Dean brought Brandt and Leigh on stage to cut their multitiered wedding cake in front of an enthusiastic Vegas audience.

Walt and Brandt were the most high-profile respondents to the Forest Service prospectus for Mineral King, but others were in Porterville to deliver their bids as well, including Los Angeles architect Ragnar Qvale and his brother Kjell, the largest distributor of imported cars in the United States. The Qvale brothers' proposal for Mineral King called for the formation of an artificial lake in the valley, on its banks a deluxe hotel with a price tag of $1 million. Inside the Sequoia National Forest headquarters building, located just a half mile from the Porterville airport, Walt, Brandt, the Qvales, and the other bidders took turns presenting their visions for Mineral King to members of the Forest Service and a group of curious journalists. Walt's large-scale maps and colorful concept drawings, set up on wooden easels, showed the locations of ski runs—the most of any resort in the Western hemisphere—hotels, restaurants, tram stations, and more, and Walt talked proudly about how no cars would be allowed. Visitors would park at the entrance to the valley, he said, and travel to the resort in a new transportation system being developed by Disney engineers.

Outside the building, Brandt, dressed casually in a button-down shirt, open at the collar, invited the foresters and journalists into his trailer-turned-plush salon to view the concept drawings and scale models for his proposed Mineral King resort. They had been created by influential Southern California architect Harry Gesner, who had studied for a time under Frank Lloyd Wright, and his futuristic domes and peaks looked like something out of a Batman comic book. Brandt envisioned a Nordic-inspired theme for the resort, with Viking architecture, a fifteen-foot bronze statue that would welcome visitors at the valley's entrance, and a glass-walled restaurant at the top of White Chief Peak. Leigh stood nearby, dressed in faded jeans and sneakers, and told the reporters she had been skiing for about three years. "I can get down most any ski hill, although I'm not a bomber," she said, adding that her two daughters—Kelly and Jamie Lee Curtis, nine and six respectively—were pretty good on the slopes as well.[2]

Speaking with journalists after their presentations, Walt and Brandt each made the case for his version of a Mineral King ski area, Walt trying to quell fears that his proposed resort would be anything like the "mountainside Disneyland" environmentalists were fearing. "We will stay close to God in our development and try to complement the work He has done in this magnificent place,"[3] he said at the time, weeks later assuring another journalist that Mineral King would be "a recreation project, not an entertainment center. There will be no Hollywood flourishes. And the name Disney won't be a part of it. Of course, our company will run the operation. But it is strictly a natural theme based on the beauty of the country."[4]

At the end of the day, the Forest Service had received six bids to develop Mineral King for skiing—much more interest than it had expected—and the agency's staff had a lot of work to do to make sure they picked the right company for the job. It was the largest response the Forest Service had ever received to a prospectus, and a decision—based on the applicants' experience and reputation, as well as their detailed proposals—was promised within thirty days. Sequoia National Forest Supervisor Larry Whitfield was impressed by the bids—Walt's and Brandt's in particular—but he had to admit to being a little overwhelmed by the proposals that were brought to Porterville. Brandt was proposing a $15 million project; Disney's bid came in $20 million higher. Given that the prospectus the Forest Service had issued in February called for a $3 million outlay, Whitfield began to worry that the clear front-runners in the Mineral King ski resort battle might be too big for the valley. He knew the Sierra Club had similar concerns, and he invited Michael McCloskey, who had just been named the Sierra Club's first conservation director, and Kern-Kaweah Chapter chairman John Harper, head of the Sierra Club's Mineral King Committee, to Porterville for a private review of the proposals.

The two men spent the afternoon of September 3, 1965, poring over plans, maps, charts, photographs, models, and more, trying to envision how each concept would alter the character of their cherished valley.[5] They were still opposed to development, but they wanted to see for themselves exactly what the impact might be. Two of the submissions, they felt, were hardly worth considering, but Harper and McCloskey found some redeeming qualities in the plans submitted by the Qvale brothers and by Marcon Construction in Glendale. Disney's proposal far surpassed the others in terms of total capacity, but the two Sierra Club members didn't find it especially innovative. Brandt's, on the other hand, "seemed to render minimum impact and maximum architectural and aesthetic grace," Harper later wrote. "Brandt's designers fragmented the overnight accommodations into numerous small clusters of aesthetically pleasing units scattered through the woods on lower slopes and valley bottom. . . . In addition, their lift lines and ridgecrest facilities blended much more imperceptibly into the natural surroundings."[6] Harper and McCloskey gave their recommendations to Whitfield, but the decision as to who would develop Mineral King would ultimately be made on the other side of the country.

※ ※ ※

Regional Forester Charles Connaughton and his team were in charge of the final review of the Mineral King proposals from Connaughton's office in San Francisco, where the Forest Service staffers took their time looking over each proposal. Taking the same view of the submissions as Harper and McCloskey, the foresters soon eliminated four of the weaker bids, leaving only Disney's and Brandt's remaining. The two men continued to lobby for their selection—Walt invited Forest Service employees Slim Davis and Roy Feuchter to the Disney studios in Burbank, where a scale model of Walt's vision for the resort, its miniature peak-roofed buildings surrounded by fake snow and tiny evergreen trees, took up part of a soundstage. On October 24, 1965, Brandt brought his trailer to the Mineral King–adjacent town of Visalia to show locals his model and get them excited about his concept. He even brought along a stenographer, who took sixty-five letters in support of his project. But since media coverage of the Disney-Brandt battle over Mineral King was heating up, attracting the attention of California Governor Pat Brown and other politicians in California, and given that Brandt and Walt both had political connections that went all the way to Washington, news of the bidding war soon made its way over Connaughton's head. Orville Freeman, President Lyndon Johnson's secretary of agriculture and overseer of the U.S. Forest Service, reached out to Connaughton, suggesting that Freeman and his team review the two bids. The decision on the fate of the Mineral King ski resort would now be made in Washington.

※ ※ ※

Early in his career, Walt didn't seem to have much interest in politics. Campaigns and elections were part of the outside world from which colorful animated realms like Alice's topsy-turvy Wonderland and Peter Pan's fairy-filled Never Land were meant to be an escape. But a well-publicized 1941 animators strike at the Disney studio changed things. Instigated by the Screen Cartoonists Guild, a labor union for animators in Hollywood, the strike saw more than three hundred artists picket for nine weeks over unequal pay and benefits.[7] Following the thinking of the time that labor unions were of Communist origin, Walt—who six years later would testify before the House Un-American Activities Committee about union activity at his studios, as well as individuals he believed to be Communists—blamed the strike on Communist influence.[8] The whole ordeal spurred him to get more involved in the political realm. He joined the Hollywood Republican Committee, formed in 1939 by conservative actors Ginger Rogers, Robert Montgomery, and George Murphy, and he raised funds for the presidential campaigns of Dwight Eisenhower, Richard Nixon, and Barry Goldwater. When Murphy decided to run for the U.S. Senate in the early 1960s, Walt helped with his campaign, making generous donations, chairing a fundraising dinner, taking out full-page ads in California newspapers, and even loaning the campaign furniture for its headquarters.[9] Walt also was close with Governor Brown, as well as with Ronald Reagan, a former Hollywood actor who had gained popularity as a conservative figure after delivering a powerful speech during the Goldwater campaign in 1964 and who was now campaigning against Brown in the 1966 California gubernatorial election. In July 1955, back in his acting days, Reagan had been one of the cohosts of ABC's live TV coverage of Disneyland's grand opening. Though Walt had publicly supported Goldwater's campaign against Johnson (in a note to his daughter Diane, Walt likened it to "taking up the gun against the enemy"),[10] he had traveled to Washington in September 1964 for a ceremony in which Johnson conferred on him and twenty-nine other notable Americans the Presidential Medal of Freedom—the highest honor bestowed on civilians. Feeling mischievous, Walt reportedly hid a Goldwater pin under his lapel.[11]

Walt had an in with the Republicans, but Brandt's political connections extended even further—to the Oval Office. Brandt had made significant contributions to Johnson's 1964 presidential campaign, and Leigh had campaigned for LBJ as well as Governor Brown—who later asked her to serve on the California State Recreation Commission. Johnson appointed Leigh to the National Advisory Council for the Peace Corps, and in 1964 he asked her to be ambassador to Finland. (She turned the assignment down, as she had recently wed Brandt and wanted to spend time with her new family.)[12]

Connaughton thought Brandt might have the edge when it came to the Mineral King bid, given his ties to the highest office in the land (there were even rumors that the Kennedys were interested in investing in a Brandt-developed ski area at Mineral King),[13] but he was happy to move the whole mess out of California and put it in the hands of a higher authority.

"The plans that these two presented weren't done on the back of an envelope, so they weren't going to be turned down by just stating that one was better for the public than the other, based on opinion," Connaughton said later. "We made what analysis we could [in California], but in the final go-round there had to be a basic choice, a basic judgment of the prevailing factors. Freeman agreed to make the decision—he could see that he was going to have to make it eventually anyway."[14]

The move drew lots of speculation among Mineral King locals, many of whom assumed Disney had the project in the bag from the beginning because of its reputation and the success of Disneyland. But Walt's and Brandt's politics were well-known, and others assumed that the Johnson administration, as a November 1965 editorial in the *Tulare Advance-Register* put it, "wasn't about to hand such a plum" to a political adversary like Walt.

The newspaper had been in favor of Disney getting the bid all along, both because of the quality of entertainment for which the company was known and the publicity the Disney name was sure to bring to the Mineral King development, but both proposals were outstanding, the editorial said, and "whichever of the two final contenders—Disney or Brandt—wins the lease, Mineral King will get a more than satisfactory treatment and will become one of the real winter sports meccas of the West."[15]

But not everyone involved in the Mineral King situation was as enthusiastic about Freeman's involvement and what a D.C. endorsement would mean to the area's development. McCloskey took the opportunity to remind the secretary of agriculture that the club's demands for a public hearing on the matter had yet to be satisfied. In a telegram to Freeman on November 3, McCloskey wrote that the decision to go ahead with the evaluation of Brandt's and Disney's bids "raises disquieting questions about the Department's policies of providing for public participation in the decision making process. . . . (A)dministration proposals for the area have been withheld from the broad public until lines of commitments were already undertaken. These commitments are still not irrevocable. The public has a right to know and express itself before such critical decisions are made. If hearings are not held on questions as momentous as the future of Mineral King, then there is little hope that they will be held on other questions too."[16]

Secretary Freeman didn't bother with a reply to McCloskey's message, but he did welcome Walt and his brother Roy—along with Hicks, Price, Schaeffler, and Disney executives Donn Tatum and Card Walker—to Washington in early November to present their Mineral King proposal to a three-man panel that had been hand-picked by Freeman. Walt began by talking about his interest in Mineral King and his experience with winter sports, including his multiple roles at the 1960 Winter Olympics and his help in financing the Sugar Bowl resort. During the second part of the two-and-a-half-hour, closed-door meeting, the panel fired off detailed questions about Disney's proposal—its budget and financing, how the company planned to carry out its plans, scheduling details, and Disney's envisioned minimum and maximum capacities. When Walt didn't know the answer to a question, he tapped Hicks's right thigh under the table as a cue for him to answer. If Hicks didn't know, he tapped Price's thigh. The system worked brilliantly.[17]

Brandt brought his plans and scale models to D.C. just days later, presenting to the panel his vision for a resort he said was better than Disney's in several ways—most notably that it would be sited in an area his studies had shown to be avalanche-free. Although Disney's planned resort was just a quarter mile away from the site Brandt had chosen, his research had shown that avalanches had been known to occur there. Brandt brought his avalanche expert along to confirm the findings.[18]

Once both companies had presented their Mineral King plans in Washington, the panel began to evaluate the submissions on four criteria: the ability of the proposed development to meet the public need; proof that the applicant had sufficient financial resources to take on the project; verification of the applicant's ability to provide public services in an "efficient and satisfactory manner"; and the fee the winning bidder would pay the Forest Service based upon percentage of receipts. Brandt offered the government 5 percent of total receipts; while Disney offered a sliding scale between 3 percent and 8 percent on ski-lift income, and 2.5 percent of all other receipts.[19]

* * *

Walt and other Disney executives waited while Freeman and his team made their final deliberations on Mineral King, but in the meantime, they had plenty to keep them busy. The company was ready to make its biggest reveal since Disneyland had opened ten years earlier: Disney was planning a new theme park on the other side of the country—one that would be much, much bigger than its West Coast predecessor. On November 15, 1965, Walt appeared at the Egyptian Room in the Cherry Plaza Hotel in Orlando, Florida, to announce that the company had purchased twenty-seven thousand acres of land for its next endeavor. Tipped off to Walt's last-minute arrival, Orlando reporters staked out the hotel the night before, waiting up late to catch a glimpse of the famous entertainer. But Walt and his entourage, which included his brother Roy, were staying under fake names at a motor lodge up the street.[20] The team toured the proposed park site by air the morning before the press conference, and the following day they climbed into a fleet of Land Rovers to more closely examine the area.[21]

Walt had been thinking about a second park ever since Disneyland had become a smash hit practically from its opening day. He had offers from Niagara Falls, Kansas City, Monterey, California, and the new Brazilian capital, Brasilia, and in 1958 Walt asked Price to conduct a feasibility study for a marshland area off the New Jersey Turnpike.[22] That idea went nowhere, but another proposed location in downtown St. Louis—which would have included a New Orleans–style French district, a haunted house, an Audubon bird room, a walkable pirate ship, and a Davy Crockett cave— got as far as the planning stages before falling apart. Walt turned again to Price, whose recent economic research on Disneyland had yielded some interesting information: Disneyland, while extremely popular in Southern California, was relatively unknown to Americans in the East. Just 5 percent of Disneyland visitors came from east of the Mississippi River, Price found, though 75 percent of the U.S. population lived in the eastern part of the country. Factor in the balmy weather and plentiful sunshine needed to run a year-round enterprise, and Florida seemed like the perfect spot for Disney's second theme park.

Again using dummy buyers—Disney-owned companies including Bay Lake Properties and the "Ayefour Corporation," punnily named after nearby Interstate 4—Disney began buying up tracts of swampland near Orlando and Ocala in 1964. Eventually, *Orlando Sentinel* reporter Emily Bavar caught on to the subterfuge, and on a press trip to Disneyland in October 1965, she asked Walt point-blank if Disney was the unknown entity buying up huge parcels of land in Central Florida. Walt "looked like I had thrown a bucket of water in his face" before denying the rumor, Bavar later recalled,[23] and after the *Sentinel* printed a story on October 24, 1965, with the headline "We Say: 'Mystery' Industry Is Disney," the November 15 reveal was hastily planned. Walt appeared with Florida governor Haydon Burns in two separate presentations—one a luncheon for business leaders and legislators, the other an afternoon press conference that drew some five hundred reporters and photographers—to announce the impending arrival of a second Disney park in Florida: a $100 million "fantasy attraction with the same basic tourist-family appeal as Disneyland," as the *Tampa Bay Times* put it.[24]

"We've still got a lot of work to do before we can even begin to think about starting construction," Walt told the reporters. "You just can't go out and build a whole new world of entertainment without a lot of studies and before our people solve a lot of problems."[25] The new park would take eighteen months to plan and another year and a half to implement, Walt said, anticipating an opening day in early 1969.

Walt's plans for the Florida Project were grander than just another collection of rides and attractions. Long interested in city planning, Walt wanted to use some of the vast acreage the company had purchased in the Southeast to build his vision of a self-contained city featuring futuristic technology. Called the Experimental Prototype Community of Tomorrow, or EPCOT, the city would feature houses run by their own power plants. Deliveries and trash collection would be made via a system of tubes that ran underground, and—as he envisioned in Mineral King—the streets would have no cars. Modern public transportation would take residents where they needed to go.

"I would get stagnant if I didn't do new things," Walt had told his wife, Lillian, in 1963, when she expressed doubts about his Florida plans,[26] and at the end of 1965, his chances of stagnation were virtually nil. The Florida Project was already in the early planning stages, Walt Disney Productions had just given the California Institute of the Arts—a private arts college Walt had helped to found in 1961, when he oversaw the merger of two longtime Los Angeles arts organizations, the Chouinard Art Institute and the Los Angeles Conservatory of Music—thirty-eight acres of its backlot to build a new campus, and on December 17, it became official: Disney was entering snow business. Walt was elated to receive the long-awaited news that Disney had been selected as the company that would turn Mineral King, California, into one of the country's premier ski destinations. To an entertainment empire that had transformed animation, reinvented the amusement park, and helped to form the landscape of television, Walt could now add outdoor recreation as another American amusement to be enhanced by Disney magic.

"After extensive analysis of the proposals I find that Disney offers the best facilities for the vacationing public and the possibility of the largest monetary return to the taxpayers for the use of public lands,"[27] Freeman said, adding that he also selected Disney because of its ability to finance the development, as well as the company's proven experience in serving the public at Disneyland. Disney was to be awarded a three-year planning permit to conduct research and finalize its plans; once its final master plan was accepted, Disney would receive a thirty-year term permit to construct its resort on the national forest land.

Disney issued a press release the following day: "We are all very grateful for the confidence the secretary of agriculture, Orville Freeman, his associates, and the Forest Service have shown in us and our plan for the

"When I first saw Mineral King five years ago," Walt Disney said in 1965, "I thought it was one of the most beautiful spots I had ever seen." National Park Service.

development of Mineral King," it quoted Walt as saying. "It is a challenge and responsibility that we enthusiastically accept."[28]

Walt said the company and its consultants planned to meet soon with Forest Service officials to finalize details of the plan, noting that no construction could begin before "definite commitments" had been made to construct the all-weather road leading to the new resort. The facility would include fourteen ski lifts, several of which would run in summer and winter alike; parking facilities at the valley's entrance; a high-capacity transportation system for moving people from the parking area to the valley proper; and a self-contained village to include an ice-skating rink, a chapel, restaurants, shops, a variety of lodging options, a ski school, conference center, fire station, and heliport. The resort would add more than $600 million to California's economy during its first ten years of operation.

Mineral King was a brand-new challenge that would stretch the company in ways it had never been stretched before. It would require new types of design, new ways of thinking, a new team of experts, planning for all types of weather, and a focus on comfort and safety that would make it unlike any project Disney had ever tackled.

Walt couldn't wait to get started.

6

BEAR NECESSITIES

1966

Hunched over his desk, gazing intently, Marc Davis allowed himself a smile as he pressed his pencil to paper and put the finishing touches on his drawing of a tuba-playing, chubby brown bear, one of the members of the all-bear band he had been tasked to create for Mineral King. The bear, blowing into the brass instrument that was nearly twice his size, was one of dozens of musical bears Davis, the then fifty-three-year-old Imagineer, had drawn for Walt, always a perfectionist who demanded options. Davis drew Dixieland bears, a bear marching band, a jazz band, a one-bear band, a country band, a mariachi band of bears—all of them fun and painstakingly detailed, per Davis's usual style—hoping to meet Walt's exacting specifications. Walt didn't have to say much; he simply arched his eyebrow to say it wasn't right.

But as Davis detailed the animal's soulful expression, he wondered if this iteration would stay. He wanted to hit on the perfect kind of bears to entertain guests at Mineral King and bring a Disney-style level of entertainment that would set the resort apart from others. It was 1966, and the planning of Disney's Mineral King was officially underway.

Although Walt was convinced the bulk of the appeal of Mineral King would be environmental—the lush trees, the mountain views, the animal watching, the nature talks, the snow-capped slopes that would glide skiers along—he also thought some type of entertainment would help to distinguish the resort. After all, spectacle was an area Walt was known for, especially with Disneyland thriving as it went into its eleventh year. Although Walt had repeatedly said Mineral King wouldn't be another Disneyland—no Matterhorn or Mickey Mouse—he wondered: If guests weren't interested in skiing, would they be interested in Mineral King? What would entertain the kids? What would make them laugh?

Buzz Price's 1965 feasibility report on Mineral King had an interesting finding that fueled Walt's thinking: "One of the most critical deficiencies of ski areas and summer resorts alike," Price wrote, "is a lack of evening activities appealing to the various visitor segments. Although the ski area normally has its night club and beer hall activities, these may not appeal to family groups"—the exact audience Walt was looking to target. "Similarly," Price wrote, "after-dinner activities in summer are seldom found at resorts." Walt's intent at Mineral King, Price wrote, is "that a sufficient number and variety of evening activities will be available to provide participation potential for all ages and tastes." It would take careful research and evaluation, Price said, "to ensure an attractive program compatible with the concept and setting of Mineral King."[1]

Walt knew the resort needed a bit of pizazz and magic—and fun—the same way he felt the Olympics had needed the extra spectacle that won the world over when he reimagined the opening and closing ceremonies in 1960. Simply put, guests needed entertainment and they needed to laugh, especially in the evening, when the mountaintops could only be seen by the faint glow of a sky full of stars.

With Price's advice in mind, Walt came up with the idea of a show hosted by bears who would sing and perform for guests. They would say the bears came out of the sequoias and were trained to be entertainers. Silly, sure. But it was a concept that would fit with the mountain surroundings of Mineral King. Yes, bears would work, Walt thought. And he knew exactly whom he would task with creating them.

❖ ❖ ❖

Davis, born in 1913 in Bakersfield, California, was one of Disney's "Nine Old Men"—the group of essential animators hired at the studio in the 1920s and 1930s who formed the young art of animation and gave life to Disney's early feature films. For Davis, it was the culmination of a lifetime love of art. He started drawing as a child, first as an avenue to ward off schoolyard bullies. His family moved around a lot in search of better employment opportunities, and as a result, Davis went to dozens of schools as a child. As the new kid, Davis was often the target of bullying boys; to escape the torture, Davis found solace in doodling. Not only did his drawings preoccupy his mind; they also preoccupied the bullies: everyone wanted one of his sketches. The more he drew, the less likely he was to become a victim.

Davis didn't stop drawing as a young boy—he embraced it with intent as he grew. After graduating from high school, he began taking classes at the Kansas City Art Institute, later enrolling at San Francisco's California School of Fine Arts and the Otis Art Institute in Los Angeles. He would spend hours at the zoo teaching himself to draw animals, which became one of his signatures. Davis got by in his early career creating artwork—posters, signs, advertisements, and other pieces—for a newspaper in Marysville, California, near Sacramento. In 1935, he found unexpected inspiration when he saw the Disney cartoon *Who Killed Cock Robin?*, a Silly Symphonies animated short in which a judge and jury of birds try to determine who committed the titular crime. It wasn't the first time Davis had seen a Disney cartoon—he had fond memories of *Three Little Pigs*—but *Who Killed Cock Robin?* had him mesmerized. Davis returned to the theater to see the short three more times, each time examining how the characters jumped off the screen, their comedy as they moved, the vibrant colors, the songs that synced with the characters in perfect rhythm. It was at that moment that he had a new career goal.

Later that year, Davis came to Los Angeles to try to break into animation. With Disney at the top of his list, he sent a letter to the studio only to get a confusing reply that read: "Dear Miss Davis, Sorry, at the present time we are not hiring women artists."[2] Dejected, Davis threw the letter in the trash and began working his contacts in an effort to find potential gigs in the motion picture industry. But his fellow artists kept telling him that Disney was hiring, and that Davis seemed like a perfect fit for the budding studio. So he tried once more, and this time had success. He joined the Walt Disney studio in December 1935, beginning as an apprentice animator on *Snow White*.

After *Snow White*, Davis caught Walt's eye with his sparkling designs and attention to detail, and he was assigned the important tasks of animating some of Disney's most identifiable characters: Mr. Toad and the *Wind in the Willows* gang in *The Adventures of Ichabod and Mr. Toad*, Cinderella, Alice from *Alice in Wonderland*, *Peter Pan*'s Tinker Bell, Aurora and Maleficent from *Sleeping Beauty*, and *One Hundred and One Dalmatians* villainess Cruella de Vil.

Animation was the company's bread and butter for years, but animation took a backseat in the mid-1950s, when Roy Disney tried to persuade Walt to abandon animation and shift his focus to Disneyland, live-action movies, and WED Enterprises, the company's design and development arm. The shift didn't spell the end for Davis; it gave him another opportunity to shine. Davis was transferred to WED in 1962, and he brought his spirit and animation know-how to bigger plans for the Disney company, starting off by reevaluating Disneyland at Walt's request.

Essentially, Davis was able to do anything, and Walt trusted him immensely. Walt said of him, "Marc can do story, he can do character, he can animate, he can design shows for me. All I have to do is tell him what I want and it's there. He's my Renaissance man."[3]

Davis's biggest assets, perhaps, were his candor and sense of humor—traits he exhibited even to Walt, whom many Disney employees saw as demanding and intimidating. Davis provided an honest voice at Disney's growing experiential entertainment empire. A few years after Disneyland opened, Walt began to worry about keeping the park fresh and entertaining for visitors. About the Jungle Cruise, he overheard one guest say, "Oh, we've been on that. We don't need to go again," and he turned to Davis for ideas on how to get the park experience out of a slump.

When Walt asked Davis to survey the park and suggest what could be done differently, Davis was frank—he told Walt the park lacked originality and humor, comparing it to just another world's fair. He suggested adding some humor to several of the attractions, including Frontierland's Mine Train Through Nature's Wonderland and Adventureland's Jungle Cruise.

Davis's candor swayed Walt, but it didn't make Davis many friends at WED. His harsh feedback and dissections of the park's attractions made the Imagineers angry and resentful. Not only did Davis rip their creations apart, pointing out flaws in each one, but Walt celebrated him for it. Walt's preference for Davis's designs created hostility—one WED executive walked by Davis's desk while he was drawing and asked, condescendingly, "And what are you doing with your little pencil now?"[4]

But it was Davis who got the last laugh. Per his suggestions for a reimagined Jungle Cruise, the attraction was updated in 1964. A completely different version than the original, which was themed more seriously after the True-Life Adventures nature film series, it now incorporated puns and jokes ("This formation on the right is actually sandstone; most people take it for granite").[5] Many Imagineers sniffed at the idea of humor being brought in. It even made Walt nervous to change an attraction that had been based on his educational wildlife films. But the joke ended up being on the naysayers. The reimagined Jungle Cruise was a hit.

Davis would surely bring the same entertainment value to Mineral King. And, of course, comic relief. The bears he was designing would embrace the same kind of humor as the Jungle Cruise, and they would perform for visitors as well. And, Walt believed, they would keep guests coming back.

The musical bears attraction, too, Walt decided, would utilize a new technology the company had begun pursuing with gusto over the past few years: Audio-Animatronics. Walt became obsessed with the technology—a form of robotic animation—when he discovered an antique mechanical singing bird in a shop in New Orleans while on vacation in the late 1950s. He was intrigued by the machine and its simplicity, but he immediately began thinking of ways to make it even more lifelike. Walt asked a group of Imagineers to take the bird apart to see how it worked—and then figure out how to make it better.[6] The first attraction using the new technology, fittingly, also featured birds: The Enchanted Tiki Room, which opened at Disneyland in 1963, featured tropical birds and other creatures whose eye, mouth, and body motions were perfectly synchronized to a musical score. It was an impressive feat that delighted audiences. But the technology was perfected further when Imagineers turned their attention to one of the most celebrated figures in American history—and Walt's own boyhood hero—Abraham Lincoln. It took the designers a year just to perfect Lincoln's head, then they had to program the body for dozens of different movements. The Imagineers devised a way of recording voices and music onto electronic tape, then used the tape to trigger movement from the Audio-Animatronic Abe.

Walt was planning to use the Lincoln figure for a "Hall of Presidents" attraction he was envisioning for a new part of Disneyland called Liberty Street, but the technology would debut in front of an altogether different audience.

✿ ✿ ✿

When the city of New York hit on the idea of holding a world's fair in 1964 and 1965 to celebrate its 300th anniversary,[7] event president Robert Moses—a former New York City parks commissioner and planning commissioner known as the city's "master builder" due to his role in the construction of much of its highway infrastructure and parks system[8]— approached Walt early on to see if he would be interested in playing a role in the event. Early rumors said Disney would be in charge of all the entertainment at the fair—and even that the fair site would eventually become the "East Coast Disneyland." Though Walt ended up playing a smaller role in the 1964 world's fair, it was one that would have a big impact on the Disney company.

Seeing the event as a chance to get his ideas and technology in front of an East Coast audience that didn't have easy access to Anaheim—as leisure air travel was less common and more expensive in the 1950s and 1960s, Disneyland's attendees were primarily from the West Coast— Walt approached several companies in 1960 about using WED to design their exhibits. His pitch was simple: "Look what I've done at Disneyland." General Motors turned him down, but three companies—Pepsi-Cola, General Electric, and the Ford Motor Company—took Walt up on the offer.[9] Not only was it his introduction to an East Coast audience; it also was a clever way to use someone else's money to further develop Audio-Animatronic technology—and to create new attractions to bring back to Disneyland.

"Walt really didn't hold much with world's fairs," remembered Jimmy Johnson, a longtime Disney staffer who at the time was head of the Walt Disney Music Company and Disneyland Records. "He felt they were terribly wasteful of creativity, energy, and money. To build all these multi-million-dollar pavilions and shows for just a one- or two-year run was anathema to him, so he instructed his people to write the contracts very carefully, providing that the attractions would become his property when the fair was over."[10]

When Moses visited WED in 1962 to check on the progress of the attractions the company was designing for the fair, he was immediately struck by the prototype of Lincoln. He asked Walt to speed up development in time for the event, and the state of Illinois agreed to act as sponsor. The exhibit began with a short feature on the Prairie State, followed by the main event: the Audio-Animatronic Lincoln delivering an oration that included excerpts from multiple speeches that had been given by the sixteenth president. It was a sensation, and it ran for the entirety of the fair.

For Pepsi-Cola and its salute to UNICEF, Disney created It's a Small World, in which visitors took a boat ride through different countries around the world while a host of Audio-Animatronic children in native garb sang the infectious song written by Richard and Robert Sherman. Disney's songwriting siblings also penned "There's a Great Big Beautiful Tomorrow" for the Carousel of Progress, an exhibit for General Electric that took audiences through the history of electricity in the home. (Housed in a unique rotating theater, the attraction was updated in 1967 for its move to Disneyland.) For the Ford Motor Company, Walt and his Imagineers created the Ford Magic Skyway, a ride that featured motorless, convertible Ford vehicles (including the brand new Ford Mustang) that glided fairgoers on a journey through time, starting in a world of life-sized, Audio-Animatronic dinosaurs and cavemen and ending in "Space City," a vivid vision of the future. Walt provided a portion of the narration.

Thanks in part to the Audio-Animatronic technology, Disney's attractions were some of the most popular at the fair, which ran in two six-month seasons over the course of two years—April to October 1964 and 1965—and welcomed more than fifty-one million visitors to Flushing Meadows in Queens.

"The world's fair was really a big lesson, a big proving ground in many ways for us," Imagineer Marty Sklar remembered. "The main thing that we learned from the world's fair was that the audience was there for Disney-style entertainment. Out of the five most-visited shows, we had four of them."[11] For Walt, it was more proof that the appetite was there for both the Florida Project and Mineral King.

* * *

The Audio-Animatronic bear band show was just one aspect of the Mineral King planning that had begun under Walt and other Disney leadership in 1966. Davis was working on the musical attraction at WED Enterprises in Glendale, three miles east of the Disney studios on South Buena Vista Street, but other Disney employees were going much farther from home for their inspiration for the resort. Walt sent several executives to the Swiss skiing village of Zermatt, which Walt wanted to use as a model for Mineral King.

Having visited Switzerland years before for various ski trips, Walt returned to the city in 1958 for the filming of *Third Man on the Mountain* (released the following year), a Disney family adventure film about a young Swiss man who conquers the mountain where his father died. Based on a 1954 novel by James Ramsey Ullman called *Banner in the Sky*, the movie starred James MacArthur—who went on to play Fritz Robinson in Disney's 1960 adventure feature *Swiss Family Robinson*—as the young climber out to find the secret path to the top his father was rumored to have discovered.

During filming, Walt became fascinated with the 14,692-foot Matterhorn, the mountain that towered over Zermatt. One of the most famous peaks in the world, the Matterhorn—which juts into the Swiss skies like a giant fang—had drawn climbers and explorers for decades. After first witnessing it, Walt sent a postcard to Disney art director Vic Greene. On the front was a photo of the Matterhorn, and on the back, a note from Walt that read: "Build this."[12] As usual, the Imagineers complied. Disneyland's Matterhorn Bobsleds, a steel roller coaster inspired by the alpine geography, opened in June 1959, five months prior to the release of *Third Man*.

But it wasn't just the towering peak that inspired Walt; he was enthralled with Zermatt, a quintessential European ski town that sat at the base of the Matterhorn in a narrow valley. The quaint village was surrounded by awe-inspiring, snow-capped mountains, in a scene that looked like something out of one of Walt's fairy tales. The area was a magnet for skiers and visitors, but it wasn't the kind of tourist trap that Walt hated—instead, its streets were clean and uncrowded. No cars were allowed, adding to the village's timeless feel. The area attracted families who rode gondolas in the winter and hiked along alpine trails in the summer. Streets were lined with picturesque chalets and shops. When the Disney executives Walt had sent to Zermatt set eyes on the town, they finally saw Walt's vision of what Mineral King could be: skiers swooping down from the peaks, families strolling through a scenic shopping district. The team—which included Bob Hicks, Willy Schaeffler, and Walt's daughter Diane and her husband, Ron Miller—visited other ski town destinations across Europe, as well as resorts in the United States, to study how other companies handled the transportation, safety, and environmental aspects of their businesses.

Traveling to other ski resorts for inspiration was far from the only Mineral King planning underway in 1966. Doing what he could at the start of the three-year period before his final master plan would be due to the Forest Service, Walt in early February sent a two-man snow survey team into Mineral King to begin accumulating data on snowfall, day and nighttime temperatures, winds, avalanche potential, and snow safety. Reporting to Schaeffler, young skiers and snow scientists Gary Poulson and Willy Stark spent two days hauling equipment into the snow-packed Mineral King village, which had been recently battered by storms. After taking a helicopter tour of the entire valley to get the lay of the land, the two set to work establishing testing and measuring stations and plotting out preliminary ski runs.[13] With two cabins and a dining hall as their base of operations, Poulson and Stark woke early each day to climb into the high bowls surrounding the valley, measuring snow depth and water content before skiing their way back down.

The Forest Service sent some of its experts to Mineral King as well, to work alongside Disney to conduct assessments of the area. They conducted lift-line, ski-run, and snow-depth surveys in the valley before the snow melted for the season and conducted a soil study in the area, warning of the potential for erosion and landslides if construction was not carried out with care.[14]

To further ensure his planning was up to snuff, Walt gathered additional experts at Mineral King and the company's planning headquarters in Burbank, including geologists, hydrologists, soil scientists, ecologists, winter-sports planners, water rights specialists, flood control, construction and sanitation engineers, foresters and resort operators, and architects and landscape architects.

Walt, Schaeffler, Hicks, and other executives were not just planning their recreation dream; they were also in the throes of a large PR blitz to promote Mineral King, looking in part to counter economic and environmental concerns that were cropping up around the project. Disney's marketing team put together an eight-page brochure, *The Disney Plans for Mineral King*, that quoted Walt:

> We believe that Mineral King should be much more than the best place to spend a vacation or holiday. We want it to be an *experience* with the outdoors for those who love nature—or who want to learn to love it. . . . Our plan for the area is being guided by one other very important consideration: Mineral King's great natural beauty must be preserved at all costs. . . . With its development, we will prove once again that man and nature can work together to the benefit of both.

The brochure went on to tout Mineral King's natural splendor ("perhaps more similar to the European Alps than any other area in the United States"), its lengthy snow periods, and the fact that it eventually would be home to some of the longest ski runs in North America—some more than four-and-a-half miles long. In addition to its Swiss chalet-style architecture, the booklet said, the year-round recreation development would include hotels and lodges, "oriented to views of mountain gaps, river gorges, ski slopes, and sports activities"; ten restaurants; and a snow play area where "several hundred people may engage in their favorite snow activities— tobogganing, sled rides, and fun with specially designed equipment."

The Disney Plans for Mineral King also referenced the January 1969 deadline for a contract for construction of the twenty-mile, all-weather road into the area, and behind the scenes, Disney staffers were keeping a close eye on legislative action around the proposed highway. Robert Brandt had gotten the ball rolling the previous year, when he convinced the state legislature to put the road into the valley under state jurisdiction, and Governor Pat Brown was working on securing federal funds for part of the construction. So confident was the Disney team that the state would move ahead with the road that in June, Walt, Hicks, and Schaeffler held a press conference at Disney studios in Burbank to give an update on the project's progress. Walt let Schaeffler and Hicks take the lead as curious reporters crowded into a meeting room where Disney staffers had placed a large photo of the valley and its surrounding peaks, with proposed ski runs outlined in white. When fully operational, the resort would have room for twenty thousand skiers at one time and be able to accommodate 2.5 million people annually.

Disney crews would soon begin setting up a "summer camp" at the Mineral King site, Hicks said, from which workers would begin conducting experimental earth-moving projects and setting up special fencing to control avalanche conditions.

"What avalanche activity exists in Mineral King will be as easy to control and live with as that found in the European Alps,"[15] Schaeffler told the journalists, who also were treated to a short film on the project.

Though Mineral King would have the timeless feel of a European ski village, its transportation system would utilize a futuristic technology simultaneously being designed for use in Disneyland; one that felt like an attraction all on its own: "WEDway," a new mass transit system based on the Ford Magic Skyway attraction WED had created for the 1964–1965 New York World's Fair. (The concept would later become the PeopleMover, a popular attraction that gave guests a "grand circle tour" of Disneyland's Tomorrowland between 1967 and 1995. In 1975 it opened as the ever-moving snake of blue cars circling above Tomorrowland in Walt Disney World's Magic Kingdom; the system is still in existence today.)

Passengers boarded via a circular moving platform that matched the speed of a series of cars traveling on its outer rim. They could step into the cars, which were constantly in motion, without the system needing to be stopped and started like a traditional train. The cars were not powered by internal motors but were pushed along by powered rotating tires that were embedded in the track every several feet. Walt excitedly ushered the journalists into the moving cars for a demonstration of the new technology. Like the cog railway into the Mineral King valley, WEDway would be an experience unto itself—another touch of Disney magic that would set Mineral King apart from other ski resorts.

"We could build the towers as high as necessary to match the terrain and snow conditions," Schaeffler said, pointing out that the transportation moved on an elevated track. "The cars and structures can be blended into the terrain so they won't be ugly."[16]

✻ ✻ ✻

The Mineral King planning was happening amid a largely fruitful half-decade for the Disney company—part of a 1960s resurgence after the company had closed out the 1950s on the ropes, both financially and in regard to employee morale, due to the financial failure of the 1959 animated movie *Sleeping Beauty*. Disney spent nearly a decade and $6 million on *Sleeping Beauty*—the last Disney animated film to feature a princess, or even a female lead character, until 1989's *The Little Mermaid*. *Sleeping Beauty* was visually stunning, but it lacked humor, character depth, and story development—mostly because it lacked Walt Disney. "Walt lost touch with the project and also seemed to resent spending time to discuss *Sleeping Beauty*,"[17] said Bill Peet, one of the film's writers.

Instead, Walt's attention was focused on other projects, including Disneyland and a slew of live-action films, including the surprise hit *The Shaggy Dog*—a comedy about a teenage boy who is transformed into an Old English Sheepdog—which had been released in March 1959. The *Sleeping Beauty* animators felt neglected by Walt, and it was apparent in the final product. The reaction to the film didn't do much to boost morale, either. *Sleeping Beauty* premiered on January 29, 1959, at the Fox Wilshire Theater in Los Angeles, opening to lukewarm or negative reviews from critics, who railed on the film for imitating its predecessors—such as *Snow White and the Seven Dwarfs* and *Cinderella*—only less successfully.

"This *Sleeping Beauty* follows closely the pattern of *Snow White*, it being a story of a beautiful princess who is menaced by a dark and jealous witch," wrote Bosley Crowther in the *New York Times* in February 1959. "And the three good fairies could be maiden sisters of the misogynistic seven dwarfs. . . . The trouble is there are only three of them, instead of seven, and there's no Dopey. That's bad. There are other things about *Sleeping Beauty* that compare less favorably with *Snow White*. The musical score is sorely lacking in notable melodies. Even though it is liberally adapted from Tchaikovsky's 'Sleeping Beauty Ballet' and does afford effective background music, it is shy on singable songs."[18]

Disney lost nearly $1 million on the project, and the film didn't turn a profit until its first rerelease in 1970. The company, which earned a record profit of $3.4 million for the 1958–1959 fiscal year, lost $1.3 million the following year, due largely to the poor performance of *Sleeping Beauty*. It was the first time in ten years that Walt Disney Productions had lost money.[19] Walt briefly considered shutting down Disney's animation arm altogether, but instead, pink slips were delivered throughout the animation department, and the animated films that followed would be created using the cheaper xerography process in which drawings are transferred directly onto animation cels, without the more expensive inking process that until then had been standard practice.

Walt eventually brushed off the failure, instructing his staff to stay positive and reminding them the company had been there before. "Why, we
were just one step ahead of foreclosure when we lost our foreign market
before the war," Walt said. "We might have gone under after the war if the
bank hadn't agreed to carry us. We'll get out of this slump, too."[20]

It didn't take long for Disney to once again strike box office gold. The
studio had primarily turned its attention to live-action movies in the late
1950s and early 1960s, churning out Americana-themed titles such as *West-
ward Ho the Wagons!*, *Johnny Tremain*, and *Old Yeller*, but it would take
a trip across the pond for the company to ready one of its biggest film hits,
Mary Poppins. After more than two decades of trying to purchase the film
rights to P. L. Travers's series—he had promised his daughters he would
make their beloved books into a film back in the 1930s—Walt finally struck
a deal. In 1961, Travers agreed to give Disney the movie rights to her novel.
Robert and Richard Sherman were tasked with the songwriting and crafted
timeless tunes including "Chim Chim Cher-ee," "A Spoonful of Sugar," and
one of Walt's all-time favorite songs from any of the movies he had made:
"Feed the Birds."

Walt was not only very invested in the film from start to finish; he became
obsessed with *Mary Poppins* in a way he hadn't with the studio's other
recent pictures. That obsession was contagious: he, along with the entire
company, was excited about *Poppins*'s progress.

"As the original *Mary Poppins* budget of $5 million continued to grow,
I never saw a sad face around the entire studio," Walt said later. "And this
made me nervous. I knew the picture would have to gross $10 million for us
to break even. But still there was no negative head-shaking. No prophets of
doom. Even Roy was happy. He didn't even ask me to show the unfinished
picture to a banker. The horrible thought struck me—suppose the staff had
finally conceded that I knew what I was doing!"[21]

Mary Poppins premiered on August 27, 1964, at Grauman's Chinese
Theatre in Hollywood—the audience cheered when it finished. The *New
York Times* called it "irresistible," with reviewer Crowther singing a much
different tune about the latest Disney film than he had back in 1959 with
Sleeping Beauty.

"In case you are a Mary Poppins zealot who dotes on her just as she is,
don't let the intrusion of Mr. Disney and his myrmidons worry you one
bit. Be thankful for it and praise heaven there are such as they still making
films," Crowther wrote. "For the visual and aural felicities they have added
to this sparkling color film—the enchantments of a beautiful production,
some deliciously animated sequences, some exciting and nimble dancing,

and a spinning musical score—make it the nicest entertainment that has opened at [Radio City] Music Hall this year."[22] Philip Scheuer, in the *Los Angeles Times*, called *Mary Poppins* "the complete fantasy. It will amaze and delight more people than you can count, and I imagine quite a lot of them won't be kids, either."[23]

Astonishing box office figures and thirteen Academy Award nominations—including a nod for best picture—followed. Julie Andrews was named best actress, and the film also picked up awards for best film editing, best visual effects, best score, and best original song (the latter two honoring the Sherman brothers and "Chim Chim Cher-ee"). It was Disney's biggest film success, and *Mary Poppins*'s net profit of more than $28 million gave Walt the financial confidence he needed to pursue the Mineral King and Florida projects. Walt's passion for those and other forward-looking endeavors was evident in late 1966, when he wrote, in the Disney annual report: "Many people have asked, 'Why don't you make another *Mary Poppins*?' Well, by nature, I'm a born experimenter. To this day, I don't believe in sequels. I can't follow popular cycles. I have to move on to new things—there are many new worlds to conquer."[24]

In addition to its film successes—other hits of the early 1960s included *One Hundred and One Dalmatians*, *The Parent Trap*, and *The Absent-Minded Professor*—the Disney company also was becoming known for experiential entertainment. By 1966, Disneyland was thriving, with 6.7 million annual visitors.[25] The park's newest land, New Orleans Square, opened in July of that year. Planning was underway for the new theme park in Florida—now known officially as Disney World—which would feature Disneyland-style attractions as well as a futuristic "city of tomorrow."

In Denver, Colorado, meanwhile, Walt was testing out a new concept for recreational entertainment—one that featured bowling and swimming in place of the skiing and sledding that would be on the menu at Mineral King. Celebrity Sports Center, which had opened on a seven-acre site in 1960 with investors including Walt and Roy, Jack Benny, George Burns, Bing Crosby, Burl Ives, and Art Linkletter, put an Olympic-sized swimming pool and an eighty-lane bowling alley under the same roof, along with midway games, bumper cars, a shooting gallery, slot car racing, billiards tables, and food and drink options including an English-style pub, a cocktail lounge, and a dark-paneled, high-end eatery. The first in a proposed nationwide chain of indoor, all-weather recreation centers, Celebrity also was envisioned by Walt as an eventual training ground for employees of Mineral King and Disney World.[26]

Mineral King was set to be a key addition to Disney's ever-expanding portfolio of experiential entertainment, and the triumphant September 19, 1966, press conference at which Walt and Governor Brown sat at a make-shift conference table under the valley's tall trees to announce financing for the all-weather road was a high point of the ski resort planning process. But for Walt, things took a turn shortly after. He had been ailing for months, shedding weight and struggling to breathe, and an old polo injury was causing so much pain in his neck and leg that a surgeon recommended an operation to reduce pressure on the surrounding nerves. On November 2, Walt entered St. Joseph Hospital, located directly across the street from the studio in Burbank, for a presurgical workup. X-rays revealed a concrete reason for his persistent cough and shortness of breath: a spot the size of a walnut on his left lung. Surgery was planned for the following week. Walt tried to downplay his concerns, telling Lillian that he could drive himself to the hospital for the surgery and that she needn't bother coming. Still, Walt's and Lillian's daughter Diane insisted the family be there. She, her sister, Sharon, and Lillian sat in the hospital for hours, half-expecting the good news that Walt, always a dynamo, would be fine following the surgery. He would need to rest, of course, but he would rally. He had projects to complete. Grandchildren to play with. Places left to explore. Legacies to leave.

But when the three saw the surgeon enter the waiting room, meeting their eyes and looking long-faced, any optimism they had about the outcome dissipated. Walt's left lung was cancerous, the surgeon explained, and had been removed during surgery. Lymph nodes were enlarged, indicating the cancer had spread. "I would give him six months to two years to live," the surgeon said.[27] Lillian couldn't process the news. His daughters were stunned. Walt, though, was hopeful and wasted no time in joking about his diagnosis. After regaining consciousness in the intensive care unit to find Lillian beside him, he took his wife's hand: "Sweetheart, I'm a new man," he said. "I've only got one lung, but otherwise I'm good as new."[28]

Over the next several days and weeks, Walt did seem better—he appeared more energetic and joked with the hospital staff and visiting family members. It was decided that he wouldn't tell the world of his diagnosis, but that didn't stop rumors from flying about the true seriousness of his health issues. Soon, the media caught wind of his condition and the company was forced to issue a press release: "Walt Disney was initially admitted to the hospital November 2 for treatment and preliminary examination of an old polo injury. During the preliminary examination a lesion was discovered on his left lung. Surgery was decided upon and performed the next week. A tumor was found to have caused an abscess, which, in the opinion of the doctors, required a pneumonectomy. Within four to six weeks, Mr. Disney should be back on a full schedule. There is no reason to predict any recurrence of the problem or curtailment of his future activities." A Disney spokesman, a UPI wire story noted, "declined to disclose whether the tumor was malignant."[29]

During his two weeks in the hospital, Walt's mind kept wandering back to work. He was anxious about the next film, about Disney World in Florida, and about Mineral King. With his mind on business, he decided he had had enough boredom and angst in the hospital. He was ready to make a visit to the office. The same day he was discharged, he strode into the Disney studios to rally the troops. During lunch, a few employees asked about his diagnosis, concerned for their leader. But Walt was bored of talking about himself and changed the subject back to what interested him—his work. He met with producer Winston Hibler, who was working on the upcoming live-action comedy *The Horse in the Gray Flannel Suit*, and read through reports on some of the company's other current projects.[30]

After lunch, before he returned to the studio to watch a rough cut of Disney's new musical, *The Happiest Millionaire*, Walt took a trip to WED headquarters in Glendale, where he checked in on Davis's progress with Mineral King's musical bear attraction—the first time he had. He walked into Davis's office and flopped down in a chair. Davis was immediately struck by Walt's appearance. He wasn't just skinny—Walt had always been thin—but he was gaunt, his voice hoarse. He looked like he could barely get out of his chair. Davis couldn't believe the man looking back at him was the same man he had worked with for the past thirty years, the same man who ran through the studio like a bomb. "God, they sure knocked a helluva lot of weight off of you," Davis told Walt. Walt didn't reply; he just looked at Davis with his thin face. Davis immediately regretted the comment.

Walt's eyes scanned Davis's wall, which was decorated with several drawings of the bears. One of them was blowing on a harmonica; another was strumming a cigar-box banjo. Walt let out a hearty laugh.

Afterward, Walt told Davis he was getting tired and needed to make his way back to the studio. Davis stood in his office doorway, watching him leave, when Walt turned back.

"Goodbye, Marc," Walt said.[31]

Walt never said goodbye. It was always, "See you tomorrow," or "I'll check with you next week."

Davis said goodbye back, worried it would be the last time he would see his boss.

Davis was right.

7

THE MAGIC FADES

1966

In a cold, white, unadorned hallway in St. Joseph Hospital in Burbank, just outside the room where Walt had been staying for the past two weeks, Roy Disney stood, shaking. His shoulders trembled as he let out large sobs, his face wet from a steady stream of tears that seemed like they would never cease.[1] Ever-stoic Roy was filled with gut-wrenching emotion. He couldn't believe what he had heard, what he had seen: Walt was gone.

Over the past several weeks and months, perhaps no one had been more worried about Walt than his older brother. Roy had witnessed Walt's physical appearance changing rapidly: his ever-present tan fading, his frame getting slimmer, his breaths becoming shallow.

Walt reentered the hospital on November 30, 1966, not long after his lung surgery, due to increasing amounts of pain and weakness. Roy visited him daily, sitting next to Walt and regaling him with tales of what was happening just across the way at the Disney studios at 500 South Buena Vista Street, the colorful, lively rooms where animators chatted and laughed feeling a world away from the confines of a cold hospital that carried dread, diagnoses, and worry.

Walt was eager to hear about Mineral King, about Disneyland and the progress on Disney World. When Roy arrived for his daily visit on the evening of December 14, he found Walt weak, as he had been the past several weeks, but lucid and even excited. Walt's mind had clearly been racing, filled with ideas about the new projects the company was building, and he eagerly wanted to talk about them. The ceiling of the hospital room was covered with one-foot-square acoustical tiles, and Walt stared up at them from his hospital bed, pointing to different tiles as he mapped out the design of the Florida property to show Roy: "Now there is where the highway will run. There is the route for the monorail."[2]

Roy left the hospital buoyed by Walt's enthusiasm for future plans. When he returned home from the visit, he told his wife, Edna, that he thought Walt could recover: "I think he's got a good chance of making it."[3] If anyone could beat the health problems Walt had been dealt over the past couple of months, it was Roy's stubborn baby brother—a man always motivated to complete his passion projects. But Roy got word early the following day: Walt had died at 9:30 that morning, on December 15, 1966, ten days after his sixty-fifth birthday. Roy and the family met at the hospital, stunned but attempting to sort out the pieces of what would happen next.

Roy's grief was shared by the world, and the news was splashed across the front pages of every major international newspaper, along with words and phrases like "beloved," "restless genius," "legend," "entertainment's most versatile creator," and "Hollywood's only authentic genius." Many of the articles were accompanied by a drawing created by editorial cartoonist Karl Hubenthal, of the *Los Angeles Herald Examiner*, depicting the globe adorned with two round ears on top and overlaid with the face of Mickey Mouse, eyes closed, a stream of tears falling. The man who touched millions was gone, and the world was in mourning.

Sympathies and accolades poured in from around the globe, including a *Los Angeles Times* epitaph that hailed Walt as "Aesop with a magic brush. [Hans Christian] Andersen with a color camera. Barrie, Carroll, Grahame, Prokofieff, Harris—with a genius touch that brought to life the creatures they had invented."[4] The *New York Times* wrote:

> Starting from very little save a talent for drawing, a gift of imagination that was somehow in tune with everyone's imagination, and a dogged determination to succeed, Walt Disney became one of Hollywood's master entrepreneurs and one of the world's greatest entertainers. He had a genius for innovation; his production was enormous; he was able to keep sure and personal control over his increasingly far-flung enterprise; his hand was ever on the public pulse. He was, in short, a legend in his own lifetime.[5]

Roy acted strong following Walt's death—he knew he had to, as company shareholders needed reassurance and the company's four thousand employees needed a leader—but he too was stunned by Walt's passing.

Aside from grief over his younger brother's death, Roy worried about what Walt's absence meant for the company—and for his own plans. Now seventy-three, Roy was reluctant to take control. His dark hair had thinned and turned white, and he had been trying to retire for the past couple of years, hoping to travel, spend time with Edna, and slow his hectic pace. But Walt's sudden passing, with no leadership succession plans in place, demanded that Roy take charge in a way he had never planned to, and work harder than he ever had. Although he was reluctant to step into the spotlight, he knew it had to be done. The entertainment empire Walt had made famous now depended on him.

Roy's first order of business was to assure people that Walt's priorities would continue. Roy made a statement to the press, which also went out as a memo to all Disney employees around the world on the day Walt died. "There is no way to replace Walt Disney," it read. "He was an extraordinary man. Perhaps there will never be another like him. . . . The world will always be a better place because Walt Disney was its master showman. . . . All of the plans for the future that Walt had begun—new motion pictures, the expansion of Disneyland, television production and our Florida and Mineral King projects—will continue to move ahead. That is the way Walt wanted it to be."[6]

Privately, however, Roy had his doubts about Mineral King. Walt had been the big skier, not Roy, and Roy wasn't sure it was the right move for the company. "We're not in the skiing business," he told Bob Hicks. "We're in the movie and amusement park business."[7] Roy also had begun to get letters from conservationists and was reading articles about the growing environmental opposition to the resort, and he was worried about sullying Disney's good name. But when it came to Walt's dreams, Roy had been proven wrong before. He opted to do what his brother would have done and stay the course, putting the ski-resort planning in the hands of Hicks, who had made it a personal mission after Walt's death to see Mineral King completed.

Roy also better acquainted himself with WED—which was working on attractions for Disney World as well as Disneyland—and he decided to leave the company's film production in the hands of several individuals with whom Walt had worked closely, including Card Walker, Ron Miller, and Roy's son, Roy E. Disney, then thirty-six, who had joined Walt Disney Productions as an assistant editor in 1954, working primarily on Walt's beloved True-Life Adventures series.

With film production and Mineral King in capable hands, Roy focused his attention on one specific goal: to complete the new Florida park in honor of his brother. In spring 1967, Roy was by the side of Florida governor Claude Kirk in Tallahassee as Kirk signed a set of bills that allowed Disney to move ahead with development and construction of the new park. Roy also announced a change in the project's name from Disney World to Walt Disney World—a small change, but one, Roy said, that would remind people "that this was Walt's dream." Roy was dedicated to Walt Disney World—he made frequent trips to the Orlando site, and he even was spotted several times driving a Jeep around the construction site, at least once looking to the sky and saying, "Walt, what have you gotten me into?"[8] Roy was a pro at raising millions of dollars to help fund the Florida entertainment mecca, and the company's stock soared under his leadership. After all, he had spent his adult life making sure there was enough money, time, and resources for Walt to build his dreams.

* * *

Roy Disney, born June 24, 1893, and older than Walt by eight years, grew up viewing his little brother as many older siblings did their younger counterparts: with equal parts protectiveness and annoyance. The two bickered throughout the years, but they were close despite their age difference. Roy pushed Walt around in a baby carriage on the streets of Chicago and bought him toys using the money he had saved in his piggy bank. And when the Disney family moved to the farm in Marceline, the brothers shared not just a room, but a bed. Four years later, after the Disneys left for Kansas City, Roy and Walt worked together delivering newspapers on father Elias's route (he bought a distributorship for the morning *Kansas City Times* and evening and Sunday *Kansas City Star* newspapers), often lamenting over their father's stern behavior, short temper, and strict rules—including the fact that although they each got small allowances, their father did not pay them for their work delivering newspapers, considering the labor a fair trade for their room and board.

After graduating from high school, Roy began working as a teller at the First National Bank of Kansas City. He joined the Navy in 1917, two days before his twenty-fourth birthday, and served in Chicago; Charleston, South Carolina; and Bremerton, Washington—even making three Atlantic crossings over seas filled with German U-boats—before returning to Kansas City. After being diagnosed with tuberculosis he had apparently acquired while in the Navy, he was sent to hospitals in the dry climates of Santa Fe, New Mexico, and Tucson, Arizona. When he felt well enough to leave, he decided to try his luck in nearby California. After a short stint as a door-to-door vacuum cleaner salesman in Glendale, he suffered a relapse of TB and was admitted to the veterans' hospital at Sawtelle in west Los Angeles. He corresponded regularly with Walt, who was trying to get an animation studio off the ground in Kansas City. When the business went bust, Walt jumped on a train and went west to join his brother. In 1923, the Disney Brothers Cartoon Studio was born, establishing the first animated cartoon studio in Hollywood.

Walt was the dreamer, always with a new and better idea that transcended what he had done before—moving from animated shorts to full-length feature films, then diving into experiential ventures like Disneyland. Roy was the realist, crunching the numbers, telling Walt what made sense from a financial perspective, and trying to bring his brother back down to Earth. Many of Walt's fancies hadn't made financial sense: Roy had been hesitant about *Snow White* and the foray into feature films—especially when the estimated quarter-million-dollar budget ballooned to $1.5 million—and he was even cautious about Disneyland early on, allowing Walt just a fraction of what he needed for the park's planning and design. But Walt's enthusiasm for projects and new ideas—and his stubbornness to not let them go—usually convinced Roy not only to listen, but to finance each of Walt's dreams. For *Snow White*, Roy made multiple visits to the Bank of America to extend the studio's loan, even persuading Walt to screen a rough cut of the film for a banker sympathetic to the Disneys' cause. (The banker's response? "That thing is going to make you a hatful of money.")[9]

Walt soon became the face of the organization, and as the company grew and became a bigger success than anyone could have predicted, he became a celebrity almost as well-known as Mickey and Donald, drawing attention, putting his name at the top of the film credits, talking to fans directly every week during the *Walt Disney's Wonderful World of Color* TV program, and indulging fans' requests for autographs. Roy was in the shadows, but that was the arrangement he preferred. Much quieter and more reserved than Walt, whose gregariousness and charisma charmed the public, Roy had never aimed to be in the spotlight. He liked being behind the scenes, doing the work and doing it well. Walt was the dreamer, but it was Roy who ensured those dreams came true. "I always go and check with my brother. Always. But I don't always agree with him," Walt said. "Roy had faith in me. I think that Roy has done a lot of things against his better judgment because he felt that I wanted to do it. Most of our arguments and disagreements I think have been because Roy has felt that he had to protect me."[10]

At a luncheon a few months before Walt died, First National Bank at Orlando president Billy Dial, who had helped with the financing for Disney

World, asked what would happen to the Florida park if Walt got hit by a truck. "Absolutely nothing," Walt said. "My brother Roy runs this company. I just piddle around."[11]

❋ ❋ ❋

Even with Walt gone, Roy was still committed to ensuring his brother's dreams came true. As 1967 dawned and he tried to wrap his head around the competing priorities of Mineral King, the California Institute of the Arts, and Walt Disney World—not to mention a slew of new attractions planned for Disneyland and film projects including *The Jungle Book* and *The Happiest Millionaire*—he was happy to put Mineral King in Hicks's capable hands. Under Hicks's supervision, Bob Allen, head of resort research for the company, and Willy Schaeffler—still reeling from Walt's death but determined to carry the vision of a Disney-run, world-class ski resort forward—took off for a five-week tour of European ski resorts in mid-January, traveling to five different countries to look for ideas they could translate to Mineral King. The final plans were due to the Forest Service in less than two years, and there was no time to waste.

Disney was confident moving ahead on the project, but public opinion was beginning to turn against the Mineral King development. The conservationist movement was growing, and some of the same newspapers that had hailed the ski area when it was first announced in 1965 were now publishing letters from readers who echoed the Sierra Club's call to keep Mineral King wild. In the California legislature, bills were proposed to block the highway into Mineral King for environmental and economic reasons. One lawmaker, California congressman Phillip Burton, even submitted a short-lived bill to transfer the Sequoia National Game Refuge—of which Mineral King was a part—into Sequoia National Park to protect it from development.

Many California skiers, however, resented the efforts to block access to such prime terrain. Pro-skiing organization the Far West Ski Association, in the January 1967 issue of its *Western Ski Time* magazine, railed against the Sierra Club, informing readers that if the conservationists got their way, Mineral King "may be lost to skiers forever. And with it would go the opportunity for Walt Disney and the collective genius of his organization to, in Disney's words, 'prove once again that man and nature can work together to the benefit of both.'" The Far West Ski Association urged readers to write letters to Interior Secretary Stewart Udall and President Lyndon Johnson, as well as senators, congressmen, and the National Park Service, asking them to let Disney build its resort in Mineral King.

The Far West Ski Association spoke for many like-minded skiers in California who wanted to see the Disney resort realized. But the conservationist movement was growing in numbers, and it was fighting not just for Mineral King, but for all of America's unspoiled wilderness areas.

* * *

Whether they were working to protect the glory of towering redwoods, the tranquility of open space endangered by encroaching development, or the quiet majesty of the Grand Canyon, conservationists in the 1960s were united in their efforts to preserve the power and beauty of nature. Fueled by books like *Silent Spring* and Donald Carr's *Death of the Sweet Waters*, a treatise on water pollution, ecology clubs formed in cities and college towns around the country. Sierra Club membership, just seven thousand in 1950, doubled in the 1950s and doubled again between 1960 and 1965 to nearly thirty thousand (Disneyland, by contrast, welcomed more than five million visitors in its first year alone).[12] The issue even made its way to the White House: in 1962, President John F. Kennedy invited 250 delegates—governors, members of conservation organizations, representatives from universities, and more—to a White House Conference on Conservation that was the first such gathering in Washington since 1909. Calling the conference "a step forward in a long journey which began, fortunately, many years ago and which will continue throughout our lives," Kennedy spoke of the importance of improving and protecting natural resources, his hopes of applying recent scientific discoveries to the problem, and the coming challenges of a growing U.S. population—projected to reach 300 million people by the end of the century. "We do not want, for example, this eastern coast to be one gigantic metropolitan area stretching from north of Boston to Jacksonville, Florida, without adequate resources for our people to participate and see some green around them,"[13] Kennedy said.

In September 1963, two months before his voice was silenced by an assassin's bullet, Kennedy set off on a five-day, eleven-state "Conservation Tour" that took him to Utah to talk about water conservation, to Montana to talk about the importance of preserving public land, and to Wyoming to describe how protecting natural resources such as land and water would help keep the country strong. For many Americans, news coverage of Kennedy's speeches was their first exposure to issues around conservation and preserving the environment.

Kennedy's successor, Lyndon B. Johnson, had spent the first four years of his life on his family's farm on the Pedernales River in Texas before moving to the small town of Johnson City in the rugged Texas Hill Country. Johnson's wife, Lady Bird, had likewise grown up exploring the woodlands and meadows near Karnack, Texas, and when Johnson took over the presidency in 1963, the couple put a focus on conservation. Lady Bird was the driving force behind 1965's Highway Beautification Act—which limited billboards and took other measures to preserve the natural beauty around the areas visible from the growing interstate highway system—and Johnson made the environment a major part of his "Great Society" initiative, convening a White House Conference on Natural Beauty and asking his science committee to put together a report on ways to restore the quality of the environment.

"We have always prided ourselves on being not only America the strong and America the free, but America the beautiful," Johnson said in a 1964 speech. "Today that beauty is in danger. The water we drink, the food we eat, the very air that we breathe, are threatened with pollution. Our parks are overcrowded, our seashores overburdened. Green fields and dense forests are disappearing."[14] Johnson signed close to three hundred conservation bills during his presidency, including the Clean Air Act, Water Quality Act, and Pesticide Control Bill. He wouldn't add Mineral King to his list of environmental priorities, but one of his cabinet members and closest advisors would soon become the biggest obstacle Disney's Mineral King development had faced so far.

⁕ ⁕ ⁕

As tenacious in the halls of Washington as he had been on the court as a member of the University of Arizona basketball team, Secretary of the Interior Stewart Udall was firmly opposed to building a highway over Sequoia National Park for any purpose—let alone to bring visitors to a privately owned ski resort built in a valley known for its natural wonder. In March 1967, the California Highway Commission had begun discussions on the $20 million highway to Mineral King—a major improvement to the existing road—but when Udall heard about the plan, he urged Disney and the state of California to look into the possibility of a monorail or some other electronic railway to protect the area's scenery and "park values." A railway from the parking structure to the resort was already part of the Disney plan, but Udall wanted a longer railway that would keep cars out of the park. The Park Service—part of the Department of the Interior—would ultimately have to approve the highway route, giving Udall the upper hand. He had already witnessed the "blighting influence" that heavy automobile

Secretary of the Interior Stewart Udall speaks at the White House Conference on Conservation in May 1962. Udall was adamantly opposed to the Mineral King highway that would run through Sequoia National Park. Abbie Rowe. White House Photographs. John F. Kennedy Presidential Library and Museum, Boston.

traffic brought to other national parks, most notably Yosemite, and he did not want the blight to extend to Mineral King. Park developers in California "will be more honored twenty-five years from now for the roads they do not build than for the roads they do," he said in March 1967.[15]

With his athlete's physique and a closely cropped, military-style haircut, Udall had become a formidable presence in Washington. He was one of the most visible conservationists in the country in the 1960s and played a key role in the passage of the Clean Air Act, the Wilderness Act, and other environmental legislation. A longtime conservationist who had grown up on a farm in Arizona, Udall had been appointed secretary of the interior by Kennedy in 1961, and in 1963 he published *The Quiet Crisis*, a book that rivaled *Silent Spring* in its catalyzing effect on the growing environmentalist movement. A brief environmental history of the United States, *The Quiet Crisis* warned of the coming dangers of pollution, dwindling open space, and overuse of natural resources if the country did not change its ways.

"America today stands poised on a pinnacle of wealth and power," Udall wrote in the book's introduction, "yet we live in a land of vanishing beauty, of increasing ugliness, of shrinking open space, and of an overall environment that is diminished daily by pollution and noise and blight."[16]

Hicks and others at Disney already knew a railway to Mineral King would be prohibitively expensive, and they continued to press the highway commission to build the road as promised. To the company's relief, the commission finally approved the highway to the resort in April 1967, with a projected completion date of October 1973.[17] Route planning could now begin—but the state still had to get Udall's okay to build the section of the road that would pass over national park land. And although that okay still hadn't come by August 1967, the California Division of Highways held a meeting on August 10 to unveil the proposed layout of State Route 276. More than two hundred people—including Mineral King property owners, public officials, and TV and newspaper reporters—packed the Veterans Memorial Building in Three Rivers, down the winding road from Mineral King, to voice their support for or opposition to the plan, and to listen as a highway planning engineer explained the lengths to which the department had gone to preserve the area's natural beauty. A 1966 study by a San Jose State College biology professor had mapped out all the giant sequoias along the route, the engineer explained, and the plan called for the construction of five bridges over grove areas to protect the endangered trees. The division also was conducting cooperative studies with the California Fish and Game Commission to find ways to protect wildlife along the proposed route.

Despite all the planning, Udall continued to push for a study of alternative transportation options, and on August 30, 1967, Secretary of Agriculture Orville Freeman—who oversaw the Forest Service—sent Udall a letter scolding him for dragging his feet. "The conspicuous failure of our two great Departments to reach agreement on as simple a matter as improving a few miles of existing road must be a growing source of embarrassment to the Federal Government, just as it increasingly frustrates and angers the State and local people and others who are directly concerned,"[18] Freeman wrote.

Freeman wasn't the only one reaching out to Udall to voice his concerns—the interior secretary was also getting an earful from Walt's old friend Ronald Reagan, who had begun his first term as California governor several months earlier, as well as California Lieutenant Governor Robert Finch and senators Thomas Kuchel and George Murphy, not to mention assorted congressmen, legislators, mayors, newspaper reporters, and businessmen from all over California. By the time November 1967 rolled around, the Forest Service began to consider extending the January 1969 deadline for Disney to deliver its final plans for Mineral King, worried that the company might simply walk away from the project if the delay continued.

"What the hell do they want?" one Forest Service official said of the interior department. "We've given them everything they have ever asked for, including a tree-by-tree walkthrough with a redwood expert."[19]

* * *

Now living in Colorado temporarily while he pursued a PhD in geography at the University of Colorado, Boulder, Sierra Club member and Mineral King crusader John Harper stayed in touch with Michael McCloskey and others in the Sierra Club as the highway controversy continued. He watched with some amazement as Udall finally lifted his objections to the road in December 1967, only later coming up with a theory as to the secretary's change of heart.

Since 1964, President Johnson had been looking to create a redwood national park in California, inspired by a proposed plan by the National Geographic Society to save the giant trees from logging and environmental destruction. Johnson tasked none other than Udall with devising a plan to create such a park.

"The redwoods are one of nature's masterpieces in North America—and in the world," Johnson said in a White House meeting in June 1964. "Yet, at the present rate of logging and with destruction resulting from inadequate conservation practices, the future of the redwoods is in doubt."[20]

By early 1967 Senator Kuchel had a bill in place to create the park, but holding things up this time around was Reagan, who was concerned about the impact of a redwood park on California's lumber industry and famously commented, "Once you've seen one redwood, you've seen 'em all."[21] In what to Harper appeared like a bit of backroom dealing, Reagan offered a trade of sorts: his support for the redwood national park in exchange for federal assurances the Mineral King highway would be built. The move put further pressure on Udall, and in December 1967 Freeman convened a high-level meeting in Washington to move the Mineral King road forward. On one side of the table sat Freeman, Senators Kuchel and Murphy, California congressman Bob Mathias, Nevada senator Alan Bible, chair of the interior department's parks and recreation subcommittee, and Deputy Budget Director Phillip Hughes, who was working to secure Reagan's blessing for a redwood national park. Alone on the other side of the table was Udall.

Udall made no statement after the closed-door meeting, but Kuchel immediately let it be known that the stalemate had finally ended and the highway had been approved. "Now that the decision has been made," he added, "I look forward to the Forest Service and Disney giving California the finest ski area in the world."[22]

Stalled out for a good part of 1967 (at one point Hicks told the Fresno Chamber of Commerce that Disney had ceased operations in Mineral King altogether until the road question got resolved),[23] the Disney company seized on this new development, pulling together Imagineers and executives for a planning meeting the day the news broke to figure out whether it was even possible to meet the original deadlines, and bringing in Freeman to talk through road placement and construction. "This removes the last obstacle," an optimistic Hicks said, adding that the company would strive to have at least one ski lift up and running by 1970.[24]

Perhaps in a show of solidarity with Disney after the drama over the road, the Far West Ski Association around the same time presented Walt, posthumously, with its second annual Hans Georg Award in honor of Walt's "lifelong interest in and contributions to the sport of skiing."[25] These included Walt's early support of California's Sugar Bowl ski resort, his wide-ranging duties at the 1960 Winter Olympics, and of course the wonders the proposed Mineral King resort offered to California skiers.

With the highway back on track, things seemed to be coming together for Disney's Mineral King plans after what felt like a long series of unwanted derailments. It was a welcome respite, especially in light of Walt's death one year earlier. But the road to completion was starting to look as winding and rocky as the primitive path into the Mineral King valley. Resistance to the development was growing at an alarming pace—much of it coming from inside the area's perimeters.

8

RISE OF THE RESISTANCE

1968

Jean Koch sat down at her black manual typewriter, ready to fire off another missive. Stacks of carbon copies of letters she had sent previously sat close by, neatly arranged. Some had been typed, some written out in neat, careful cursive, when the words came to her faster than she could type. Although each letter was different, tailored to its recipient with opinions, facts, impassioned anger, and poetic descriptions of the precious, peaceful area she loved, the larger message of all the letters was by now written in the sinews of her hands. Her words came with ease as she punched each key, each letter, resulting in a satisfying clack-clack-clack. Koch crafted sentences that, when added up, created one unmistakable message: development in Mineral King could not happen.

Her letters had come fast and furious in the months and years since 1965, when she first heard about the Forest Service's plan to develop Mineral King, and she reached out to anyone who could, and should, save her cherished area: the National Wildlife Federation, state legislators, the Forest Service, newspaper editorial pages, California Governor Pat Brown, the Disney company. How could they stand by as one of the remaining largely unspoiled lands in California was about to become another Yosemite—a once-tranquil refuge that, with a sharp increase in visitors and popularity in recent years, had become crowded, smoggy, and noisy?

Koch and her husband, Richard, had owned their cabin in Mineral King since 1958, and it had become a treasured place—as much a part of the

Mineral King activist and cabin owner Jean Koch at her typewriter, where she spent much of her time writing letters in her fight to save Mineral King. Courtesy of Jean Koch and Jill Tovey.

family as a building can be. And it was being threatened in the name of progress.

"We feel that those of us who enjoy the winding mountain road and the reward of a degree of isolation and quiet are being sadly overlooked," she wrote to Brown in an April 1965 letter. "Once the damage is done, it cannot be corrected. The delicate Alpine meadows, the giant Redwoods, the beautiful limestone caverns and the fragile ruins of log cabins and other relics of the romantic mining history of Mineral King are irreplaceable."[1]

Koch, a housewife in her mid-forties with dark hair she often kept well-coiffed, knew the area better than most. She had memorized the songs of the birds and the gentle rippling of the nearby river; the feeling of the crisp mountain air on her skin; the sweet smell of gooseberries that grew on sticky bushes outside; the sound of fallen leaves and dry pine needles crunching under her shoes as she and her family hiked and explored the area. It was all just outside her front door.

Born and raised in Orange County, California, Koch had a long history with Mineral King that began long before Walt ever set foot in the valley. In 1933, her father and some of his friends, all of whom worked for the Orange County assessor's office, decided to take a fishing trip in the mountains. After unrolling a large map of California and weighing their options, they picked out Mineral King and contacted a packer there. They went on a ten-day pack trip, riding horses during the day and camping at night. The men rode over Franklin Pass, down Rattlesnake Creek, and up the Kern River, admiring the dramatic landscape and taking in the wide vistas. In the meantime, Jean, her brother, and her mother camped in Sequoia National Park. It was love at first sight for the entire family. After that, her father never

Jean Koch in Mineral King's Cold Springs Campground in the early 1940s, before she and her husband bought their cabin there. Courtesy of Jean Koch and Jill Tovey.

wanted to go any place other than Mineral King for vacation, so every summer they packed up their tents and other camping equipment and headed
for Cold Springs Campground, a camping site nestled amid the trees near
the Mineral King ranger station.[2]

Soon, Jean felt the same pull to the area. After she married Richard
Koch, a pediatrician and researcher, in 1943, the couple visited Mineral
King often and began looking for a cabin to call their own, especially when
kids started to enter the picture. When a cabin came up for sale in 1958,
they jumped at the chance, borrowing money from Jean's parents to make
the purchase. The cabin, painted green, was small—just one room with a
kitchen extension on the east side. But the Kochs maneuvered old furniture and moved heavy curtains from around the bed and pushed it to the
corner to create more room. They bought a wood-burning stove from Sears
Roebuck after one too many close calls with the old butane stove installed
by the previous owner. An attic provided a sleeping area for the Kochs'
five children. Best of all, a wide porch on the south side of the cabin overlooked a small stream that wound through the flat valley like a glistening
silver ribbon. Sometimes the family slept on the porch, drifting off to the
gentle sounds of flowing water and the soothing glow of stars above. It was
the perfect, cozy sanctuary for the Kochs, away from the hurried pace they
experienced while living in their modern, spacious home in Los Angeles
during the other parts of the year. A five-hour-plus drive from the backed-
up highways, the school routines, and Richard's hectic job as a doctor lay
an oasis of quiet reprieve.

The Kochs were one of just sixty-seven families who had permits to own
and maintain summer houses on national forest land in Mineral King—a
privilege they didn't take for granted. The family backpacked in the Sierra
during parts of their summer vacations, embarking on treks that included a
110-mile round-trip hike from Mineral King to Mount Whitney—the tall-
est mountain in the lower forty-eight states—and a 150-mile hike on the
John Muir Trail.[3] Named for the Sierra Club founder, the route snaked
through the Sierra Nevada mountain range in Sequoia, Kings Canyon, and
Yosemite national parks. In the fall, when gooseberries were ripe and red,
Jean picked them and made wild gooseberry jelly. The kids often spent time
fishing and swimming in the river, hiking to one of the many lakes in the
area, or walking to the general store to buy candy.

It was a mountain paradise they felt needed to be saved from development, and Jean was part of the vocal grassroots movement that was forming
from inside the Mineral King valley to do so. She was a founding member
of the Mineral King District Association, a coalition of cabin owners that

The Koch family cabin in Mineral King. Courtesy of Jean Koch and Jill Tovey.

was fighting against the Disney project, and she was the leader of the Sierra Club's Mineral King Task Force. Unlike other members of the Sierra Club, who spent maybe a few weekends each year hiking, backpacking, and camping in the area, Koch and the other cabin owners had much to lose if the Disney development was built. Not only would their backyard turn into a nightmare of whirring chairlift machinery and crowds of tourists, but she and her neighbors feared their cherished summer cabins would be destroyed to make room for the resort.

Koch's passionate letters and thoughtful analysis—she repeatedly said her grievance was not with Disney, but with the Forest Service, which she felt "misled" the company into "thinking this development is feasible and desirable," as she wrote to Disney executive vice president Card Walker in July 1969—almost always elicited a reply. But she didn't always get the response she wanted.

Some of the organizations she wrote to argued that not only was Mineral King not a true wilderness area—it had a general store and a post office, after all, in addition to the cabins—and thus didn't need to be preserved, but also that there was a great demand for skiing in California. Worse yet, some of the organizations claimed the Kochs' argument was self-serving, as they were one of the only families who owned a cabin in the primitive area.

In March 1967, for instance, after another letter to the National Wildlife Federation, Koch got an upsetting reply:

> Our information indicates that this particular area is not now, and has not been for many years, a true wilderness area. As we understand the facts (though admittedly no member of our staff here has been able to personally see or investigate the area), there are approximately sixty persons or families who have cabins, cottages, or other permanent structures at Mineral King. The town, largely a summer colony, has a store, post office, and other facilities not associated with wilderness areas.

Given those facts, the letter said, it was difficult for the organization to understand the position of those who opposed the Disney resort because of its threat to unspoiled wilderness.[4]

After a few more months of back-and-forth correspondence, Koch wrote in August 1967 to the National Wildlife Federation that she was canceling her membership in the organization due to its position on Mineral King and would encourage other conservationists to do the same. She also had a sneaking suspicion that the National Wildlife Federation was refusing to get involved since Walt Disney had served as a spokesman for the organization's National Wildlife Week back in the 1950s and early 1960s. It was a claim the federation denied: "There is no point in making any further attempt now to explain our position, or lack of one," an organization representative wrote to Koch. "I do want to correct one misunderstanding, however, with relation to Mr. Disney. At no time has the fact that the late

Walt Disney served as an honorary president and chairman of our Wildlife Week effort had any influence on our thinking or actions."[5]

* * *

While her husband also was involved in the fight against Disney's Mineral King project—passionate about the environment, signing his name to dozens of letters penned by his wife, and helping to raise funds for the cause—Koch was comfortable taking the lead. Like her, women across the country were getting more vocal and more involved. The 1960s were becoming a turning point for women in more ways than one. Females were entering the workforce in unprecedented numbers, and awareness was growing around sexual harassment in the workplace, as well as gender disparities in pay and promotions. That helped spur the Equal Pay Act of 1963—signed by President John F. Kennedy—which amended the Fair Labor Standards Act and aimed to prohibit wage discrimination based on gender. And after the first birth control pill was approved by the Food and Drug Administration in 1960, scores of women embraced it, giving themselves control over their sexuality and freedom and allowing them time and energy to embrace their passions and choices—those outside of childbearing and purely family responsibilities.

For many women, that passion involved becoming part of the growing conservationist movement. Across the country, women formed groups to protect wildlife, stop pollution, and preserve open spaces.[6] For instance, the League of Women Voters, a nonprofit group formed in 1920 to encourage women to take an active role in political issues after they had won the right to vote, played a major role in the fight against water pollution. Many of its chapters launched clean water campaigns and lobbied for government action. And in an effort to stop air pollution, New York City resident Hazel Henderson cofounded Citizens for Clean Air, handing out leaflets to other moms during daily walks with her young daughter.

Like many other conservationists around the country, women, in particular, found a call to action in Rachel Carson's *Silent Spring*. And although Carson's work was intended for both genders, the author still was thrilled by the reaction it received from women. "I believe it is important for women to realize that the world of today threatens to destroy much of that beauty that has immense power to bring us a healing release from tension," Carson said in a 1954 speech to Theta Sigma Phi, a national sorority of women journalists. "Women have a greater intuitive understanding of such things. They want for their children not only physical health, but mental and spiritual health as well."[7]

The women's liberation movement was in tandem with the environmental movement as the country as a whole seemed to be shifting in its thinking. Koch straddled both lines as a female leading the charge against the Mineral King development. In addition to her environmental activism, she was vocal about other causes as well. She was known for wearing a button that read "59 cents"—and she was happy to explain to anyone who asked that for every dollar a man earned, a woman earned forty-one cents less.[8]

As her letters continued to be answered with disappointing replies, Koch decided to get more aggressive and add action to her words. If no one else would stop the Disney development, then she would. Acting as spokesperson for the Sierra Club's Mineral King Task Force, she started a newsletter that was mailed out to a growing list of people who wanted to defend Mineral King from development. *The Optimist* included the latest news on the Disney plans and the fight against them; suggested activism ideas such as distributing brochures and petitions and writing letters (accompanied by a handy list of addresses, including that of Disney executive Card Walker); and sold merchandise including "Save Mineral King" T-shirts and Sawtooth Peak-inspired patches that helped finance the resistance efforts. The newsletter also injected a bit of humor in the form of "Sawtooth Sally," an older woman who wrote a regular column about the Mineral King drama that read like a gossip column ("I've heard it rumored that a major American movie and recreational corporation is investigating potential ski development sites . . . in Colorado?" and "I recently visited Mickey Mouse's grave in beautiful Sequoia National Forest Lawn and adorned it with a lovely wreath of evergreens"). Koch later admitted she was the author of the column.

Koch placed signs, donation jars, and petitions throughout the Mineral King area (sometimes without a permit, which caused the material to be removed more than once by Forest Service rangers) and chatted with campers and other visitors to warn them of the dangers of development and encourage them to join her cause. With University of Southern California film students Bruton Peterson and Jim Rascoe, Koch established the Mineral King Film Fund to create and finance a documentary film that would tell the Mineral King story—from the area's historical background to the controversy over the Disney plan.

The resistance efforts were small to start but soon began to spread, reaching out from Mineral King like the roots of a giant sequoia. Soon, the bumpers of cars around Southern California were adorned with "Keep Mineral King Natural" stickers. Volunteers collected signatures on petitions against development. Flyers for summer 1968 and 1969 "hike-in" protests,

The poster for the second annual Mineral King "Hike-In" protest, which drew hundreds of people—and garnered attention from the caricature it used. Courtesy of University of Southern California, on behalf of the USC Libraries Special Collections.

the latter depicting an ax-wielding Mickey Mouse destroying the redwoods, were shared and posted around the area. The resistance even grew beyond the Golden State—in January 1968, the *New York Times* weighed in on the Mineral King controversy with an editorial deriding the "commercial project that will ruin one of the nation's truly majestic wilderness areas"[9] and urging President Lyndon Johnson to issue an executive order to incorporate Mineral King into Sequoia National Park. Six months earlier, the National Park Service, in its monthly magazine, had suggested that instead of a ski resort in Mineral King, Disney should consider establishing a "True-Life

Adventure area," named for the studio's wildlife documentaries, as a tribute to Walt. Rather than ski lifts and souvenir shops, the site would provide visitors with ways to photograph, observe, and study wild animals in their natural habitat.[10] The Mineral King issue had gone national, giving Koch and others in Mineral King hope that Disney's plans for the valley might yet be stopped.

Encouraged by the attention the issue was receiving around the country, Koch packed her gear in July 1968 to join the two-day hike-in and camp-in protest organized by John Rettenmayer and Al Hill, two University of California, Los Angeles, graduate students opposed to the Disney develop-ment. The students invited Sierra Club members and anyone else who was interested to see the valley before the new highway was built and Disney started construction. A group of some two hundred conservationists, which in addition to Koch included several other Mineral King cabin owners, hiked through the area and then gathered for a debate on the development.

Sierra Club director Martin Litton, whose short-sleeved button-down shirt, complete with pens in the breast pocket, was a washed-out blue compared to the deep green mountaintop he stood in front of, addressed a group of activists sitting on the hillside among jagged rocks, many wearing hats to shade them from the beating sun. Litton took issue with the Forest Service more than Disney, slamming the agency for opening the door to development without any public input. "The problem is that we're indi-viduals; we're paying the bills for the very agencies that would destroy the beauty of these places," Litton said. "This is our dilemma. . . . How are we served by public agencies which we must support, and how can we in any way have an influence or a voice in what they do, except very indirectly and very slowly? In a battle of this kind, we must have an adversary. We have an adversary: the United States Forest Service. Not Disney, and not the ski people, but the United States Forest Service."[11]

Although the hike-in was in protest of the development, the activists did invite those from the other side to join the conversation. Jim James, super-visor of Sequoia National Forest, for instance, spoke in favor of a recreation facility in Mineral King, saying, "I'm for human conservation first and plant conservation second. And I feel that the half a dozen or a hundred people who see [Mineral King] every year now aren't enough."[12]

* * *

By late 1968, as the end of its three-year preliminary planning period approached, Disney's Mineral King team was putting the finishing touches on its final master plan to deliver to the Forest Service in January. After all their preparation, they were ready to start building Walt's dream recreation project. But as word of the resistance began to spread throughout the company, it seemed to many that without Walt there to guide the project and talk through the controversy, the Mineral King development was beginning to go off the rails. Still, Disney leaders, determined to finish Walt's dream, remained undeterred in their progress. All of the company's snow studies, soil analysis, international research trips, highway surveys, and ski-run planning coalesced in a final master plan that was quietly submitted to the Forest Service on January 8. Disney saved the fanfare for January 27, the day the plan was officially approved by the Forest Service, holding a press conference at studio headquarters in Burbank to announce the next steps in the Mineral King development process. Reporters swarmed around concept drawings and a large-scale model of the resort that depicted ski runs, a bustling village area, and buildings designed in the Swiss chalet style, just as in Walt's beloved Zermatt in Switzerland. The press conference was led by Donn Tatum, who had been named president of Walt Disney Productions in November, after Roy stepped down to focus on securing financing for Walt Disney World.

"The challenge Walt Disney saw at Mineral King was to make it an example of man's determination to meet an ever-growing public need in a manner that will, at all times, be in harmony with the area's natural beauty and unique alpine environment," Tatum said. "This will be the realization of one of Walt Disney's last and greatest dreams."[13]

Also in Burbank to celebrate the delivery of the master plan were California Senator George Murphy and John Deinema, regional forester for the Forest Service.

In estimates that had been scaled down slightly from Disney's original 1965 proposal, the company projected some 5,000 skiers per day when the resort opened in 1973, Tatum said, the number climbing to 8,500 by 1978. Mineral King would be one of the few ski areas in the country offering uninterrupted ski runs as long as four miles, with a vertical drop of more than 3,700 feet. Food-service facilities were planned for the two major lift terminals, and the bowls would be linked via interconnecting trails. Visitors would park in an eight-story underground garage located outside the valley, from which day skiers would be whisked by gondolas to the slopes, while overnight guests would take a relaxing ride on a cog railroad a little over a mile to reach the alpine village, where their luggage and skis would be waiting for them in their rooms. The village area was slated to include 465 guest rooms—a mix of hotel, apartment, and dormitory-style accommodations—as well as five restaurants, a convention center, theater, railroad station, pet lodge, and specialty shops. Twenty acres near the village would be developed for snow play activities including sledding and ice skating; in the summertime—which Tatum noted would be just as busy, if not more so, than the winter months—the area would be home to volleyball, shuffleboard, and badminton courts, horseback riding, and a heated outdoor pool.

Southern California skiers and business owners were elated at the announcement, the latter group touting $22 million in homes, motels, service stations, and more they anticipated being built along the roads leading into Mineral King. Tax revenues and employment numbers were expected to rise as well.[14]

Disney was ready to move ahead with engineering studies and additional planning in advance of beginning construction in 1971, but the company's pledge to preserve the "area's natural beauty and unique alpine environment" didn't impress the Sierra Club. President Edgar Wayburn said the organization was considering legal action to block the development. The club feared for the fate of the valley, he said, since Disney planned to "put as many people into Mineral King on a given day as enter Yosemite Valley at any one time . . . and Mineral King is one-sixth to one-third the size of Yosemite."[15]

❖ ❖ ❖

But before Disney could even think about a battle in the courtroom, it had another major battle to contend with—one with Mother Nature. It was the company's first taste of what could happen at Mineral King if things didn't go to plan.

Disney believed it had everything figured out when it came to predicting and controlling avalanches in the Mineral King valley, at one point claiming, with a bit of swagger, that "we can make [the snow] move when we want, not when it wants."[16] Its final master plan for Mineral King went into detail on the avalanche studies the company had conducted, explaining that the village center was planned for an area that had proven to be free from avalanche exposure.[17] But those with insider knowledge of the valley knew otherwise. Even Jean Koch had warned Card Walker and others in a letter about the dangers of avalanches at Mineral King.

In February 1969, Koch's predictions came true when an avalanche roared into the valley with fatal results. Disney employees David Beck and Wally Ballenger were living in primitive cabins on the former Ray

Mineral King project manager Bob Hicks, center, tours Mineral King with Senator George Murphy, left, and Representative Bob Mathias in February 1969, weeks before the avalanche that claimed the life of Randy Kletka. Behind the trio is Jim James, supervisor of Sequoia National Forest. © Tulare Advance-Register —USA TODAY NETWORK.

Buckman property in Mineral King, conducting snow surveys and other research in advance of resort and ski lift construction. While they were used to heavy snow in the area, the 1968–1969 winter had been particularly rough, with a late February storm dumping five feet of new snow on top of the twelve feet that had fallen previously. A few weeks earlier, Hicks had toured the area with Murphy and California Representative Bob Mathias, and just before that, a CBS television camera crew had come to Mineral King from New York to shoot some footage on the development for an upcoming segment on the Sierra Club.[18] A storm cut the filming short, however, and the camera crew was stranded for several days before being flown out by helicopter. By February 21, the snow had gotten so bad that Hicks ordered an evacuation due to the hazardous conditions. Beck and his wife, Susan, got out, but Ballenger and a visiting friend, Randy Kletka, opted to stay. The two decided to sleep in separate cabins in case one had to dig the other out, staying in touch by telephone. They were talking by phone on the evening of February 24 when an avalanche came thundering down from the mountain above, severing the phone line. Ballenger was able to create an airhole from the back door of his cabin, digging nearly fifteen feet up to the surface. Kletka tried to do the same, but a fire that had started when the avalanche upended a potbelly stove in the corner of his cabin quickly consumed all of the oxygen in the room. Rescuers recovered his body—along with the remains of several asphyxiated dogs and cats—on February 26.[19] The avalanche also destroyed multiple cabins. Beck called the disaster a once-in-a-hundred-years event and said that the cabins—some a century old—had "never been hit by anything like this before."[20] Hicks assured the public that the proposed Mineral King village area remained safe, though the disaster might alter some of the plans for its development.

For those opposed to the Disney resort, the event, as Koch wrote to the editor of the *Los Angeles Times* in 1969, was "further evidence of the poor planning of the proposed development there by Walt Disney Enterprises. Unless the site of the proposed Alpine Village has been changed following the tragedy, avalanches did indeed occur at the site of the planned village. Avalanches were widespread throughout the valley, as they have been throughout the entire history of Mineral King."[21]

* * *

A storm of a different kind was brewing within the Sierra Club, where a power struggle was taking place between longtime executive director David Brower, known for his militant environmental ways, and Ansel Adams, who was looking to return the club to its hiking roots. Brower, now fifty-six, was known for his brash, confrontational style, and for taking on public and private companies and government entities—often at no small expense—to save the redwoods, the Grand Canyon, various forms of wildlife, and, he hoped, Mineral King. Adams, on the other hand, longed for the days when the club was run on $9,000 or $10,000 a year and wasn't in the newspapers every week taking a stand against the latest environmental injustice. "The Brower group has a tendency to resent every intrusion into the wilderness and to overlook the realities of life," Adams said. "They forget that utilities and highway people have their own obligations. . . . If the Disney people put a resort in Mineral King, I don't see anything wrong with that. Brower is trying to set up an Eden. The Sierra Club has to roll with the [punches], because the world is getting very tough."[22]

In 1968 the club had begun looking more closely into Brower's book publishing program, which had produced close to twenty large-format, coffee-table-worthy books of nature photography that, while beautiful, had lost money for the organization. Brower also had opened a London office of the Sierra Club in 1968, tied to the publishing program, without bothering to get permission or let other members of the organization know of his plans.

On October 19, 1968, the Sierra Club board of directors met to discuss Brower's fate. Some, including Adams, thought he should be fired. Brower sat stoic and quiet as he was accused of financial irresponsibility, including diverting book royalties to himself and taking out an unauthorized page-and-a-half ad in the *New York Times*. Brower was given some time to write up a defense of the charges against him, but in early 1969, he went on the offensive, taking a leave of absence as executive director to prepare a run for the board of directors, where he and his supporters—if victorious—could run things the way they wanted to. The club temporarily split into two factions: Brower's Committee for an Active Bold Constructive Sierra Club; and the Adams-led Concerned Members for Conservation. Brower campaigned for months, getting a fair amount of ink in California newspapers, but when the final votes were tallied in April, the entire Committee for an Active Bold Constructive Sierra Club had been defeated.

Brower left the Sierra Club to form a new environmental organization, Friends of the Earth; named as his replacement was Michael McCloskey, who was appointed to a new position, chief of staff. McCloskey, then thirty-five, had become the club's conservation director in 1965, and among his priorities was the fight against development in Mineral King, which he had helped to lead for the past four years. McCloskey, who had a law degree from the University of Oregon and had once run for public office, had a new strategy in mind for blocking Disney's ski resort plans.

* * *

Just upstairs from the Sierra Club's main offices in downtown San Francisco was the headquarters of the Conservation Law Society of America, a nonprofit law firm created by Brower and longtime Sierra Club director Richard Leonard to provide low-cost legal services to conservation groups. McCloskey had grown friendly with its executive director, attorney Robert Jasperson, over the years, and one day McCloskey asked him if he thought the Sierra Club had any legal options when it came to fighting Disney on Mineral King.

McCloskey was encouraged by the 1965 Storm King Mountain case in New York, in which a group of concerned citizens calling themselves the Scenic Hudson Preservation Conference successfully sued the Federal Power Commission to block construction of a hydroelectric power plant on a section of the Hudson River considered to be among the most scenic river areas in the world. In a first-of-its-kind decision, the U.S. Court of Appeals, Second Circuit, ruled that aesthetic beauty alone was justification enough for an environmental group to file suit to block construction. Plaintiffs traditionally had to demonstrate economic or other harm in order to have legal "standing" to sue, but in the appeals court's decision, McCloskey saw a shift in thinking he thought might make the Mineral King battle an easier one to fight in the courts. Hoping Jasperson would feel the same way, McCloskey gave him everything the Sierra Club had on Disney's Mineral King development and the proposed highway.

Jasperson and another young environmental lawyer, Greg Archbald, set to work. Jasperson made a visit to Mineral King to see firsthand what the valley looked like and what impact a giant ski resort project might have, and in April 1968 he sent McCloskey a seven-page letter outlining the legal strategies the Sierra Club could consider using to halt the Disney development. In Jasperson's view, there were three ways in which the Mineral King ski resort was technically illegal. Firstly, by its own regulations the Forest Service was only permitted to grant thirty-year leases to private companies if the area being leased was eighty acres or less. That covered Disney's proposed "village" area, where hotels, restaurants, and shops would be located, but if the actual ski slopes were included, the acreage far exceeded what was allowed. The Forest Service was attempting to comply by issuing one-year leases for the ski slopes and other land, but Jasperson thought they were on shaky legal ground.

Jasperson also saw potential for a lawsuit against the Park Service, which had in place a requirement that roads built in national parks were to be constructed only for the convenience of park visitors. Roads that carried visitors from the park to national forest lands beyond—as was the case with the proposed section of highway that would run through Sequoia National Park—were not allowed. Finally, there was the issue of Mineral King's status as a national game refuge, which it had been designated by Congress in 1926. As Jasperson saw it, a major ski resort was incompatible with an area designated specifically as a sanctuary for deer, bighorn sheep, and other creatures.

McCloskey brought Jasperson's recommendations to the Sierra Club board of directors, and at a December 1968 meeting in San Francisco, the club authorized funds to pursue a lawsuit against the Mineral King project. The Sierra Club's legal committee, headed by young attorney Phillip Berry, agreed there was enough in Jasperson's report for a lawsuit, but they had neither the time nor the resources to handle it. Legal committee member Don Harris knew of another San Francisco lawyer, Leland Selna, who liked to camp and was interested in the environment; in February 1969, the Sierra Club hired Selna, thirty-five, to start building the legal case against the Disney development and the yet-to-be-constructed highway. By May 1969, when McCloskey officially took on his new Sierra Club post, that case was nearly complete.

The stage had been set by Koch—her petitions, her letter-writing campaign, her *Optimist* newsletter, and the documentary she was helping to fund—and by Rettenmayer and Hill and the participants at their hike-in protest. None of it, however, had stopped Disney from proceeding with its plans. Now it was time to raise the stakes even higher. It was time for the Sierra Club to take the Mineral King fight to the courtroom.

9

DAVID V. GOLIATH

1969

It was an overcast day in San Francisco, the brick-red towers of the Golden Gate Bridge barely visible down the hill and a misty fog settling in over Chinatown and the Tenderloin. As Michael McCloskey took a seat in the cozy, book-lined library at Sierra Club headquarters inside the city's historic Mills Building, he read through his notes one more time. It was June 5, 1969, and the room would soon be packed with journalists clamoring to hear about the lawsuit the Sierra Club had just brought against the federal government to block Walt Disney Productions' recreation project in Mineral King.

Attorney Leland Selna had filed the case that morning in the U.S. District Court for Northern California in downtown San Francisco. He knew he was taking an important legal step for the Sierra Club, which by 1969 had fully embraced its conservationist mission. The Mineral King lawsuit was one of the first the Sierra Club had ever filed on behalf of an environmental cause, and Selna had worked closely with McCloskey to put together a case the two felt had a good chance of succeeding.

McCloskey had been at the Sir Francis Drake Hotel on that May day in 1965 when the organization drafted its statement of opposition to the Disney development at Mineral King, and he had helped to lead the fight against the project since then, issuing press releases, writing the Forest Service to request a public hearing, and urging Interior Secretary Stewart Udall to stay strong in his opposition to the proposed highway. For

McCloskey, Mineral King was the latest conservation challenge in a career that had been devoted to preserving America's wild places.

⁕⁕⁕

Born in 1934 in Eugene, Oregon, where he grew up exploring the outdoors both on his own and as a member of the Boy Scouts, McCloskey wasn't aware, as a young boy, of the environmental hazards lurking in gasoline fumes and soldered pipes. It wasn't until after college that he would realize the threats modern civilization posed to the wilderness areas he loved so much.

"Parents kept warning us to stay away from the nearby Willamette River, which was then grossly polluted from the untreated local sewage that flowed into it," McCloskey wrote in his book *In the Thick of It: My Life in the Sierra Club.* "Refuse at the lumber mills was burned in so-called wigwam burners, producing wood smoke that we now know was full of carcinogens. And pulp mills were built later that sent sulfurous fumes into the wind. The late summer skies were clotted with choking smoke as farmers burned seed-grass fields following harvests to kill insects."[1]

Sierra Club executive Michael McCloskey, who led the organization's fight against the Mineral King development, pictured here in the 1970s. Courtesy of Michael McCloskey.

McCloskey was introduced to the legal world when he served in the Army in the late 1950s, after graduating from Harvard with a degree in American government. He moved through the military ranks and eventually was appointed to serve as defense counsel in courts-martial cases. He won every case he handled, then switched sides to work for the prosecution, where he was equally victorious. Inspired, McCloskey returned to his hometown of Eugene to attend law school at the University of Oregon, but his studies in business law left him cold.

McCloskey soon concluded that his interest in law would be best channeled into environmental advocacy. He was a longtime member of local outdoor organization the Obsidians, and during law school he began serving on the group's conservation committee, where he worked to block dams on the upper McKenzie River and preserve the natural setting of Waldo Lake. During his first year after law school, McCloskey ran for the state legislature in Oregon's Lane County, home to Eugene, and while he lost by 2,500 votes, he gained valuable experience in crafting messages and winning over a crowd.

It was through the Obsidians that McCloskey met Sierra Club executive director David Brower, who in 1960 hired him to investigate a plan for logging in northeastern Oregon, then brought him on as the Sierra Club's first full-time field organizer. McCloskey traveled the Northwest in a Volkswagen, and sometimes on horseback, to learn about environmental issues. He helped stop development in Minam Valley, blocked a pumice mine at Rock Mesa, and helped create North Cascades National Park in Washington before the Sierra Club board of directors asked him, in 1965, to move to California to become assistant to then president Will Siri.

Now it was 1969, and Brower had made a dramatic exit from the Sierra Club. McCloskey was determined to move past the infighting and refocus the organization on conservation—including the fight for Mineral King.

✧ ✧ ✧

As that fight headed toward the courtroom, McCloskey knew he had to be very thoughtful about whom the Sierra Club actually named in its lawsuit. Club members felt like scrappy Davids going after a Goliath—without question, Disney had become one of the most powerful companies in America, with its enviable profits, ever-expanding portfolio, and powerful name recognition. But the club also knew Disney was more than just a powerful company—it was a beloved one. Walt had been a sort of father to the country, and his popularity had been unmatched by pretty much anyone, even celebrities or politicians. It was rivaled only by that of his own famous creations.

His characters were innocent, purehearted princesses and wide-eyed animals whose worst qualities were mischievousness and unbridled curiosity. It was an ethos that seemed to define the entire company. Sure, the Sierra Club had been more than vocal against Disney's Mineral King plans, holding protests, sending letters to legislators, and speaking against the development at public meetings. But taking Disney to court—that was a different story. The club's executives and legal team worried that might go too far and paint the Sierra Club as the villain rather than the underdog hero. Suing Disney, they worried, could harm the club's reputation and instead sway public opinion to Disney as a sympathetic victim of the evil environmentalists. "To sue Disney would be like suing motherhood, the flag, and the Boy Scouts all at once," joked one Sierra Club member.[2]

That's why the club instead focused the suit on five government officials and the offices they oversaw: Walter Hickel, who had succeeded Udall as secretary of the interior and oversaw the National Park Service; Orville Freeman's successor, Clifford Hardin, secretary of agriculture, who oversaw the U.S. Forest Service; John McLaughlin, superintendent of Sequoia National Park; John Deinema, regional forester for the Forest Service; and M. R. James, forest supervisor of Sequoia National Forest.

In the brief submitted that June morning, McCloskey and Selna presented a number of justifications for the injunction, including Mineral King's status as a national game refuge, the fact that the highway through Sequoia National Park was illegal because it crossed the park for non-park purposes, the fact that avalanche danger in the area had not been adequately considered, and the fact that the proposed highway was a serious threat to giant sequoias in the area. Also at issue was a sixty-six-thousand-volt electrical line that would stretch across the park to power the resort. Most importantly, they argued, both the Disney resort and the highway, if built, posed a severe threat to Mineral King's natural state—a threat that would only get bigger with time. The motion included quotes from Disney's 1966 brochure on the resort, including a line from Walt that the Sierra Club used often in its anti-Mineral King materials: "All of us promise that our efforts now and in the future will be dedicated to making Mineral King grow to meet the ever-increasing public need. I guess you might say that it won't ever be finished."[3] A hearing on the injunction request was scheduled for June 30.

For Deinema, who had been one of the featured speakers at the Disney press conference in January 1969 announcing the Forest Service's approval of the company's master plan for Mineral King, the suit was an unwelcome surprise. "(It) comes as a real disappointment to me and I think to the general public who have given their support for the Mineral King project," Deinema said.[4] "I have repeatedly asked the Sierra Club for constructive advice and to work with us to make an outstanding public recreation area even better. My offer still stands today."[5]

The conservation movement celebrated the Sierra Club's move on Mineral King, but many others shared Deinema's views, especially California skiers who had been eagerly awaiting a world-class ski resort—with a touch of Disney magic—in their backyard. The argument played out in letters and editorials in newspapers across California in the coming weeks as McCloskey and Selna waited for their June 30 hearing before judge William

Sweigert. Sweigert had grown up in San Francisco and was a protégé of then Supreme Court Justice Earl Warren, having served as Warren's executive secretary when Warren was governor of California in the mid-1940s.

Sweigert heard both sides of the Mineral King dispute during two days of testimony starting in late June. Selna reiterated the Sierra Club's arguments on the temporary permits, the road through Sequoia National Park, and the violation of the area's status as a game refuge, and pointed out how much the Disney proposal exceeded the original Forest Service prospectus. The prospectus had called for a $3 million facility accommodating 100 overnight visitors, he said, while Disney's $35 million plan would have enough rooms for 3,300 to stay overnight. Selna also told the court he believed the secretary of the interior was planning to grant a final right-of-way permit for the highway in a matter of days.

Defending the government agencies was assistant U.S. attorney Paul Locke, who told Sweigert there was no urgent need for an injunction, as the state wasn't planning to request bids on the highway until May 1970 at the earliest. If the Sierra Club wanted a permanent injunction against the Mineral King resort, Locke said, the government was ready to go to trial. Most importantly, Locke said, the suit was invalid from the start because the Sierra Club hadn't shown how its individual members would be harmed by the Mineral King project—and therefore had no legal standing to sue.

Locke submitted affidavits from several individuals involved with the resort's planning and approval, including McLaughlin, assistant regional forester Slim Davis, and Walt Disney Productions president Donn Tatum, who said the company already had spent more than $750,000 on research and planning for Mineral King, including reports on ski run and resort siting, vertical photography, and topographic mapping, as well as the snow survey teams who had lived at Mineral King each winter since 1966. Would that planning continue, or would the Sierra Club be victorious in its first legal strike? Both sides waited anxiously while Judge Sweigert weighed the evidence.

* * *

Three weeks later, the verdict was in. David had felled Goliath. Pinocchio had escaped the whale. The Mineral King resort, four years in the making, was officially blocked. Judge Sweigert granted a temporary injunction on July 23, finding that the Forest Service had violated its own rules by attempting to grant Disney access to land outside of the eighty acres covered by its permit, and that the highway through Sequoia National Park was illegal because it went against interior department rules. Crucially, he found that the Sierra Club did indeed have the legal standing to file for an injunction due to its interest in preserving nature, particularly in the Sierra Nevada. The matter was urgent, Sweigert found, because the Department of the Interior could grant the highway permit to the state at any time. The Sierra Club, Sweigert wrote in his decision, "should not be left to 'watchful waiting' upon the state of California."[6] The organization had raised enough questions around the approval of the resort and the highway—including possible excess of authority—Sweigert said, to justify the preliminary injunction. Next up would be a trial.

The injunction was only temporary, and there was still a lot of legal work to do, but for now, McCloskey and Selna were elated. There would be no bulldozers clearing trees to make way for the highway, no dynamite placed among the rocks on the hillside to make a smooth surface for skiers. The Disney plan wasn't dead, but at the very least, the Sierra Club had bought itself some time.

While the Sierra Club celebrated the courtroom victory, Locke immediately began working on the government's appeal, determined not to let a small band of environmentalists put an end to what could turn out to be one of the country's finest ski areas. At Disney, Tatum and other executives worried about what the decision could mean for the company's image. The studio behind *Bambi* and the True-Life Adventures documentaries couldn't find itself on the wrong side of an environmental controversy. To help right the ship, the company in fall 1969 put together an advisory council of six nationally recognized conservationists to give the Mineral King development a sheen of environmental respectability. The advisory council—tasked with modifying the resort plans in hopes they would meet environmental muster, as well as developing an environmental education program at Mineral King—included Horace Albright, former director of the National Park Service and one-time superintendent of Yellowstone National Park; Thomas Kimball, executive director of the National Wildlife Federation; Eivind Scoyen, former superintendent of Sequoia and Kings Canyon national parks; and, in an appointment that came as a surprise to the Sierra Club, Bestor Robinson, a former Sierra Club president and director who also had served as a member of the Secretary of the Interior's Advisory Committee on Conservation in the 1940s and 1950s.

Robinson, an avid skier since he had served abroad in World War II, had skied and camped in most of the Sierra Nevada. He was part of a smaller, more conservative group of environmentalists—including some members of the Sierra Club—that saw skiing at Mineral King not as a violation of the area's natural wonder, but as a way for the mountains surrounding the valley to serve their highest purpose. The Disney resort could be a good thing for skiers as well as the environment, were it to be built the way Walt had envisioned it.

"I had no use at all for the argument that there was something superior in the wilderness use and that the skiers should be considered a second-class use. To me they were both very valuable forms of outdoor recreation," Robinson said later. "Some people want to ski, and some want to camp in the wilderness. Others, like myself, wanted to do both. And I had no use at all for the argument that some corporation is going to make money, as if the conflict on Mineral King was between the Disney corporation making money and the campers in Mineral King being purists."[7]

❖ ❖ ❖

Although Disney was not officially named in the lawsuit, the company found itself defending its ski-development plans as it were. Mineral King became a topic at center stage during Disney's annual stockholders' meeting on February 3, 1970, at Hollywood's Pantages Theatre, a glitzy, art-deco movie house with red velvet chairs and lavish gold-and-silver kaleidoscope designs on its vaulted ceiling. Although the company had plenty of good news to share at the meeting—including strong Disneyland attendance and a rise in earnings—several of the 1,600 stockholders present peppered Tatum with questions about the Mineral King lawsuit and the protests against the development. A group of concerned investors distributed leaflets throughout the theater that called attention to "major financial hazards in the Mineral King project."[8] One stockholder rose from the audience to question the financial implications of the Mineral King development, expressing concern about what the controversy was doing to the company's image. Another urged Disney leaders to drop the project and sue the government for persuading them to get involved with Mineral King in the first place. (The suggestion wasn't popular among attendees.)

Outside the meeting, on the sidewalk in front of the Pantages, was exactly the type of scene some investors were worried about. Around twenty-five picketers—hoisting colorful signs with slogans like "Put Mineral King in the Park," "Make Love, Not Resorts," and "All Disney's artists and all Disney's men can never put Mineral King together again"—circled the sidewalk in front of the venue's entrance and marched in protest. Another sign depicted a caricature of Mickey—not as a mouse, but as a rat, his snout long and sharp—holding an ax, surrounded by trees and dollar signs.

Conservationists may have been against the Mineral King project, but Disney and the government were at least hoping to get the legal system back on their side. Just six days after the stockholders' meeting, oral arguments for the government's appeal of Judge Sweigert's temporary injunction took place in San Francisco. A panel of three judges was asked to consider if the ruling against the Mineral King project should stand, and if the Sierra Club had the legal right to pursue the case. Back in the courtroom on behalf of the Sierra Club was Selna, who reiterated the organization's belief that the Forest Service was violating federal law by allowing Disney access to more than the eighty acres its permit allowed.

"They could put up the darndest resort they could think of—Ferris wheels and all—but only on eighty acres," Selna told the judges.[9]

The Justice Department had filed the appeal in December 1969, arguing that the Sierra Club lacked legal standing to request the injunction in the first place, as it hadn't shown any injury to its interests. "The club may not employ the federal courts as a forum in which to air its generalized grievances about the management of federal lands," the motion read.[10] Lending its support to the government's appeal by filing a brief as a "friend of the court"—a party with a stake in the case who is not actually part of the proceedings—was the Far West Ski Association, whose members worried about what a permanent injunction against the Mineral King development might mean for current and future California ski areas. Under fire in the Sierra Club's suit was the Forest Service's use of a mix of short- and long-term permits to accommodate development in Mineral King—a system that was already in place in many of the state's ski areas. If the dual-permit arrangement was found to be illegal, the existing ski areas could be threatened as well—not to mention any future developments planned for national forest land. Also weighing in on behalf of the government's case were the United States Ski Association and representatives of Tulare County, who reminded the court of the $1.5 million in taxes the resort was slated to bring in each year to finance school programs and road construction.

The appellate court justices took the case under advisement after one day of oral arguments from Selna and the government's attorney, Walter Kiechel, and Disney, the Sierra Club, and the government waited throughout the spring and summer for the court to make its ruling. Disney project manager Bob Hicks did his best to keep the project in the public eye, appearing in front of various rotary clubs and chambers of commerce around Southern California to defend Disney's position on Mineral King. Walt Disney had been a pioneer in conservation, Hicks reminded the Fresno Rotary Club in March, and the Mineral King development was going to be a "vast laboratory" to study how people could enjoy the outdoors without causing environmental harm.[11]

Also working to keep the Disney project alive was the Far West Ski Association, which in April 1970 started a series of "ski-ins"—in contrast to the "hike-ins" environmentalists had held there the previous two summers—bringing groups of skiers into Mineral King each weekend to give them a taste of what would be lost if the Sierra Club succeeded in blocking the resort. Participants were pulled by snow tractors to the tops of the peaks, where they bombed down the huge bowls through fresh powder. "I've never seen anything like this," said one ski-in participant. "It's like the Alps."[12]

The ski-ins also aimed to show California skiers that the Mineral King area was not the unspoiled paradise the Sierra Club claimed it to be. "Because of the Sierra Club opposition, most people have the idea this is wilderness," said Far West Ski Association president Dick Goetzman. "It isn't. It is a beautiful area, but it has been mined and logged and people have built cabins and summer homes here for a century. The only way people can know this is to see it."[13]

* * *

The ski-ins notwithstanding, McCloskey's hopes that the Sierra Club would win the Mineral King appeal were growing by the day. He was amazed by the growing interest in environmentalism that had resulted from press coverage of the Mineral King campaign and other Sierra Club initiatives. The organization had seen its membership soar by 23 percent in 1969, and the numbers looked to be increasing even more in 1970. Also helping to fuel the movement in the early part of 1970 was the tremendous media attention being given to the impending arrival of the very first Earth Day in April. The event had been conceived the previous year by Wisconsin senator Gaylord Nelson after two high-profile ecological disasters—a January 1969 oil spill off the coast of Santa Barbara, California, and a June 1969 fire on the Cuyahoga River in Ohio—caused many Americans to realize just how bad things had gotten from an environmental standpoint. From their living rooms, they were horrified as they watched television coverage of rescuers attempting to save birds and animals coated in oil in California, and as the flames rose off the water in Ohio. Inspired by the growing number of student protests against the Vietnam war, Nelson envisioned a one-day teach-in at universities across the country on issues of air and water pollution. He recruited others to the cause and set the date for April 22, which fell between spring break and final exams for most college students. McCloskey spent the very first Earth Day at the University of Minnesota, where he appeared as the day's keynote speaker before an audience of three thousand students, urging them to commit their lives to environmental work.[14]

❖ ❖ ❖

McCloskey also had been part of environmental history a year earlier, in April 1969, when he had traveled to Washington to deliver the lead testimony in support of a bill that would become one of the most powerful tools environmentalists could use to protect nature. Signed into law by President Richard Nixon on January 1, 1970, the National Environmental Policy Act of 1969 (NEPA) required any federal agency looking to start a project that could significantly affect the environment to first create a detailed examination of its potential environmental impact. In a statement attuned to the consciousness and environmental problems of the time, the act confirmed that Congress recognized "the profound impact of man's activity on the interrelations of all components of the natural environment," including population growth, urbanization, industrial expansion, and expanding technological advances.[15]

It was a law that would profoundly alter the way federal projects were planned and conducted, though few—including McCloskey—realized it at the time. "I must confess that even I did not foresee the importance of its requirement that agencies document the impact of their proposals on the environment and inform the public of their findings," he later wrote. "In future years, however, the Sierra Club would make repeated use of that provision in court."[16]

It did occur to McCloskey when the law was signed in 1970 that since Mineral King was a joint project between Walt Disney Productions and the Forest Service, chances were good that the Forest Service would have to provide an environmental impact statement on the development, were the project to move forward. That was likely to cause further delays, no matter how the appeals court ruled.

McCloskey held onto hope throughout the summer of 1970, but on September 17, 1970, the appeals court dealt a crushing blow to the Sierra Club's case. The justices ruled unanimously that the organization did not have legal standing to sue. Nothing in the club's original suit, the appellate court wrote, showed that its members would be affected in any way by the construction of the Mineral King development and its accompanying highway, "other than the fact that the actions are personally displeasing or distasteful to them."[17] The Sierra Club had alleged its "special interest" in the conservation of national parks and forests, particularly in the Sierra Nevada, the judges wrote, but the departments of agriculture and the interior had a special interest in those areas as well. After all, they had been charged by Congress with a direct responsibility to protect and conserve national parks and forests. The Mineral King development might be displeasing to the Sierra Club, but the United States Ski Association, the Far West Ski Association, and Tulare County were all in favor of it. "We do not believe such club concern without a showing of more direct interest can constitute standing in the legal sense," the court opined.[18]

The court also rejected all of the club's legal arguments. A combination of term and revocable permits was indeed allowed, the judges wrote, as evidenced by the fact that at least eighty-four recreational developments on national forest land were currently under such arrangements—many of them ski areas. As to the highway, the appeals court noted that no previous cases were cited to prove the illegality of the road—and the existing road largely followed the same path as the one yet to be built. The plans for the highway showed a great deal of concern for "preservation of aesthetic and ecological values," including sequoia trees, the justices wrote, and the secretary of the interior should have wide discretion in improving roads through national parks. "We know of no law and find little logic in a contention that a twisting, substandard, inadequate road through 9.2 miles of the park is legal but that an improved all-weather two-lane highway along a new but approximately parallel alignment is illegal."[19]

The appellate court judges were similarly dubious about the Sierra Club's claim that the Forest Service had held no public hearings on the Mineral King development—the record showed such a meeting in 1953, they said, and a "well-publicized hearing" had been held in August 1967 by the California Division of Highways. "It does not appear that the proposed roadway was any clandestine project," the court wrote.

In the summary of their decision, the appeals court judges pointed out that overpopulation was becoming a problem in the United States, and that the issue was creating a myriad of environmental problems. Even so, the court saw no problem with federal agencies "determining to make available a vast area of incomparable beauty to more people rather than to have it remain inaccessible except to a rugged few."[20]

McCloskey had expected better from a California court in 1970, especially with the momentum of NEPA and the first Earth Day on his side. The appeals court's judgment on standing, he said, was "completely out of harmony with the judicial climate of the '70s."[21]

After the verdict, Disney president Tatum—happy about the court decision, but still wary of environmental backlash—asked the Sierra Club to work with Disney and the government to ensure an ecologically sound development.[22] But the Sierra Club wasn't ready to throw in the towel just yet. The organization still had one arrow left in its quiver—and to some, it was a hell of a long shot.

The Sierra Club decided to appeal the case all the way to the Supreme Court—a request that even to some of the club's executives felt like a far-off dream. McCloskey, for one, knew the chances of the Supreme Court taking the case were slim; after all, in 1971, the high court agreed to hear just 5.8 percent of the cases it was asked to review.[23] Selna was more optimistic, as he thought the environmental implications of the Mineral King case would interest the court. But even if the Supreme Court opted not to hear the case, at the very least, the move kept Mineral King from being despoiled for a while longer.

The appellate court gave the Sierra Club until November 6 to file its final appeal—agreeing to keep the temporary Mineral King injunction in place until the high court made a decision on whether or not to hear the case. Getting in just under the wire, the club filed its petition on November 5, asking the court to hear the suit. At stake was not just the Mineral King development, but the future ability of the Sierra Club—and other environmental organizations—to sue to protect public lands, without having to show how the club or anyone else would be personally damaged by the development.

If the Supreme Court did in fact decide to hear the club's case, it would be a turning point for environmental lawsuits: a sign that environmental cases were worth fighting for; that trees and mountains and wildlife and the areas they called home that couldn't fight for themselves deserved to be protected. It was undoubtedly a Hail Mary, but McCloskey, Selna, and others had what felt like some momentum on their side. And they had been surprised before. The appellate court ruling was a disappointment, but they hadn't lost all hope. Recent cases like Storm King in New York had shown that the "door to legal standing is three-fourths open,"[24] McCloskey said. The Sierra Club was ready to kick the door open all the way.

10

TAKING A STAND

1971

Day was breaking over William Douglas's private refuge. The dew was drying on the blades of grass in the yard, and the sun had begun to peek through the fall leaves still hanging onto the tree limbs outside the front window.

Though Douglas lived just outside of urban Washington, D.C., with its bustling sidewalks and crowded commuter trains, he had found a cozy house that faced more than an acre of lawn, garden, and woods. He kept a bevy of quail on the property and welcomed visitors like raccoons, cardinals, and muskrats. Behind his back fence was a reservoir on whose banks Douglas once saw more than one hundred turkey vultures drying their wings.[1]

This natural backdrop inspired the seventy-three-year-old Supreme Court justice in the early morning hours of November 17, 1971, as he thought about one of the cases the court was scheduled to hear that day— one he had been anticipating for weeks—*Sierra Club v. Morton* (as in Rogers Morton, now secretary of the interior). The Sierra Club had sued to block a ski development the Disney company was looking to build in Southern California, and the appeals process had landed the argument in front of Douglas and his fellow justices. The Sierra Club, Douglas knew, was looking for official confirmation of its legal standing to sue on behalf of the environment, and he was curious to see what the rest of the high court had to say. Standing was a complex issue that had taken the spotlight in a

Supreme Court Justice William Douglas. Courtesy of the Supreme Court of the United States.

number of recent environmental cases, and Douglas had his own thoughts about how it might be interpreted.

Douglas knew a landmark environmental law case would eventually make its way to the Supreme Court, and he wanted to be there when it happened. It was why the longtime Sierra Club member, who had been appointed to the Supreme Court in 1939, had stepped down from the Sierra Club board of directors in 1962, after serving as a director for just one year. He knew the organization even then was contemplating litigation that could someday reach the high court, and he didn't want his involvement with the Sierra Club to disqualify him from ruling. He had given up his membership altogether the previous December, writing to Sierra Club president Phillip Berry, "The problems of the environment are so numerous and so great and the Sierra Club is, or may be, in many of them. Nobody knows what the future will bring forth."[2] Resigning from the Sierra Club was a big step for Douglas, as his involvement in the group was an important way for him to stay connected with others who shared his passion for wilderness and the mountains.

⋆

Born in 1898, Douglas developed his love of the outdoors when he was young. After his father died of a sudden illness in Portland, Oregon, when Douglas was six, his mother bought a small house in Yakima, a scenic south-central Washington town ringed with foothills. Yakima is forty miles east of the Cascades, a mountain range that includes the snowy peak of Mount Rainier and the volcanic rise of Mount Adams. As a young man, Douglas hiked the foothills around Yakima, in the summer keeping an eye out for rattlesnakes and in the spring making his way through shoots of western ryegrass and patches of green sage streaked with yellow bitterbrush. It was on one of these hikes that a teenage Douglas felt the Cascades calling—their distant ridges offering "streams and valleys and peaks to explore, snow fields and glaciers to conquer, wild animals to know."[3] Over the next ten years he got to know the range well, hiking, camping, and fishing in its solitude and majestic beauty. After attending Whitman College in Walla Walla, Washington, on a full scholarship, Douglas headed east to attend Columbia Law School in New York City, but he never forgot his time in the mountains and the spiritual feeling it gave him to hear the song of the wind through the conifers, to discover his relationship to the larger universe in a blade of grass or the song of a willow thrush at sunset, or to "worship God where pointed spires of balsam fir turn a mountain meadow into a cathedral."[4]

After graduating second in his class from Columbia in 1925,[5] Douglas took a job at a Wall Street law firm for a few years, then became part of the faculty at Yale Law School. He left Yale for Washington, D.C., in the early 1930s, after President Franklin D. Roosevelt nominated him to the Securities and Exchange Commission, which Roosevelt had created in response to the Wall Street crash of 1929. Douglas became chairman of the SEC in 1937, and in 1939, Roosevelt nominated Douglas to fill the seat of retiring

Supreme Court Justice Louis Brandeis. Douglas joined the high court months later, at the age of forty. Known as "Wild Bill," he was an outspoken supporter of civil liberties and environmental causes both behind the bench and in his personal life. He badgered government officials—senators, congressmen, the secretaries of the interior and agriculture—to support his causes and help preserve the wilderness.[6] As a justice, he granted a stay of execution to Julius and Ethel Rosenberg—an American couple convicted in 1951 of spying on behalf of the Soviet Union—and authored landmark decisions around free speech, privacy, and criminal procedure.

Douglas traveled back to Washington state often over the years, in 1964 building a cabin in the Goose Prairie area, near the Yakima foothills he wandered as a boy. An early environmentalist, Douglas in 1954 led a protest hike against proposed construction on the Chesapeake and Ohio Canal near Washington, D.C., and in 1965 he published *A Wilderness Bill of Rights*, a manifesto for "those whose spiritual values extend to rivers and lakes, the valleys and the ridges, and who find life in a mechanized society worth living only because those splendid resources are not despoiled."[7] He knew the time was right for a lawsuit like the one the Sierra Club had filed against the government on behalf of Mineral King, and he was excited to be part of the history of environmental law.

❊ ❊ ❊

The Sierra Club had filed for a writ of certiorari—the fancy Latin name for the Supreme Court's official declaration that it would hear the case—on November 5, 1970, and the high court had accepted the case on February 22, 1971. It would be the Sierra Club's first time in front of the Supreme Court. The hearing had twice been delayed due to unfilled vacancies on the court, but when Chief Justice Warren Burger opened oral arguments at 11:06 a.m. on November 17, Douglas was ready to hear the testimony. Seated with six other justices against a regal background of tall marble pillars and floor-to-ceiling red drapes, he listened as Leland Selna, lawyer for the Sierra Club, made the case for the organization's standing to sue: its work over the decades to protect the Sierra Nevada and draw the boundary lines of Sequoia National Park; its yearly trips to the valley. The problem was, nothing in the record showed the club's involvement with Mineral King. The group wanted to make its argument purely about protecting nature, and its case spoke of Mineral King's "fragile ecology," its alpine setting, its vulnerable native deer herd. The justices probed Selna, examining his standing argument from every angle. How long had the Sierra Club been around for? How many members did it have? Were those numbers relevant to standing? Could an individual with a deep interest in Mineral King make the same case the Sierra Club was making? Would removing the condition that a plaintiff had to show actual damages to claim legal standing result in a flood of environmental lawsuits across the country?

But then again, if the Sierra Club—longtime defender of the wilderness and protector of the Sierra Nevada—wasn't qualified to bring a case like this one, asked Justice Harry Blackmun, who was?

"In many instances," Selna told the court, "nobody."

Because the club represents the public interest, Selna said, "any questions regarding standing should be resolved in its favor because in these cases, conservationist organizations may be the only people who will step forward to challenge the illegal acts."[8]

Satisfied he had made the case for the Sierra Club's right to sue over Mineral King, Selna moved on to the merits of the case, starting with the high-speed access highway through Sequoia National Park, which, he told the justices, was clearly illegal.

"[Are] there no roads in Sequoia National Park?" Burger asked. "Is it just for hiking and horseback parties and that sort of thing?"

There was an existing road, Selna allowed, but it predated Sequoia National Park. Either way, the fact that a primitive road was already in Mineral King wasn't a "legalizing effect for the proposed new highway."

"A new highway would be huge by contrast, would be on a different route, with new cuts, fills, and structures," Selna said. "The record shows that its effect would be to wipe out 220 acres of virgin park land and to endanger sequoia trees."[9]

Selna closed by talking about the eighty-acre limitation Congress had put in place for leases on park land—a limitation the Forest Service was trying to get around in Mineral King, he said, by issuing revocable permits for the portions of the resort that stretched beyond eighty acres.

"In the entire history of this case, no one has explained the purpose of that limitation if not to restrict developments to eighty acres," Selna told the justices. And even though the appeals court had found that eighty-four other ski resorts used a combination of term and revocable leases, that did not "require this court to choose between closing them down and making Mineral King legal," Selna said. The court could focus its decision only on Mineral King.[10]

After Selna's testimony, Erwin Griswold, solicitor general for the United States and defender of the government's position, made his case. He looked at the issue differently from Selna: the Sierra Club's connection to Mineral

King, he said, was purely aesthetic. A ski resort there wouldn't cause a bit of harm to the club or its members. If the Sierra Club was found to have standing in its case against the Mineral King development, "then I believe it is fair to conclude that anyone who asserts an interest in a controversy has standing," Griswold said. In its initial complaint, he reminded the court, the club did not allege that it had a financial interest in the controversy, or that any of its activities or property were threatened by the Disney resort.

"[The Sierra Club's] sole allegation is that it has a large number of members and that it has exhibited a special interest in the conservation and sound maintenance of the national parks, game refuges, and forests of the country," Griswold said.

Justice Byron White asked Griswold a question that caught Douglas's attention: What would happen if the Sierra Club amended its suit to say that its members regularly camped out in Mineral King?

"That would help," Griswold said, "but they have not done it."[11]

Burger gaveled the hearing to a close after a little over one hour of testimony, and Douglas and his fellow justices were left with much to think about. In addition to the oral arguments, they had the amicus curiae, or "friend of the court," briefs to consider. On the government side, there was the brief that had been submitted to the Ninth Circuit Court of Appeals two years earlier by the Far West Ski Association and the United States Ski Association, as well as the brief filed by representatives of Tulare County. Weighing in on behalf of the Sierra Club were the Wilderness Society, the Izaak Walton League, and Friends of the Earth, who joined forces to write a brief that attempted to more explicitly establish the Sierra Club's connection to Mineral King and Sequoia National Park and make the case for the club's standing to sue. John Muir and the Sierra Club had been responsible for the creation of Sequoia National Park and the establishment of the Mineral King game refuge, the brief said, and since the Sierra Club made yearly camping trips into the area, it would in fact be impacted by the Disney project. "It is clear that the Sierra Club is both a national organization and a local organization with particular interest in the Sierra Nevada Mountains. Its headquarters is in San Francisco and 27,000 of its 78,000 members live in that area," the brief said. "The Sierra Club itself is a user of the refuge and park."[12]

Douglas read the briefs carefully, finding himself in agreement with the environmental groups who said the Sierra Club did indeed have standing to bring the suit against the Mineral King project.

* * *

Douglas wasn't the only legal mind in 1971 thinking about standing as it related to the environment. Some 2,600 miles away from Washington, D.C., on the sunny campus of the University of Southern California in Los Angeles, Christopher Stone—a thirty-three-year-old law professor at USC's Gould School of Law—had been paying attention to the Mineral King case as it made its way through the courts. When the Ninth Circuit Court of Appeals rejected the Sierra Club's standing to bring suit against the government, he had what he thought was a pretty simple idea: If the Sierra Club couldn't or wouldn't show how it would be injured by the Disney development, why not show how Mineral King itself would be injured? Ships and corporations were regarded as individual entities with legal rights; why not trees and rivers?

Stone began writing an article on the topic in October 1971, just a month before the Supreme Court hearing, with hopes of getting it in front of the justices before they made their final decision in the Mineral King case. The *Southern California Law Review*, the flagship journal of the Gould School of Law, had a special issue on law and technology coming out in March 1972, and Stone convinced the editor to make room for his environmental treatise. By cosmic coincidence, Justice Douglas had been tapped to write a preface to the special issue, and all of the articles were due to him by December so that he could begin writing his introduction. Stone worked at a breakneck pace to finish his paper, and on November 17, 1971—the same day as the Supreme Court hearing on the Mineral King case—Douglas received brief synopses of all the articles slated for the March issue, including Stone's "Legal Rights for the Environment, Too?" (It was later retitled "Should Trees Have Standing? Toward Legal Rights for Natural Objects.") The law review editor included a one-paragraph overview of each article, adding to the section on Stone's paper that "Professor Stone's draft has not yet been edited but because of its extraordinary nature, we are sending along a draft of the first sixty paragraphs."[13]

Douglas devoured all sixty, and inspired by Stone's argument, he began writing his dissent just hours after the oral arguments in *Sierra Club v. Morton*. Like Stone, Douglas believed that valleys, meadows, lakes, rivers, and trees ought to be given standing—through human intermediaries—to sue for their own preservation.

✳ ✳ ✳

Five months was a long time to wait for a decision, but the Supreme Court moved by its own slow clock, and on April 19, 1972—three days before the third annual Earth Day—the Sierra Club, the Forest Service, Disney, and the Department of the Interior got the word: The Supreme Court was ready to rule.

The environmental movement had only grown in the two years since the appeals court ruling on Mineral King, giving the Sierra Club hope that the Supreme Court might find in its favor, but the justices, by a slim margin, handed the organization another loss. By a 4–3 vote, the court found that the Sierra Club had failed to make its case for standing. The justices declined to weigh in on the actual merits of the case—whether the road was illegal, the permits invalid, the game refuge being violated.

Writing for the majority, Justice Potter Stewart wrote, "Aesthetic and environmental well-being, like economic well-being, are important ingredients of the quality of life in our society, and the fact that particular environmental interests are shared by the many rather than the few does not make them less deserving of legal protection through the judicial process." But legal standing, Stewart wrote, "requires more than an injury to a cognizable interest. It requires that the party seeking review be himself among the injured." The Sierra Club, Stewart wrote, had not shown how it or any of its members "would be affected in any of their activities or pastimes by the Disney development. Nowhere in the pleadings or affidavits did the Club state that its members use Mineral King for any purpose, much less that they use it in any way that would be significantly affected by the proposed actions of the respondents."[14] The appeals court, therefore, was correct in its ruling, he judged, and its reversal of the temporary injunction was affirmed by the highest court in the land.

Disney celebrated the decision as the end of a three-year legal delay on the Mineral King project, during which public demand for outdoor recreation facilities had only continued to grow. Card Walker, now Disney's president, urged "all parties to work together" as the company moved forward to make Mineral King one of the best ski areas in the country.[15]

The Supreme Court decision was an immediate victory for Disney and the government, but the Sierra Club, too, saw a win in the dissents written by Douglas, Blackmun, and William Brennan Jr., all of whom recognized the urgency of updating legal processes in response to the environmental crises of the early 1970s.

"If this were an ordinary case, I would join the opinion and the Court's judgment and be quite content," Blackmun wrote. "But this is not ordinary, run-of-the-mill litigation. The case poses . . . significant aspects of a wide, growing, and disturbing problem, that is, the Nation's and the world's deteriorating environment with its resulting ecological disturbances. Must our law be so rigid and our procedural concepts so inflexible that we render ourselves helpless when the existing methods and the traditional concepts do not quite fit and do not prove to be entirely adequate for new issues?"[16]

In the final draft of his dissent—which would become a touchstone of environmental law in the decades to come—Douglas echoed Blackmun's sentiments, citing the "contemporary public concern" for protecting the ecological balance of nature.

"The critical question of 'standing,'" Douglas wrote, "would be simplified and also put neatly in focus if we fashioned a federal rule that allowed environmental issues to be litigated before federal agencies or federal courts in the name of the inanimate object about to be despoiled, defaced, or invaded by roads and bulldozers and where injury is the subject of public outrage.

"Mineral King is doubtless like other wonders of the Sierra Nevada such as Tuolumne Meadows and the John Muir Trail. Those who hike it, fish it, hunt it, camp in it, frequent it, or visit it merely to sit in solitude and wonderment are legitimate spokesmen for it, whether they may be few or many," Douglas wrote, referring in his dissent to Stone's article in the *Southern California Law Review*. "Those who have that intimate relation with the inanimate object about to be injured, polluted, or otherwise despoiled are its legitimate spokesmen."[17]

The dissents indicated a new way of thinking when it came to protecting the environment. It was much bigger than Mineral King—it was the hope that every tree, every flower, had the right to exist and be beautiful and pure, and it didn't matter if a human would suffer from its loss. The loss alone was enough to cause injury.

Douglas's and Blackmun's opinions were a hopeful sign for the Sierra Club, but even more encouraging was a small footnote that Michael McCloskey later learned had been added just a week before the decision was published. The court noted that the amicus curiae brief written by the Wilderness Society and other environmental groups did make a compelling case for the Sierra Club's standing in the Mineral King affair, but that the case as presented did not include that information. "Our decision does not, of course, bar the Sierra Club from seeking in the District Court to amend its complaint"[18] by adding more information about its use of Mineral King and how the Disney development would impact its activities there, the footnote said.

It was all the club needed to hear.

✿ ✿ ✿

Armed with the Supreme Court decision that in McCloskey's words, "has virtually given us an invitation to refile our pleadings,"[19] the organization returned to Judge William Sweigert's courtroom in San Francisco in July 1972 with an amended suit that claimed the club and its members regularly conducted outings in the Mineral King area and would be deprived of "wilderness experiences they have enjoyed since the turn of the century"[20] were the Disney resort to be constructed. The Sierra Club also added a new complaint based on the National Environmental Policy Act, which had become effective on January 1, 1970, while the litigation was pending. The Forest Service would now have to complete a lengthy environmental impact statement before moving forward with the resort project.

For good measure, the club added the Mineral King District Association, the alliance of cabin owners in the area, as coplaintiffs. Among those cabin owners was Jean Koch, head of the association, who was happy to be included in the suit along with many of her neighbors, all looking to save their treasured community and the land they loved.

Sierra Club attorney James Moorman, executive director of the newly formed Sierra Club Legal Defense Fund—founded when the organization realized how much it was paying outside lawyers to work on the Mineral King case—traveled to Mineral King to give the district association an update on the legal proceedings. He later remembered the "wonderful little community" he had discovered there.

"I learned as I talked to them that they viewed Mineral King as their place in the world," he said. "I stayed in the cabin of a woman who had met her husband there as a teenager. Their families both had cabins, as did their fathers. The various members lived in different places around California, but they all came together at Mineral King each summer and renewed their friendships. Mineral King was incredibly important to these people. It was their 'place.'"[21]

The Sierra Club was going to keep fighting to save that sacred place, not just for the cabin owners, but on behalf of every hiker, camper, and fisherman who found Mineral King a site of refuge and restoration. The club would do its damndest to keep a Disney development out of the fragile valley.

※ ※ ※

As the Sierra Club lawsuit continued to put Disney's plans for the California wilderness on hold, the company turned its focus on what it was able to control: the project amid the Florida swamplands. The planning for Walt

Disney World had moved along swiftly and, unlike Mineral King, was relatively drama-free, with the resort opening in Orlando on October 1, 1971. The 107-acre Magic Kingdom mirrored Disneyland with its Main Street, a castle as the park's showcased icon (this time a re-creation of Cinderella's exquisite blue-and-white palace), and a mix of charming and thrilling attractions. Opening day also saw the debut of the Contemporary Resort and Polynesian Village Resort, which represented the Disney company's first foray into the hotel business. At the park's official dedication ceremony on October 25, Roy took to a podium on Main Street, U.S.A., and—with Mickey Mouse standing to his left and Cinderella Castle behind him, the royal-blue tips of its towers and turrets shimmering in the fierce afternoon sunlight—paid homage to his brother.

"Walt Disney World is a tribute to the philosophy and life of Walter Elias Disney . . . and to the talents, the dedication and the loyalty of the entire Disney organization that made Walt Disney's dream come true," Roy said. "May Walt Disney World bring joy and inspiration and new knowledge to all who come to this happy place . . . a Magic Kingdom where the young at heart of all ages can laugh and play and learn—together."[22]

Walt wasn't there to see it, but his influence in the new park was everywhere: from the charming Main Street shops that evoked Americana-flavored nostalgia to the painstaking details that made the amusement park unlike anything that existed at the time. Walt's influence even went beyond the park—with their founder's love of nature in mind, the company developed a conservation plan for Walt Disney World, setting aside 7,500 acres as a permanently protected conservation area. Bob Hicks worked with local environmentalists and government agencies—as well as the Disney conservation advisory committee that had been created to guide the Mineral King plans—to establish the preserve, home to 150 species of birds and animals including wild turkeys, wood ducks, bears, armadillos, and alligators. The nature area was one piece of a $10 million environmental quality plan that also included using treated wastewater to water golf courses, collecting trash via underground pneumatic tubes, and improving incineration facilities well beyond what was required by the Florida Air and Water Pollution Control Commission.[23]

The Magic Kingdom opened with nineteen attractions, including Disneyland favorites the Haunted Mansion and the Mad Tea Party, and such new draws as the Hall of Presidents. Another attraction debuting exclusively at Walt Disney World was the final iteration of Marc Davis's bear band show, dubbed the Country Bear Jamboree—the inclusion of which, to some company insiders, seemed to indicate Disney was losing hope that the Mineral King project would ever come to fruition.

Nestled in the park's Frontierland, a rustic-themed land that looked like an Old West town, the attraction was housed in a log cabin called Grizzly Hall. Park visitors made their way through a cozy, wooden-entranced lobby, and into a dark theater with wooden benches and three animal heads—a deer, a moose, and a buffalo—mounted on the wall. (They talked, of course.) When the curtain lifted, the sixteen-minute show began, and guests watched eighteen Audio-Animatronic bears sing a number of country hits—both original songs and old country favorites, like Tex Ritter's "Blood on the Saddle" and Wanda Jackson's "Tears Will Be the Chaser for Your Wine"—and play an array of musical instruments, from banjos and fiddles to a jug and a washboard. Henry, a friendly top-hatted brown bear, acted as master of ceremonies, making jokes and introducing the different musical acts.

A piece of Disney's Mineral King project was alive and well in 1971 after all. And it was an immediate hit. After the success of the show in Florida, Imagineers decided to replicate the attraction on the West Coast, not only bringing the Country Bears to Disneyland, but also theming an entire new land around the attraction. The four-acre, $8 million Bear Country opened in spring 1972. In addition to Country Bear Jamboree, the land included the Golden Bear Lodge, a restaurant overlooking the Rivers of America; the Mile Long Bar refreshment center, which used mirrors to create the illusion of a bar that extends forever in each direction; and Teddi Barra's Swingin' Arcade, a pay-to-play arcade named after one of the Country Bears and featuring games with a backwoods theme. Guests entered the new land to the sounds of a snoring bear—Rufus—who could be heard but never seen.

With its rustic feel and thickly planted trees, Bear Country was the closest Disney had come so far to building Walt's mountain recreation dream. But now that the Supreme Court had ruled in the company's favor—and despite the latest legal holdups—Disney was ready for that to change. And the company's new president would go directly to California residents to sell them, once again, on the idea of a ski resort in Mineral King.

HEROES AND VILLAINS

1972

Disney president Card Walker had had enough. Enough of the lawsuits, the holdups, the setbacks, the misinformation, and the public battle with environmentalists in which Disney was being painted as the villain in a man vs. nature all-out war. Although the Supreme Court had ruled against the Sierra Club, allowing Disney to progress with its plans for Mineral King, in many ways the company also lost. It lost time, it lost money, and worst of all, the world had lost the original vision of Mineral King as described by Walt, whose good intentions and grand vision seemed to be fading with each year that passed following his death. It was a distortion Walker could no longer accept.

So on May 5, 1972, just weeks after the Supreme Court ruling, Walker decided to take matters into his own hands and make a direct appeal to the citizens of California in black and white. In an effort to combat the inaccuracies in the picture being presented of the company, Walker took out a full-page ad in several newspapers throughout the state, including the *Los Angeles Times*, *San Francisco Examiner*, *The Sacramento Bee*, and *The San Bernardino County Sun*, to make the case for Disney's Mineral King development. As they drank their morning cups of coffee, California residents opened up their papers to see a message from a leader of the Disney company under large banner text that read, "I remember . . . because I was there with Walt Disney at Mineral King."

"No one seems to remember what Walt Disney *really* had in mind at Mineral King," Walker said in the ad. "What Walt Disney said was simply this: The creation of recreational services at Mineral King is a challenge and an obligation—a challenge to serve the growing public need; an obligation to preserve the beauty of the land. I remember. Because I was there with Walt Disney. . . . And I'm tired of hearing and reading the distortions, the misinformation, the lawsuits and all the press releases vilifying the concepts proposed by Walt Disney and Walt Disney Productions."

To make it clear whose idea the recreation plan was, a photo of Walt at Mineral King, plans in hands, fedora on his head, was at the top of the newspaper page. Walker stood to his left.

It was fitting that it was Walker who took a stand on Mineral King. The fifty-six-year-old was president of the company by that time, having taken over the role in 1971, after a three-month period that had seen one of the company's biggest triumphs, followed by one of its biggest tragedies. Roy Disney had worked for years to finish Walt Disney World in honor of his brother, but just weeks after the Florida theme park opened in October 1971, Roy died suddenly at age seventy-eight after suffering a cerebral hemorrhage. He passed away on December 20 at St. Joseph Hospital in Burbank, the same place his younger brother had died five years earlier. Roy's death hadn't garnered nearly as much attention as Walt's, which was news that had been splashed on the front page of every newspaper globally and spurred widespread outpourings of mourning and grief from politicians, celebrities, and fans. In contrast, coverage of Roy's death elicited just a few column inches in newspapers around the country, in articles that described him as Walt's business partner and the behind-the-scenes enabler of his brother's ambition. As it had been throughout their lives and storied careers, despite what the elder Disney brother had accomplished, despite him aligning the planets to make Walt's dreams happen, Roy's star never came close to Walt's. Roy was always in his brother's shadow, even in death.

Walt's passing five years earlier had been a tragedy, but the loss of the second Disney brother marked a different kind of sadness for the company, one that truly spelled the end of the glamorous Disney brothers era, a rags-to-riches success story that resulted in an entertainment empire that defined art and animation, movies and music, experiential escapes, fantasy and fun. Roy had been there to carry on after Walt died, not only as the primary moving force to realize Walt's dreams but also as the keeper of the Disney flame. Things were different after Roy died, though. There was no clear successor. The Disney company would move on, but without its founding fathers.

But in many ways, Walker, who had worked in various aspects of the company for decades, was as close to a natural fit for the position of company president as possible. Having worked intimately with both Walt and Roy on projects over the years—including the Haunted Mansion, It's a Small World, and Pirates of the Caribbean attractions; films including *One Hundred and One Dalmatians* and *The Jungle Book*; and the development of Walt Disney World—he knew the temperament of both brothers. He knew what drove them, what constituted a true Disney experience, and what Walt and Roy wanted and dreamed of for the company.

✿ ✿

After graduating from the University of California, Los Angeles, in 1938, Esmond Cardon "Card" Walker joined Disney as a mailroom clerk. And barring a stint serving in the U.S. Navy as a flight deck officer during World War II, he never left the company. He ascended the corporate ladder from the mailroom to the camera department, then the production and story departments, before moving into advertising and sales, where he became vice president.[1]

Most of Walker's decisions were based on what Walt would have done, and Mineral King was no exception. Walker wanted to strike the right tone in the ad. His former boss and friend was personable and affable, stopping to talk to visitors and fans in Disneyland or sharing his plans, movies, and parks with the masses on his television show. Walt was friendly, but he wasn't a pushover. He could be persuasive, stern, and even formidable when he needed to get things done.

With that in mind, Walker decided to get his message about Mineral King out directly, without the media, reporters, or other officials warping his words. He didn't want the message to get lost in another game of telephone.

If anyone knew who Walt was, what he stood for, and what he envisioned for one of his great, final projects, it was Walker, a man who had toured the Mineral King area with Walt in 1966, when Walt was sharing his vision to make the valley accessible for scores of curious tourists looking to explore the high country.

Walt wasn't trying to build a "Disneyland in the mountains," Walker wrote in the newspaper ad. He never was. He was simply trying to make the area its own adventure based on what it already had to offer—trails, snow-capped peaks, animal-watching, natural beauty. "No 'Disneyland' or 'amusement center' was ever contemplated. What Walt Disney did propose was 'to create, design and operate facilities at Mineral King that serve the public need and the interests of participants' who venture into this unique alpine environment."

For every argument against development of wilderness areas, about the permanent damage that could be done, about how the natural land would be molded and changed, there was an equally powerful argument for development that many pointed out: without development of some kind, without a proper way of getting there, or having somewhere to stay, people couldn't actually enjoy the wilderness and understand and appreciate its beauty. To build something in nature to make it far easier for visitors of all abilities and ages to see it—not just athletic backpackers or experienced back-country skiers—is to make it accessible, to make it so that people can understand its magnitude and how special it really is.

"Shall this area remain totally inaccessible in winter and available only to a select few in summer, or shall it be made available for the pleasure, benefit and enjoyment of everyone?" Walker wrote. "If you believe California needs recreational opportunities and facilities of the highest caliber, then the time has come to take a stand. Who really speaks for Mineral King? And who really speaks for you?"

After trying to lay low during the Sierra Club lawsuits—Bob Hicks had visited civic organizations throughout the region to make the case for Mineral King but rarely addressed the court drama directly—the ad was a forceful change in demeanor for Disney. Company executives like Walker were growing tired of sounding like the bad guy. Disney, after all, was used to being the hero, not the villain. It created colorful, detailed, memorable antagonists—a puppy-napper hell-bent on slaying dogs for a fabulous black-and-white spotted coat, a horned sorceress, a cruel and evil stepmother determined to punish her kindhearted stepdaughter, a captain who sought revenge against Peter Pan for leaving him with a hook for a hand—but the heroes, the good guys, the princesses, the ones who were driven by good and morals and kindness and character: those were the stars. They were the ones who defeated the villains. Disney was no bad guy, and it was intent on keeping its good name.

Walker and the Disney company were doing much more than simply paying lip service and devising a PR campaign to take back the narrative on Mineral King. In the midst of the lawsuits, as fears grew about the project's feasibility, they had been quietly working with the Forest Service to make changes to the resort plans in hopes of appeasing environmentalists and finally making Mineral King happen.

In the biggest compromise to getting the Mineral King project built, the company decided to eliminate the controversial all-weather highway that would cross Sequoia National Park, replacing it with an electrically powered, cog-assisted railway—one in which a toothed "rack rail" ran between the two main rails, allowing a cog wheel mounted to the underside of the train to mesh with the teeth and pull the train up steep grades. The narrow-gauge railway, which would cost roughly $20 million and travel some fourteen miles, would be paid for by those who used it. The power line to the resort would be buried in the roadbed of the railway, eliminating the need for an overhead electrical line across Sequoia National Park.

The railroad plan not only would eliminate automobile traffic from Mineral King, but it also would enable the Forest Service to control the number of people allowed into the area at any given time. Plus, it would remove the need for a parking structure inside the valley, as visitors would park their cars before they boarded the train that would take them into the resort.

Though a train was part of the plan all along, it also was a feature that would have pleased Walker's former boss. Walt's lifelong fascination with trains began in his childhood when Walt's father, Elias, and his uncle Mike worked for the railroad. Walt had a short stint as a news butcher in 1916, selling snacks, newspapers, and magazines on the Kansas City Southern, Missouri Pacific, and Missouri-Kansas-Texas railroads—an experience that, he recalled, was "brief, exciting, and unprofitable."[2] Railroads would bring better luck for Walt later, though: famously, Walt's biggest and arguably most important creation, Mickey Mouse, was born on the railway. Following a cross-country train trip to New York in early 1928, Walt learned he had lost his first animated star, Oswald the Lucky Rabbit, as well as half of his animation staff due to a contract dispute with his film distributor. But on the return trip to California, Walt scribbled a doodle that became Mickey Mouse—a cartoon that defined his legacy and of course spurred his empire. Trains made appearances in numerous Disney shorts and films, from the 1929 short *Mickey's Choo-Choo* to the 1941 film *Dumbo*. And when Disneyland opened in 1955, the Disneyland Railroad—a steam-powered train ride that encircles much of the park, stopping in four different lands—was among its opening-day attractions.[3]

In addition to detailing them in the newspaper ad, Walker and other Disney officials announced the revised plans for Mineral King in May at a press conference at the Tulare County Courthouse in Visalia, hoping to remove some of the Sierra Club's objections. Not only was the company adding the railway to its Mineral King plans; it also was downsizing the resort in an effort to appease environmentalists. The number of visitors was reduced from a previously estimated maximum of fourteen thousand people a day to an average of four thousand and a high of eight thousand,[4] and the resort would now have between seven and ten ski lifts, rather than the twenty-two initially planned. The company would spend $15 million to $18 million on housing, restaurant facilities, and other needed structures— considerably lower than the $35 million estimated cost when the resort was first proposed.[5] In addition to reducing Mineral King's environmental footprint, Disney likely had a secondary motive: saving the company some money. The downscaled resort would help financial matters after Walt Disney World had opened half a year earlier to the tune of $400 million, significantly higher than the initial projection of $100 million.[6]

⁎ ⁎ ⁎

For California Governor Ronald Reagan, the announcement of Disney's scaled-down plan for Mineral King was cause for some soul-searching. Reagan had been a friend of Walt's and was very much in favor of the Disney ski resort, but he knew the expensive highway that would run through scenic Sequoia National Park—now estimated at $38 million[7]—had long been a point of dissension for many California voters. Now that Disney was planning to bring visitors to Mineral King by rail, Reagan saw an opportunity to score some points with environmentalists while helping the state's budget at the same time. Soon after Disney's May 1972 announcement that it was downsizing the resort plans, a bill had been introduced to eliminate state funding for the fourteen-mile stretch of road that Disney now wanted to use for a railway. When the bill reached Reagan's desk, he asked one of his staffers to reach out to Disney to make sure the highway was no longer needed. Board chairman and CEO Donn Tatum assured the staffer it was not, and on August 18, 1972, Reagan signed a bill blocking the construction of a high-speed highway into Mineral King. "I want to stress as strongly as possible that I am firmly in support of the development of Mineral King as a recreation area," said Reagan, who had begun his second term the year prior. "However, I am convinced that proper future development will not be hampered by lack of access by a high-speed road. Alternate access methods will suffice and, in the end, better serve the needs of both conservation and recreation."[8]

Reagan's move was welcome news to antidevelopment activists, some of whom hoped the elimination of the highway was the beginning of the end of Disney's ski resort plans in Mineral King. But the death of the road alone wasn't enough to completely ease their concerns. The fight against the development continued, and in April 1973, protestors took their message straight into enemy territory.

❋ ❋ ❋

As families walked excitedly toward the gates of Disneyland, a group of demonstrators marched on the sidewalk nearby, holding up handmade picket signs painted with anti–Mineral King messages including "Disney has his mountain in the city. He doesn't need a city in the mountains."

The protestors stood in sharp contrast to the throngs of kids skipping toward the park's gates, children tugging at their parents' arms, urging them to walk faster so they could enter the haven where they could ride Matterhorn Bobsleds and Pirates of the Caribbean. It was Saturday, April 14, 1973, and dozens of Mineral King demonstrators circled the area for their "March on Disneyland."

The group of protestors, Jean Koch among them, met at 10 a.m. at nearby Stoddard Park in downtown Anaheim with a mix of trepidation and excitement. Protesting was new for many of them, so the group was nervous as they shouldered their handmade signs, gripped leaflets explaining their mission, and gathered up stacks of "Keep Mineral King Natural" bumper strips to hand out to passersby. But they were encouraged as they looked around and saw the cheesy gift shops surrounding the park. Imagining stores in Mineral King selling Mickey Mouse stuffed animals and coffee mugs touting the Disney name, they started their protest, walking past motels and restaurants before arriving at the gates of Disneyland. The sun was getting stronger and brighter with each passing minute.

Disney guards kept watch on the group, as did several police cars that cruised by during the march, making the picketers nervous. But their nervousness changed to amusement when they "heard a chugging overhead and realized that the Disneyland helicopter was also keeping us under surveillance," Koch later wrote of the march in the *Optimist* newsletter.[9]

The march on Disneyland was the brainchild of Koch and Jerrold Klatt, a twenty-four-year-old hiker, skier, and Sierra Club member who had been opposed to the Mineral King development since he first heard about it a few years prior. He had been to Mineral King a handful of times, and he knew how special the area was. When he began receiving bulletins from the Sierra Club about the proposed Disney project, he knew he had to do something. Where better to get the word out than Disneyland, where an anti-Disney protest was bound to get people talking? Klatt lived in Escondido, outside of San Diego, and in December 1971 he had written a letter

MARCH ON DISNEYLAND

WE CAN SAVE MINERAL KING
MAKE EARTH WEEK 1973 EFFECTIVE AND
HELP US STOP DISNEY PRODUCTION'S PLANNED
DESTRUCTION OF THIS BEAUTIFULL WILDER-
NESS MOUNTAIN BASIN. MEET US AT
STODDARD PARK [starting + ending (?) point] at
10:00 A.M. ON SATURDAY, APRIL 14, IN ANAHEIM.
BRING YOUR SIGNS AND
POSTERS AND RALLY TO
THE CAUSE.
     Call or write us at address
above for more info.
SEE YOU THERE!

The flyer for one of the demonstrations against Disney's Mineral King development plan—this time held on enemy ground. Courtesy of University of Southern California, on behalf of the USC Libraries Special Collections, and Jerrold Klatt.

to the editor of the city's newspaper, the *Daily Times-Advocate*, about Mineral King. It read in part, "Only the rich elite of L.A.—primarily—will enjoy this area, where costs to ski and [stay] overnight average $50-$75 per day. I am an avid skier, but a more avid enjoyer of our far-too-few beautiful places."[10]

As they marched, the protestors handed out bumper stickers and leaflets to anyone who asked. The leaflet, titled "Why Are We Picketing Disneyland?," gave an overview of the "fragile, primitive" Mineral King area and Disney's plans to "denude vast areas for ski runs and building sites" and bring in thousands of people per day.

"As surely as the Disney company can construct a Matterhorn in the midst of a city, it can destroy a natural wonderland in the midst of the mighty Sierras," the leaflet continued. "We urge that Mineral King be kept natural. What better tribute to the late Walt Disney, who after all, was a conservationist."

The Disneyland march was the latest in a series of antidevelopment actions by conservationists—including the Sierra Club's Mineral King Task Force, which was showing no signs of backing down in its efforts. The documentary film Koch had helped to create with University of Southern California students Bruton Peterson and Jim Rascoe had premiered in April 1972, and by that fall, it had been viewed by seventy thousand people in more than 500 screenings.[11] "Reaction to it has been near unanimous praise," Koch wrote in the fall 1972 *Optimist*, noting that while the film was predictably popular with conservation groups, it also was appreciated by the Boy Scouts, school classes, church organizations, and political gatherings. A print of the film, Koch wrote, was in use at the Washington, D.C., office of John Tunney, a Democratic senator from California.

The film provoked an immediate emotional response with its peaceful opening scenes—a deer eating grass in the meadow, kids playing next to a stream, a family fishing by a creek—which were soon juxtaposed with scenes of developed wilderness areas like Mammoth Mountain, with its grinding, squeaky ski lifts, and crowded Yosemite, with blasting music, rows and rows of parked cars, and noisy crowds of tourists, some smoking cigarettes. In one scene, a picnicker at Yosemite drops a plastic container into a stream, the refuse floating away as others look on.

The documentary, which also delved into the history of Mineral King and its mining past, explained the controversy over the Disney development and featured footage of one of the summertime hike-in protests, as well as an interview with Stewart Udall, who had left his secretary of the interior post in 1969. Udall said an improved Mineral King road and the resulting traffic would "unnecessarily scar the park as it went through,"[12] virtually ensuring pollution and other environmental problems in Sequoia. The documentary even had its own Hollywood connection: it was narrated by Burgess Meredith, a virtuosic actor known for an eclectic body of work including *The Twilight Zone* and the 1960s *Batman* TV series, in which he played the Penguin, one of the caped crusader's many foes. He even had a Disney credit to his name, having just starred, in 1971, in a two-part episode of *The Wonderful World of Disney* called "The Strange Monster of Strawberry Cove."

Meredith ended the Mineral King documentary with a deep thought, delivered in his practiced, resonant voice: "Man has never been in complete harmony with his environment. However, there have been times and places where this was nearly so. Mineral King is such a place."[13]

❋ ❋ ❋

The march on Disneyland and the documentary were more signs of the growing public opposition to the Mineral King project, even after Disney had scaled down the size of the resort and removed the highway from its plans. Walker may have asked the public for its support of Mineral King in May 1972, but behind the scenes, the frustration he had voiced in the newspaper ad was playing out in other ways. The legal delays and the bad publicity surrounding Mineral King had Walker, Hicks, Willy Schaeffler, and others at Disney looking for alternate sites where constructing Walt's ski resort dream wouldn't be as fraught with controversy.

Back in December 1971, a group of Disney executives had traveled to San Francisco to talk with Forest Service officials about the latest legal issues with Mineral King and the possibility of finding an easier path to creating a Disney ski area. The Forest Service suggested four alternate locations, and though it took the company a few years to fully explore all the options, the site they chose in May 1974 would open up a new world of recreational possibilities.

Some four hundred miles north of Sequoia National Park, in the Sierra Nevada near Lake Tahoe, sat Independence Lake, an area that had similar characteristics to Mineral King: breathtaking slopes, rocky terrain, stands of pine trees that decorated the area in deep green hues. But the site had its own highlight that set it apart from Mineral King: a large lake inside the valley, so rich blue it looked like Alice's dress when night fell on Wonderland. When the sunlight hit the water, the ripples danced in the glow like Tinker Bell flitting through the forest. The lake was large—two-and-a-half miles long and a half mile wide—but not too large to distract from the geography that surrounded it: towering mountain peaks that slowly angled their way toward the blue water at the bottom of the valley.

Independence Lake had a rich history: Europeans had flocked to the area in the nineteenth century, naming it on Independence Day. Its highest

The scene of Disney's second attempt to build a year-round recreation destination: Independence Lake, California. Simon Williams.

peak, the 9,148-foot Mount Lola, was reportedly named for Lola Montez, a flamboyant Irish performer who was rumored to have danced for miners at the lake in 1853. The area had been closed to the public since 1937, when the Sierra Pacific Power Company had purchased the land surrounding it, but in the early 1970s, the company became interested in finding a partner to develop the area for skiing.

Independence Lake would open up a new set of opportunities for Disney: The water would be a destination in its own right. Biking, walking, and horseback riding trails, as well as fishing and swimming, would all be part of the year-round appeal. A boat taxi would carry guests from one side of the lake to the other.[14]

Schaeffler visited the area in the summer of 1974 to conduct an onsite inspection.[15] He still had high hopes, and a soft spot, for Mineral King, but he too was growing tired of the delays and the drama that surrounded the plans there. It had already been more than a decade since Schaeffler first set foot at Mineral King, whooshing down the slopes and comparing them favorably to the best skiing he had seen throughout the world. In the years since, he had become even more enchanted with Mineral King as he planned the ski runs and better understood the site, taken by its rugged terrain and untapped potential. Now nearing sixty, his once-blond hair graying, thin, and combed straight back, Schaeffler had begun to dream about retiring in Mineral King, creating an apartment above one of the Disney hotels on the slope as Walt had done when he built an apartment above the Town Square Fire Station in Disneyland.[16]

He wanted to make magic at Mineral King, but more than that, Schaeffler wanted to be part of a world-class resort with Disney people at the helm. Although Independence Lake would be a second choice, it wouldn't be a bad one, he soon determined: It had slopes that would accommodate all sorts of athletic abilities and would provide "the greatest ego skiing available for the family. It will make everyone look good."[17] With Schaeffler's approval of Independence Lake, Disney decided to pounce on the opportunity. It didn't mean the end of Mineral King, the company made clear, but it might be a faster way to get into the skiing business. Land and snow studies and preliminary planning were soon underway.

Walker unveiled the vision for Independence Lake in July 1975 at Tahoe-Truckee High School in nearby Truckee, California, showing concept drawings depicting ice skaters on the frozen lake and horse-drawn carriages carrying families through the snow-covered village, past brightly lit shop windows. Disney's plan for the area included a lakeside pedestrian village with nine shops and a 275-room lodge, as well as ten ski lifts, underground parking, an ice-skating rink, fishing lakes, a swimming pool and spa, twelve tennis courts, a restaurant located at the top of the mountain, and outdoor activities including camping, fishing, and hiking.[18]

Walker spoke of Walt, promising to stay true to his former boss's love of the outdoors. The company's desire to get into the recreation business was born from that love, Walker said, not simply as a way to make money. To reinforce the point, his slide-show presentation included a photo of Walt, accompanied by an audio recording of the late Disney leader's voice: "We're not out to make a fast buck."[19]

But despite the excitement and optimism inside the auditorium, a familiar scene was taking place outside the schoolhouse—much to the dismay of Walker and other executives. Some residents and environmentalists in the Independence Lake area had been opposed to the project since it was first announced, and a small group of about twenty protestors, some dressed as Disney characters including Mickey Mouse and Donald Duck, marched outside the venue with picket signs relaying such messages as "Donald Duck is a Rat—and Rats Don't Ski," "Don't Mickey Mouse Sierra County," "Prevent Plague—Keep Mickey Mouse from Infecting Sierra County," "Mickey Mouse is a Louse," and "Mickey Mouse on Skis—Eeek!"[20] The protestors were members of the newly formed Sierra County Conservation

Club (no relation to the Sierra Club), and the group's spokesman vowed of Disney's Independence Lake plans: "It's not going to happen."

It was the type of scene Disney had desperately hoped to avoid at Independence Lake. In fact, seven months earlier, the company had approached a somewhat surprising group for its input on the project: the Sierra Club, which was continuing to fight the development in Mineral King. The olive branch was extended in late 1974, and the club—elated that Disney's attention was turning away from Mineral King—agreed to assist the company in studying the environmental impact of the Independence Lake project.[21]

For Disney, one of the biggest enticements of Independence Lake was that much of the land in the area was privately owned, meaning the company might be able to avoid the headaches it had experienced with Mineral King. However, a good amount of the private land alternated in a checkerboard pattern with Forest Service land, which meant the Forest Service controlled about every other square mile. It was an issue that seemed manageable at first, but soon turned more difficult. Sierra Pacific reached out to the Forest Service about a land exchange in 1973, asking the agency to swap eight thousand acres of public land on the proposed resort site for private land located within Tahoe National Forest. But the Forest Service's original approval of Independence Lake had hinged on the resort being built partially on federal land, and the agency declined any exchange until it could conduct its own land-use study.[22]

The start date for the Forest Service's study got pushed and then pushed again in the latter part of 1975, and for Walker and Hicks, the further delays were too reminiscent of what they had already endured in Mineral King. In November 1975, just four months after announcing their plans for the resort and after spending nearly $1 million on planning and environmental studies, Disney decided to suspend all preliminary work on the project until the Forest Service could complete its research.

But as one gondola door closed, another opened, and the timing was right for Hicks and Walker to turn their attention back to Mineral King. The resort was suddenly looking more possible than ever before thanks to the Forest Service, which had completed the first draft of its environmental impact statement (EIS) on Mineral King in December 1974 to comply with the National Environmental Policy Act, the 1970 law that required federal agencies to put together a detailed analysis of any project with the potential to affect the environment. The 336-page draft EIS foresaw a year-round outdoor recreation facility with enough campsites for 1,325 people, lodging for 6,000, eighteen ski lifts, and restaurants that could seat a total of 2,350 guests. The report also examined the ski resort's potential effects on everything from trees, soil, streams, rivers, and archeological sites to air quality, vegetation, and wildlife. Construction would cause temporary increases in erosion, the report said, and automobile exhaust and campfire and fireplace smoke could cause slight decreases in air quality. The resort would cause the permanent loss of around 284 acres of vegetation and wildlife habitat, and while it would pose a small threat to two endangered species (the California condor and the peregrine falcon) and one rare species (the wolverine), "the development at Mineral King will not substantially conflict with the purposes for which the Sequoia National Game Refuge was established." The Disney executives were happy to see the section titled "Why Develop Mineral King?," in which the report's authors remarked on the area's "superlative ski terrain," equal to that at established ski areas in Europe; its moderate weather, even in winter; its dependable annual snowfall; and its arrangement of bowls, which provided for maximum protection from wind. "Mineral King is the only remaining area where high quality, large scale winter sports opportunities can be provided at a location reasonably accessible to Southern California," the report read, adding that national recreational demand for skiing on national forest land was projected to increase 37 percent between 1970 and 1990. The draft EIS also made a recommendation for a new transportation option to the resort that would cause the least environmental impact while offering maximum visitor comfort, safety, and convenience: Guests would drive in on a six-mile, two-lane highway that wouldn't pass through national park land, then take a scenic, thirteen-mile cog railway journey the rest of the way in. It was a plan very similar to what Disney had already announced.

Hicks was happy to see the Forest Service was still in favor of a Disney resort in Mineral King, but he was concerned about a few aspects of the report, primarily the transportation options it presented. Despite the fanfare the company had made about a railway three years earlier, it remained unclear whether the Park Service would allow train tracks to be installed on the section of the route that would transect Sequoia National Park. Financing of such a system was also in doubt. The railway "is not likely to prove feasible," Hicks wrote in his six-page response to the draft EIS, "even though it would be the preferred system, and a spectacular and enjoyable system for the guest."[23]

A secondary option presented in the draft EIS—a combination of train and bus travel—struck Hicks as far too complicated, expensive, and time-consuming for the day visitor the company envisioned as a primary customer at Mineral King. Disney didn't want Mineral King to become a destination resort accessible only to the wealthy. If the road was to be improved for bus travel, he argued, why not improve it for cars as well? There would be no highway, just a two-lane, thirty-five-mile-per-hour, all-weather road that would deliver visitors to the parking structure at the edge of the valley, where a mechanized transportation system—likely some version of the PeopleMover—would carry them the rest of the way into the valley.

"Even though Walt Disney Productions agrees with the United States Forest Service that Mineral King can and should become the finest winter recreational site in North America," Hicks's response said in closing, "we cannot support any development concept which falls short of Disney's highest concepts of public service and convenience."[24]

Sierra Club leader Michael McCloskey submitted a thirty-one-page response of his own, lambasting the Forest Service for a shortsighted report that lacked specifics and failed to present any real alternatives to a ski development in the heart of the wilderness.

"The draft EIS is replete with references to further analysis and investigation which will have to be performed after a site-specific plan is developed," McCloskey wrote. "It is not sufficient to rely on promises that such analysis will be performed some time in the future, after permits have been issued, when the plan is so insufficiently articulated. Environmental impact analysis must be performed *before* a decision is made to proceed with the project and permits are issued; in order for such analysis to proceed, the plan must be more specific."[25]

The missives from Hicks and McCloskey were among the dozens of official responses the Forest Service received to its draft impact statement, from entities including the Federal Energy Administration, the Environmental Protection Agency, and the Federal Power Commission. The agency also received 2,150 letters from the general public, split nearly equally between those in favor of the Disney resort and those opposed to it, with "overwhelming support" for the project coming from residents of Southern California.[26]

The Forest Service went back to the drawing board in April 1975 to start putting together its final environmental impact statement. In a move that came as a surprise to Disney, the agency also began work on a new concept for the Mineral King resort in response to the feedback it had received on its draft environmental impact statement. Unveiled in August, the new version of the development would allow just five thousand visitors a day, half the number Disney had envisioned in its original plan. The village area would be reduced in size, and six to nine chairlifts would be constructed in place of the original eighteen.[27] Disney said it would examine the proposal, but the company wasn't too interested in a plan that didn't allow for enough paying guests to make the resort economically feasible. The Forest Service's new idea for Mineral King was quickly shelved.

In February 1976, without much fanfare save for a press conference that Disney declined to attend,[28] the Forest Service released its final environmental impact statement for Mineral King, this time recommending a development with a maximum capacity of six thousand people in the summer, eight thousand in the winter. Compared to the draft EIS, the final report also called for an increase in summer activities including fishing, hiking, camping, and horseback riding. The Forest Service now recommended scrapping the cog railroad idea entirely, instead envisioning an improved, two-lane road from Hammond to Faculty Flat, where visitors would board an electric bus to ride the rest of the way into the village.

At Disney headquarters in Burbank, where the scale models of Mineral King had long ago been cleared from the soundstage where they once had been visited by politicians and planners, and the colorful concept drawings of the resort hadn't graced the walls for years, the new report offered a glimmer of hope. Maybe someone did speak for Mineral King after all. An electric bus? It was nowhere near Walt's vision of a hidden underground parking lot where a romantic train ride through snow-covered pines awaited visitors, but it was a way to get skiers to the mountain. Not to mention, the company had been waiting on the Forest Service to complete its environmental report for years. It was required by law before the trial could begin on the permanent injunction, which the Sierra Club had first requested nearly seven years ago. Hicks couldn't believe the case had dragged on for so long.

For the Sierra Club, however, the final environmental impact report was just more of the same. There was no such thing as acceptable development in Mineral King, the club said, and after the feedback the Forest Service had received on its draft EIS, the organization was frankly astonished the resort was still on the table. Eleven years after the Forest Service had first issued its prospectus for a ski area in Mineral King, the whole project felt like an idea whose time had passed.

Others throughout California had their own thoughts on Disney's Mineral King development, even years after the initial announcement of the plans. Aware of—and curious about—the ongoing drama in the middle of the Golden State, plenty of skiers, environmentalists, Mineral King residents, business owners, and politicians combed through the Forest Service's long-awaited final environmental impact statement, searching for clues about the future of the controversial project. Among those who carefully read all 285 pages was John Krebs, a Fresno, California, resident who in 1974 had been elected U.S. representative for California's 17th Congressional District. And he was about to put in motion a plan that would bring the long saga of Mineral King to an end.

12

A PLACE IN THE PARK

1976

As the helicopter moved slowly over the mountains surrounding Mineral King, its whirling blades ruffling the green-needled treetops, John Krebs tried to envision it: a giant ski resort, swarming with people, multiple lifts dragging chairs up and down the mountainside, bustling hotels and restaurants, Windex-blue swimming pools, neon green tennis courts. He just couldn't see it. The area was too pristine, too beautiful.

Over the roar of the chopper's engine, Krebs—the forty-nine-year-old Democratic U.S. representative for California's 17th Congressional District—had to shout to be heard as he explained to his traveling companions the reasoning behind the bill he had written one month prior, which would place the Mineral King area into Sequoia National Park and protect it from development. Though former California governor Ronald Reagan had banned fourteen miles of the proposed highway into Mineral King a few years earlier, the Forest Service's final environmental impact statement had put an improved road through other parts of the area back on the table, Krebs said, and the area's agricultural economy would be destroyed by the air pollution that would result from the huge increase in traffic to Disney's year-round resort. Not to mention, there was still no plan in place to finance the highway, either from the Disney company or the state of California.

It was May 29, 1976, and Krebs had invited two other members of the House of Representatives' Subcommittee on Public Lands on an aerial and ground tour of the Mineral King area, where they could check out the scenery, meet some of the locals, and decide for themselves whether to support Krebs's efforts to keep major development out of the scenic region, which on this spring day was alive with colorful wildflowers nestled in the lush green grass of the valley.[1]

Later in the day the trio met up with members of the Forest Service, supervisors from Tulare County, and representatives from Disney. They traipsed up and down hills and through the valley, Krebs holding his tongue as the Forest Service officials pointed out where the ski lifts would go, and where in the valley the alpine village would be located. Krebs knew the people he needed to convince that Mineral King belonged in Sequoia National Park were in Washington, not Tulare County.

❊ ❊ ❊

Born in Berlin in 1926, Krebs had moved with his family to Palestine in 1933, along with thousands of other European Jews fleeing the rise of fascism. He came to the United States in 1946 to attend the University of California, Berkeley, then served in the U.S. Army from 1952 to 1954, returning to his native Germany as an infantry corporal. He came back to California to earn a law degree at the University of California's Hastings College of the Law in San Francisco before moving to Fresno in 1957 to start practicing law. Krebs became involved with the local wing of the Democratic party and eventually was appointed to the Fresno County Planning Commission, then the Fresno County Board of Supervisors.[2]

In 1974 Krebs had defeated four-time incumbent Republican Bob Mathias—a longtime supporter of Disney's Mineral King project—to become representative for the 17th District, which included the area around Mineral King. Long aware of the ski-development controversy, Krebs began gathering information on the Disney resort and the opposition to it almost immediately after taking office. He received an avalanche of letters from constituents worried about the project, and in summer 1975 he reached out to the Sierra Club for help, asking the organization's Northern California and Southern California regional conservation committees for their recommendations for an ecologically sound Mineral King master plan.[3] The groups put together a list of eleven guidelines, including keeping lake basins and high ridges free from development, relocating existing parking areas to less fragile ground, and paving the remaining dirt surfaces of the Mineral King road. Krebs studied the recommendations and spoke with other constituents, and in March 1976 he took an official position: like Michael McCloskey, Jean Koch, John Harper, and many other environmentalists and Sierra Club members, he was against development in Mineral King, which he said would cause disfigurement of the valley, along with excessive commercialization.[4]

"Clearly, the environmental toll which would be exacted as a result of the proposed development would far outweigh the short-term economic benefits it might bring to the county of Tulare,"[5] Krebs said. He promised legislation within thirty days to incorporate Mineral King into the national park system.

In late April 1976, Krebs submitted his bill that would put Mineral King into Sequoia National Park, drawing praise from constituents who thanked him for his foresight and conscientiousness.[6] Joining Krebs in the effort was Alan Cranston, a Democratic California senator from Palo Alto who had introduced a nearly identical bill in the Senate a few weeks prior. Cranston was a California native who was aware of Mineral King's history, and while he wasn't completely opposed to skiing in Mineral King, he favored a recreation facility on a much smaller scale than what Disney had planned. His bill looked to transfer jurisdiction of Mineral King from the Department of Agriculture to the Department of the Interior, where some development might be possible, but any such project, his bill said, would require full public participation.[7] Cranston's and Krebs's bills both eventually died in committee, but the two lawmakers were undaunted, quickly drafting new legislation to introduce in the next session of Congress, set to begin in January 1977 under a new president whose commitment to conservation was the most progressive the White House had seen in decades.

❋ ❋ ❋

Even before being elected president in November 1976, Jimmy Carter had been dedicated to protecting the environment for much of his life. Growing up on his family's farm outside of Plains, Georgia, and playing in the nearby Choctawhatchee River and Kinchafoonee Creek, Carter developed his love of nature early.

"I have never been happier, more exhilarated, at peace, rested, inspired, and aware of the grandeur of the universe and the greatness of God," he wrote, "than when I find myself in a natural setting not much changed from the way He made it."[8]

Shortly after serving in the Georgia senate in the late 1960s, Carter helped to create the Georgia Conservancy, which protects the state's natural environment. As governor of Georgia from 1971 to 1975, Carter established the Georgia Heritage Trust, and when he ran for president in 1976, ecology was a large part of his platform. "Environmental protection is not simply an aesthetic goal," he said, "but is necessary to achieve a more just society."[9] As president, Carter installed solar panels on the White House and created the Department of Energy to implement the country's first comprehensive national energy policy. He also established the Chattahoochee River National Recreation Area in Georgia, expanded conserved federal lands in Alaska, and signed the Endangered American Wilderness Act of 1978, which created new designated wilderness areas on national forest land in California, Utah, Wyoming, New Mexico, Idaho, and Oregon.

Carter's election coincided with a nationwide growth in environmental consciousness that had started with the first Earth Day in 1970 and had led to the creation of the Environmental Protection Agency and the National Oceanographic and Atmospheric Administration in 1970, as well as passage of the Clean Water Act (1972), the Endangered Species Act (1973), and the Safe Drinking Water Act (1974). When Carter took office in January 1977, leaded gasoline was starting to be phased out nationwide to reduce tailpipe emissions, and the effects of "acid rain" on plants and aquatic animals were beginning to be studied.

McCloskey, the Sierra Club's executive director, had a direct line to Carter on environmental issues and was part of a group of conservation leaders who met with the president every six months. He knew the Georgian's administration offered new possibilities for environmentalists. "While his predecessors gave lip service to environmental values, Carter came into office really meaning it," said McCloskey, who gave his personal endorsement to Carter during Carter's reelection campaign in 1980. "We found that whenever we could talk directly to him, we got somewhere."[10] If ever the political climate was right for a bill like the one Krebs and Cranston were proposing for Mineral King, it was in the early days of the Carter era.

✸ ✸ ✸

It had been eight years since the Sierra Club first filed a lawsuit in U.S. district court asking for an injunction against the Disney development in Mineral King—and five years since the club refiled its case following the Supreme Court decision. Though the mountain slopes around the valley remained free of ski lifts, the case had still neither gone to trial nor been dismissed. The Sierra Club had waited first for the Forest Service to complete its environmental impact statements, then for the agency to formally approve the project. And even though that formal approval had yet to come, Judge William Sweigert—on the brink of retirement and looking to clear his docket—decided in March 1977 to dismiss the refiled 1972 lawsuit for "failure to prosecute."[11] It was a surprise move that temporarily revived interest in Mineral King at Disney and the Forest Service, but Disney, wary of more delays, ultimately turned its attention back to Independence Lake in the northern Sierra, in August 1977 filing for a zoning change that would make it easier to move forward with the resort.[12] The company's new master plan for Independence Lake, based in part on its own environmental studies, included a twenty-one-acre pedestrian village on one end of the lake, with lakefront lodging, restaurants, campgrounds, and base operations for summer and wintertime recreational programs.[13] In addition to more than one thousand acres of ski slopes targeted at families and intermediate skiers, the resort would feature tennis courts, two fishing lakes, and a "year-round swimming experience."[14] "Ours is the most advanced of any such project that could come on the line by 1981," said Jim Stewart, Disney's vice president of corporate relations. "It will be the first new project here in a decade, during which time the demand has grown tremendously."[15]

The project had to await more environmental impact studies, but protestors reacted to the news nonetheless, with one group of Nevada artists vowing to use nine tons of vegetable dye to color a one-mile strip of snow on Mount Lola in protest of Disney's proposed Independence Lake development.[16]

* * *

Krebs traveled back and forth between Washington and California every two weeks, relishing the time he spent in Fresno with his wife and two teenage children. But in early October 1977, even his days in California were filled with anxiety as he awaited the first hearing on his Mineral King bill—officially titled the Sequoia National Park Enlargement Act—in front of the House National Parks and Insular Affairs Subcommittee. On October 27, twenty-six witnesses, including environmentalists, farmers, skiers, lobbyists, Disney executives, and residents of the small towns surrounding Mineral King, packed into a small hearing room in Washington to say their piece for or against Krebs's proposed legislation to place the Mineral King area into Sequoia National Park. Disney had by that point spent twelve years and $1.5 million on its Mineral King plans, Stewart told the representatives, and the company wanted the question settled once and for all.[17] Not only had Disney scaled down its Mineral King plans considerably, Stewart said, but it was now willing to bring in 65 percent of visitors by bus to cut down on automobile traffic.[18]

U.S. Representative John Krebs with President Jimmy Carter, who later signed the
National Parks and Recreation Act of 1978 that put Mineral King in Sequoia National
Park. Courtesy of Danny Krebs and Hanna Krebs.

Along with testimony from Southern California skiers pleading for the
resort to be built ("We want our children and our children's children to be
able to ski there,"[19] said one skier from Costa Mesa), the representatives
heard from former California representative Jerome Waldie, now testify-
ing on behalf of environmental group Friends of the Earth, who said the

Disney resort should be outlawed immediately. Two San Joaquin Valley farmers testified that the increased automobile emissions that would result from an influx of skiers would be harmful to their crops.[20] Also offering testimony was the chairman of the Fresno County Board of Supervisors, who remembered a camping trip he had taken with his family at Mineral King— an area even "more spectacular than what is in Sequoia National Park."[21]

Encouraged by the testimony, Krebs started planning for a second hearing on the bill in January 1978. The hopes the representative had pinned on the environmentally progressive President Carter were born out at that hearing, where National Park Service Director William Whalen testified that the Carter administration had thrown its support behind Krebs's bill, explaining that the "visual intrusion of ski lifts, ski trails and relatively dense visitor use support facilities"[22] at Disney's proposed resort would wreck the unspoiled beauty, not to mention the air quality, of the Mineral King area. With the president on his side, Krebs knew the fate of the resort was all but sealed.

When word of Carter's endorsement of Krebs's bill reached Disney president Card Walker, however, Walker was furious. In February 1978, he fired off a two-page missive to Carter, on Disney letterhead adorned with a sketch of Mickey Mouse, scolding the president for ending the company's thirteen-year effort to build a "badly needed, high quality year-round" recreation facility. Walker was livid that Carter had reversed a long-standing decision on which Disney had relied while spending a great deal of time, money, and creative energy on the Mineral King project, suffering attacks on its image and reputation along the way. Carter's "narrow and completely one-sided stance," Walker wrote, "is a classic case, which demonstrates why business is losing confidence in its government, why business executives are hesitant to commit new capital investment, and therefore, why the economy is currently stagnating."[23]

Despite the vitriol directed the government's way from one of California's most visible companies, things were finally falling into place for the conservationist crusaders who had made it their mission to ensure that Mineral King would never be developed. The state's governor, Jerry Brown— elected in 1974 and the son of former California governor Pat Brown—sent Krebs a letter a few weeks after the January hearing, indicating his support for adding Mineral King to Sequoia National Park,[24] and in February the House Committee on Interior and Insular Affairs passed the bill unanimously. Left out of Sequoia National Park decades earlier only because of old mining claims that never amounted to anything, Mineral King—that out-of-place thumb at the bottom of the park map—was finally on the way to being put back where many felt it had always belonged.

* * *

Like Krebs, other legislators were prioritizing conservation in 1978—in Texas, Senator Lloyd Bentsen and Representative Chick Kazen were working to preserve four Spanish Colonial-era missions in San Antonio,[25] while in Hawaii, Senator Spark Matsunaga had been pushing for a national cultural park at Kaloko-Honokohau on the Big Island. These efforts and some 150 similar initiatives from lawmakers around the country—including Krebs's Mineral King legislation—were put together in an omnibus parks bill that four months later would become one of the most significant pieces of environmental legislation passed by the Carter administration. One hundred and fourteen years after Abraham Lincoln signed the first-ever legislation to set aside American land "for the enjoyment and protection for future generations,"[26] Carter became part of the national park legacy continued by presidents Ulysses S. Grant, Grover Cleveland, Theodore Roosevelt, Woodrow Wilson, and Lyndon Johnson when he signed the National Parks and Recreation Act of 1978. Enacted on November 10, 1978, the act established fifteen new national parks, authorized increased land acquisition and other improvements in existing parks, and designated nearly two million acres in eight national parks as wilderness. The $1.3 billion act also expanded parks in forty-four states and created a huge number of new cultural and historic sites, including the Edgar Allan Poe National Historic Site in Pennsylvania and the Saint Paul's Church National Historic Site in New York.

"This new law reaffirms our nation's commitment to the preservation of our heritage, a commitment which strives to improve the quality of the present by our dedication to preserving the past and conserving our historical and natural resources for our children and grandchildren," Carter said in a statement. "It honors those who helped to shape and develop this nation; it acknowledges our need to receive strength and sustenance from natural beauty; and it addresses the pressing need to improve recreational opportunities in our urban areas."[27]

With the stroke of Carter's pen, Mineral King was now part of Sequoia National Park and safe from major development—from Disney or anyone else—via an act that took care to note that while Mineral King "has outstanding potential for certain year-round recreational opportunities . . . the development of permanent facilities for downhill skiing within the area would be inconsistent with the preservation and enhancement of its ecological values."

It was a bittersweet victory for Krebs—just three days before Carter signed the parks and recreation bill, the representative was voted out of office after two terms, defeated by an opponent who had made Krebs's resistance to a Mineral King development a key part of his campaign. Krebs's successor, Charles "Chip" Pashayan, an attorney and first-time candidate from Fresno, said a Disney resort in Mineral King would be good for skiers and good for business, and a majority of voters agreed. An organized group of skiers even came to Krebs's district in the weeks before the election, going door to door in an attempt to persuade voters to elect Pashayan and keep Disney's Mineral King project moving forward.

* * *

There would be sighs of relief in Mineral King in the days following the passage of the National Parks and Recreation Act, as cabin owners like Jean Koch celebrated the fact that their land would remain unspoiled. The transfer of Mineral King into Sequoia National Park created a new problem, however—the parks act said that ownership of each private cabin in Mineral King would revert to the Park Service upon the death of its registered owner. In 1986, cabin owners would form the Mineral King Preservation Society to add Mineral King to the National Register of Historic Places— they finally succeeded in 2003, though the designation only included a portion of the area. The matter was ultimately settled in 2004, when Congress passed an amendment to the National Parks and Recreation Act that allows the issuance of cabin permits to the owners of record "and their heirs, successors, and assigns."[28]

For McCloskey and the Sierra Club, the law was a huge victory after more than ten years of battling against the development—and it finished club founder John Muir's grand plan for protecting the Sierra Nevada to boot. The win at Mineral King was motivation for the club to keep on fighting for even more threatened wilderness areas to be preserved.

But in Burbank, the Mineral King news was no cause for celebration; instead it was a huge blow to Walker, Bob Hicks, Willy Schaeffler, and other Disney leaders still clinging to the hope of making Walt's year-round-recreation-destination dream happen, despite the complicated and drawn-out battle. Their plans for Mineral King, the land Walt had called the most beautiful spot he had ever seen, would never come to fruition. There would be no cog railway carrying visitors into the valley, no wilderness walks to educate children about the animals and plants that graced the area, no mountaintop restaurants, no skiers making their way down the slopes, no Winter Olympics held at a Disney property. Eighteen years after Walt first dreamed up the idea of a ski resort imbued with Disney magic and know-how, it was finally over. Disney, uncharacteristically, had lost.

Walker, who would retire five years later but would remain a consultant to Disney until 1990, finally admitted defeat, writing in the 1978 Walt Disney Productions annual report that the National Parks and Recreation Act "brings to an end our proposed Mineral King project." And with the Independence Lake development still in limbo with the Forest Service (the company would walk away from that project as well in the months to come, fed up with more delays), the idea of a Disney-run, world-class recreational resort—anywhere—seemed completely out of reach. The company's desire to create such a project was as strong as it ever was, but, Walker wrote, "we are frankly still discouraged at the prospects of achieving this objective."[29]

Disney's Mineral King dream was gone, but it wouldn't be forgotten. It was there on October 1, 1982, when Walker, Donn Tatum, and Lillian Disney celebrated the opening of EPCOT in Walt Disney World—another of Walt's final visions that did make it to reality. It was there on April 15, 1983, when the first international Disney park, Tokyo Disneyland, opened with the Country Bear Jamboree as one of its inaugural attractions. And the Mineral King dream was there when Schaeffler oversaw some of the downhill skiing events at the 1980 Winter Olympics in Lake Placid, New York—the first Winter Olympics on U.S. soil since 1960, when he and Walt had started talking about creating a ski resort of their own. That the pair's dream resort in Mineral King was never built was one of the great regrets of Schaeffler's life.

And though a Disney destination in Mineral King, California, would never see the light of day, the company's ideas and plans for the development—not to mention the years-long environmental battle that ultimately spelled the project's doom—would live on.

13

LASTING LEGACIES

1986

Mike Shannon was just twenty-seven years old when he took over as president and chief executive officer of Vail Associates, the company that owned the picturesque Colorado ski resort nestled in the heart of the Rocky Mountains. It was 1986, and Shannon—who had served as vice president of the media and entertainment division at the First National Bank of Chicago and vice president of acquisitions for the Gillett Group in Nashville before coming to Vail—was the youngest CEO of any major North American ski resort, not to mention brand new to the winter sports industry. The Wisconsin native, whose shaggy red hair and youthful appearance set him apart from other executives, had started skiing just three years prior, on business trips to Vail, but he quickly fell in love both with the sport and the mountain town. He was enchanted by Vail's European feel—by the warm glow of the lights on the Bavarian-style hotels in the village and the burbling creek that flowed through town, bisected at one point by a covered bridge. There was the Austrian-influenced Hotel Gasthof Gramshammer, where Pepi's Restaurant and Bar served up goulash and wienerschnitzel, and the Blü Cow, which specialized in Swiss hot dogs and cold draft beer. Shannon knew that Vail ski resort founder Pete Seibert, who had served in the Colorado-trained 10th Mountain Division of the U.S. Army during World War II, had taken his inspiration for the resort from one of the world's best-known and most scenic ski areas—Zermatt, Switzerland, the same alpine village that had inspired Walt Disney's designs for Mineral King.

Vail's ski resort turned twenty-four years old in 1986. The ski area located about 100 miles west of Denver had fallen on hard economic times in the early 1980s, and in 1985 it had been purchased by Gillett Group head George Gillett, a businessman and avid skier who had been visiting Vail regularly since 1963. The ski area was beautiful, but it needed a change in leadership. Shannon spearheaded the group's acquisition of Vail, then became its president.

The fact that he was a novice in the winter-sports industry didn't deter Shannon from setting lofty goals in his new position. In 1986, Vail was the fifteenth most popular skiing destination in the country, trailing much more successful areas like California's Mammoth Mountain and Colorado's Aspen. Shannon set his sights high: he wanted to make Vail number one. He just had to figure out how to do it.

Shannon's wife, Mary Sue, was a nursery school teacher who worked with kids all day, and the couple had two young children of their own. It gave Shannon an idea: Why not position Vail as a family-friendly resort? Other ski areas were targeting young, athletic skiers, but the family segment, including children, was largely ignored. Aspen, the posh town southwest of Vail that attracted the rich and famous to its slopes, could have the celebrities. Vail would welcome the families.

When it came to family-friendly entertainment, there was one company that did it better than anyone else—and Shannon happened to be friends with its president. At the First National Bank in Chicago, Shannon had worked on foreign film financing for Frank Wells, the then Warner Bros. vice chairman who in 1984 had been named president and chief operating officer of Walt Disney Productions. Wells was a longtime skier who owned a house in Vail, and when Shannon took over as president of the ski area, the two soon became fast friends—skiing together and comparing notes on travel and business trends.

Like the rest of the world, Shannon knew about Disney's movies and theme parks, about the family focus it brought to all of its projects, but he also knew that Disney had once tried to build a ski resort in the mountains of California. He approached Wells with a request: "I'd be very interested in going to WED," Shannon said, to talk with Disney Imagineers about ways to turn Vail into the country's favorite family skiing destination.[1] Wells arranged for Shannon to visit Disney's Glendale and Burbank headquarters, where Shannon spent the better part of a day meeting with Disney Imagineers. For extra inspiration, the Imagineers dusted off the Mineral King plans and concept illustrations, giving Shannon a firsthand look at the resort's cozy alpine architecture and snow play areas. Inspired by the

A young skier visits with Sport Goofy in Vail, Colorado, in 1989. Sport Goofy became the mascot of the Colorado ski area after the resort's CEO, who was friends with Disney President Frank Wells, Disney-fied the resort. Courtesy of Kelley Baskins.

Disney history all around him, Shannon made a bold request: "Frank, if there's something we could do together, we'd love to have the [Disney] characters come to visit Vail in some way."

Soon after, "Sport Goofy," the athletic incarnation of the cartoon canine who had starred in animated shorts such as *How to Play Baseball* and *The Olympic Champ* (both released in 1942), became Vail's ski ambassador, appearing at events, welcoming families to the resort, and offering encouragement to youngsters at the ski school. Walt's beloved buck-toothed character who yodeled down mountain slopes in *The Art of Skiing* was on skis once more—not at Mineral King, Independence Lake, or a Disney recreation destination, but at a ski resort in Colorado. It was a big deal: Disney rarely allowed its characters to appear outside of official Disney properties. Disney created the costume and invited a handful of Vail employees to receive mascot training at Disneyland, and Sport Goofy—wearing a ski cap and goggles on top of his head and sporting a bright red-and-yellow ski suit—made his official Vail debut at the 1989 World Alpine Ski Championships, cutting the ribbon at the event's opening ceremony at the resort's Red Tail Camp.

Sport Goofy quickly became a draw for families and a regular at Vail's ski school, which took more cues from Disney in its innovative and whimsical design. At Vail, learning to ski was a fun adventure, with characters and attractions and experiences. Kids could ski through a rumbling, roaring dragon at Dragon's Breath Mine and practice their balance on the snow-banked turns that simulated the mythical creature's tail. They got accustomed to moguls on the Mining Mounds, a series of small hills, and learned to snowplow at a strategically placed magical mine where the ski instructor would pull up a bucket of gold. It wasn't real gold, of course—it was gold-painted rocks—but the excitement and magic it created for the kids was real.

Ski lessons weren't just an athletic challenge or a class with a strict instructor leading drills that reminded youngsters of another day in school—at Vail, kids could be kids and have fun. It was like an amusement park on the slopes; a Disneyland in the mountains. Once they knew the basics of the sport, young skiers were able to go out on their own to explore Gitchegumee Gulch, the Magic Forest, and the Indian village at Fort Whippersnapper, where they could explore teepees or meet with Jackrabbit Joe and Sourdough Pete, costumed Western characters who skied the hills to share the legend of the dragon's treasure. Later, Vail opened a winter play area called Adventure Ridge, with snowmobiling, ice skating, tubing, and even a kids-only restaurant. Nearby Beaver Creek—which Vail opened in 1980 as a luxurious year-round resort—had three kid-friendly areas of its own, including Buckaroo Bowl and Hibernating Bear Cave. Shannon had succeeded in his mission—Vail garnered universal acclaim as the country's best ski area for kids and families.

Shannon and his colleagues took other pages from the Disney playbook when it came to customer service and guest relations, areas in which Vail had scored low marks under its previous leadership. Shannon and Gillett ensured that all the resort's employees were trained in a Disney-style "customer first" model of service, and they gave them name tags that listed their hometowns, giving guests more potential points of connection with the resort staff. Like Disney, Vail's new leadership focused on cleanliness throughout the resort; the company also invested in daycare and childcare facilities and even sent managers and children's instructors to Walt Disney World for inspiration. Over the course of a few years, Vail had become a Disney-inspired ski area, and it was a rousing success: in 1989, Vail was ranked number one on *Ski* magazine's annual list of the best ski resorts in the country and *Snow Country* magazine's list of the top thirty-five vacation ski resorts in the United States.

Outside of Vail, other ski companies seemed to be following Disney's lead when it came to creating European-style ski villages that would become as much of a draw for tourists as the actual ski runs. One of the most successful was Whistler Blackcomb in British Columbia, a merger of two popular ski areas that in 1998 boasted a village area with multiple hotels, ninety-seven restaurants, a nightlife scene to rival that of the world's most cosmopolitan cities, and an abundance of boutique shops and day spas. More than one industry insider likened Whistler Blackcomb to a "Disneyland of skiing"[2]— a moniker the resort's parent company, Intrawest, grew to embrace.

Disney hadn't succeeded in building its dream ski and recreation resort, but it had contributed to innovations in the ski industry. And the concepts and themes it had developed for Mineral King would also be reflected in Disney properties to come.

✿ ✿ ✿

Visitors enter the California resort through a pair of sliding doors decorated with a colorful stained-glass scene of mountain peaks, a tranquil stream, and stands of green pine trees under a colorful sunset sky. At the check-in counter, guests are greeted by tile mosaics, dark wood details, images of bears, and a recurring color palette of forest green and redwood brown.

In the grand lobby, huge wooden beams stretch out overhead like the branches of a giant tree. At the right time of day—early morning or late afternoon—sunlight shines through the hotel's high windows and sprinkles light onto the lobby floor, just as it would the ground of a forest where the light is dappled by the rustling leaves of the trees. At the end of a long day outside, guests gather in the warmth of a mammoth stone fireplace, reading and talking under the light cast by rustic, oversized chandeliers. Artifacts from California's environmental history fill the surrounding bookcases and glass-fronted display cases, and the walls are covered with framed images of wildlife and nature. The featured décor in one of the hotel's adjoining restaurants includes silhouette cutouts of gold miners and murals of California history.

A few hundred yards away sits a two-acre nature trail that loops around part of the hotel, with signs that educate visitors about local plant and animal life and the mythology of the Native American tribes that once inhabited the region. For children, there are a range of forest activities: adventure ropes courses, a natural rock slide, ziplining, rocks to climb, lookout towers to ascend. Scattered throughout the area in rough lean-tos and faux fire lookouts are topographic maps of Sequoia National Park and the surrounding wilderness—among the spots to search for are the Kern River, Mount Whitney, and the John Muir Trail.

It may sound like Walt's vision for Mineral King, but this is what it's like today at the Grand Californian Hotel & Spa in Anaheim, one of three hotels in the Disneyland resort. Inspired by the Arts and Crafts movement and evocative of the Craftsman-style architecture seen in national parks lodges, the Grand Californian opened in 2001, alongside the Downtown Disney shopping district and Disney's California Adventure—a theme park whose mission in part is to celebrate California's wild past.

In a rarity for a Disney hotel, the Grand Californian opens right into a theme park—the seventy-two-acre California Adventure, which celebrates different parts of the state's history. There is a section dedicated to the Golden Age of Hollywood (the park's fine dining restaurant is named after the movie theater where *Snow White and the Seven Dwarfs* premiered in December 1937), and Pacific Wharf, bustling with food stalls, is inspired by the waterfronts of Monterey and San Francisco. One of the park's eight themed lands, Grizzly Peak, is an homage to California wilderness and national parks. Among its attractions is Grizzly River Run, a fast-moving water ride themed partly after the California Gold Rush. Motifs of tree branches and statues of birds and bears are everywhere. The land also is home to the aforementioned Redwood Creek Challenge Trail, a forest-themed area featuring a variety of wilderness activities, including a walk-through redwood tree, bridges, rock climbing, a zipline and animal watching.

Grizzly Peak also pays tribute to a conservationist with deep ties to the national parks of California—and to the group that eventually helped shut down Disney's Mineral King plans: John Muir, founder of the Sierra Club. On the outer walls of a gift shop designed to look like a wilderness trip outfitter (inside, guests can buy seeds that allow them to grow their own giant sequoias) are emblazoned two quotes from Muir: "In every walk with nature one receives far more than he seeks," and "Come to the woods, for here is rest."

Disney's California Adventure and the Grand Californian aren't the only Disney properties that appear to have been inspired in part by the Mineral King plans and Walt's passion for the outdoors. Nature, wildlife, and the national parks lodges of the early twentieth century have had a surprisingly large influence on Disney resorts worldwide. Disney's Wilderness Lodge in Walt Disney World, for instance, has a rustic feel similar to that of the Grand Californian and is inspired by national parks lodges found in the American Northwest. Guests there can fish, explore nature trails that wind through pine forests, or relax in rocking chairs that overlook a gently flowing creek. The giant eighty-two-foot fireplace in the hotel's lobby represents the different layers of the Grand Canyon, and bold Native American imagery is a powerful reminder of the true origins of the American West. Seven miles away, at Disney's Animal Kingdom Lodge outside of Disney's Animal Kingdom—an entire theme park dedicated to the celebration and conservation of wildlife and the environment—guests can see grazing wildlife such as zebras and giraffes outside the windows of their rooms.

Disney's Fort Wilderness Resort & Campground, part of Walt Disney World since 1971, the year the park opened, offers cabins and campsites in 750 acres of cypress and pine forest, where guests might catch a glimpse of ducks, deer, or rabbits. And in Disneyland Paris, the tree-lined, forest-themed Disney Sequoia Lodge—inspired by American national parks including, of course, the park in which the Mineral King area is now located—features drawings from *Bambi* on the walls of its guest rooms. Disney's year-round resort in California's High Sierra never came to be, but the company's commitment to giving its customers authentic nature- and wilderness-inspired experiences remains.

❖❖❖

It's not a wilderness- or national parks-themed lodge, but on the Hawaiian island of Oahu, Disney's Aulani resort has its own tie to the company's Mineral King plans—in an entirely different way. Aulani was the first Disney property to be inspired by its natural surroundings and embrace true cultural authenticity—a concept that was born during the Mineral King planning, as Walt wanted the ski resort to be true to its mountain location (along with some Swiss chalet flair). Disney's resorts across the globe are known for their powerful theming, but those themes are often borrowed from other areas in far-off places. In addition to the Wilderness Lodge and Animal Kingdom Lodge, some of Walt Disney World's well-known resorts, including the Polynesian Village Resort (South Seas-inspired), the Grand Floridian Resort & Spa (inspired by Victorian-era seaside resorts), the Yacht Club Resort (a New England-influenced, nautical-themed hotel), and Port Orleans Resort (themed after New Orleans's historic French Quarter) mimic other places and spaces, not the land around them.

It was a different story in Hawaii—and like at Mineral King, the local residents made all the difference. When Disney bought twenty-one acres of land in Kapolei on the island of Oahu to build the resort in 2007, Disney fans were thrilled, but many Hawaiian people were not. They had grown tired of the overcommercialization of their land and culture—and entertainment giant Disney, they feared, would only make things worse. Seemingly heeding the lessons it had learned at Mineral King and Independence Lake, though, Disney created an advisory council of Hawaiian elders to ensure every element of Aulani—from its architecture and artwork to its restaurants, bars, and stores—would be authentic to Hawaiian culture. As it was with the panel of conservationists Disney had established in 1969 to help guide the Mineral King planning, every decision for Aulani was run by the council of elders. Disney also developed its own cultural training program for Aulani's employees, aimed to instill or enhance Hawaiian values— kuleana, laulima, malama, oluolu, and kaulike (responsibility, cooperation, caring, graciousness, and fairness). Among Aulani's Hawaiian employees, Disney's efforts at authenticity were a great success: "We have this seed in us and we were never allowed to bloom as a people, as a culture, as a nation," one employee said when the resort opened in 2011. "Disney has allowed us to bloom. It's been an awesome and wonderful journey."[3]

• • •

Beyond the Disney properties it seems to have influenced, Mineral King itself has been the source of several references and in-jokes for the company's animators and Imagineers over the years, including, in summer 2022, a revamp of the final scene of the Walt Disney's Carousel of Progress attraction in Magic Kingdom park in Florida. Along with a new pink sweater dress for Grandma and a "Progress Tech: School of Urban Planning" hoodie for the family's daughter, Patricia (a reference to "Progress City," one of the early concepts for EPCOT), James, the family's son, now sports a sweatshirt adorned with a patch featuring a mountain, a sun, and a snowflake. The design mimics the logo of Sky Crown—one of the mountainside restaurants envisioned at Mineral King.[4]

Earlier Disney references to the Mineral King project include a sign that was for many years visible to guests exiting Splash Mountain in Disneyland—an advertisement for "Brother Ted Wershbords" (a reference to the Country Bear Jamboree), based in Mineral King, California. The company's slogan was "For clean country critters."

A much more obvious reference to the company's ill-fated ski resort appeared in the 2022 animated special *The Wonderful Winter of Mickey Mouse*. In the second segment of the twenty-four-minute episode of the animated Mickey Mouse series, Mickey, Goofy, and Donald pack their red car sky-high with elaborate gear (held together by some twine) to take a trip to the slopes—in Mineral King. But when they get to their rustic log cabin atop a snowy peak, cobwebs fill every corner, bugs scatter across the floor, and the gang complains about the musty smell. Three animal heads are mounted on the cabin wall—a moose, buffalo, and deer, just like the talking heads on the wall of Country Bear Jamboree's Grizzly Hall. (The heads later come to life and taunt Goofy.) Things turn worse when the cabin gets snowed in and the famous friends nearly freeze. To a yodeling musical backdrop, they attempt to dig their way out, but don't succeed. When Donald complains to his mouse-eared pal about the situation, Mickey holds up a brochure that reads "Mineral King Deluxe Ski Resort," and says, "It's not my fault. The brochure said it was deluxe accommodations. Deluxe!"

After being dislodged by an avalanche, the cabin goes careening down a ski hill with Mickey, Donald, and Goofy inside, knocking down a "Mineral King Ski Resort" sign on its way to the bottom of the hill.

Mineral King also—appropriately—found its way into Disney's 1972 live-action comedy *Snowball Express*, starring Dean Jones, Nancy Olson, and Harry Morgan, later of *M*A*S*H* fame. Jones plays Johnny Baxter, a New York office drone who inherits a ski resort in the Rocky Mountains. In one memorable scene, Baxter takes a lengthy and acrobatic tumble down a ski hill, "leaving a wake of destruction from Farewell Gap to Aspen Flats"—a reference to two iconic Mineral King destinations.

* * *

It wasn't just the world of Disney that was transformed by the Mineral King project. The resort and the battle over its construction also had a huge impact in the field of environmental law. The Sierra Club Legal Defense Fund—which was formed in 1971 to work on the Mineral King case—in 1997 changed its name to Earthjustice. The nonprofit environmental law organization has filed thousands of lawsuits on behalf of the environment, taking on issues including climate change, air pollution, fracking, and oil drilling in the Arctic. The legal fund changed its name to signify the services it provides not just to the Sierra Club, but to more than five hundred other clients, including the American Lung Association, the Humane Society of the United States, and the Natural Resources Defense Council.

The Sierra Club may have wanted to set a major legal precedent by filing its initial lawsuit based purely on preserving the natural beauty of the Mineral King area, but ultimately, the Supreme Court's helpful suggestion that the club refile its lawsuit to show how its members would be personally affected by the Disney resort would provide a roadmap for environmental cases to come. As Oliver Houck wrote in the *Tulane Environmental Law Journal* in 2017, the case "opened the courthouse door to any individual 'adversely affected,' even aesthetically, by a government proposal, and this was a bombshell. From here on, the Sierra Club and like groups could sue if they had but a single affected member. . . . Citizen-driven environmental enforcement was off to the races."[5] Indeed, in the three years following the Supreme Court's decision in the Mineral King case, ninety-five environmental lawsuits cited *Sierra Club v. Morton*, seventy-three of those referring to the concept of standing.[6] Factor in the environmental considerations and reports that have been required by the National Environmental Policy Act since its passage in 1970—as well as individual state laws that have similar requirements—and the legal landscape for projects with the potential to do environmental harm looks much different than it did in 1965, when the Forest Service first issued its prospectus for Mineral King.

The Supreme Court ruled against the Sierra Club in the Mineral King case, but the dissents from justices Harry Blackmun and William Douglas have resonated much louder in the field of environmental law than the majority opinion. Douglas's dissent, in particular, while it hasn't resulted in a wave of lawsuits filed on behalf of natural objects, has served as inspiration for environmental groups looking to protect nature in the courtroom. In 1978, the Sierra Club filed a successful suit on behalf of Hawaii's Palila bird, an endangered species that was threatened with extinction by packs of feral sheep and goats, and other endangered species—including the coho salmon, the northern spotted owl, and the marbled murrelet—have been represented in court as coplaintiffs alongside humans.[7]

✧✧✧

The Mineral King case has had more personal results as well. More than thirty-three years after he escorted two of his fellow legislators on an aerial and ground tour of the Mineral King area in preparation for his house bill that would add the area to Sequoia National Park, John Krebs—then eighty-two—returned to the valley in July 2009 for the formal dedication of the John Krebs Wilderness. On a sunny summer day crowned by blue skies and backdropped by Mineral King's stunning peaks, Krebs, his family members, and many longtime supporters, along with various politicians and Park Service personnel, gathered at the end of the old Mineral King road to celebrate the former California representative's environmental legacy. The 39,740-acre John Krebs Wilderness—which includes the Mineral King

John Krebs in July 2009 at the formal dedication of the John Krebs Wilderness, which recognized the former U.S. representative for fighting to save Mineral King. Courtesy of Danny Krebs and Hanna Krebs.

area—was established as part of the Omnibus Public Land Management Act of 2009, signed March 30 of that year by President Barack Obama. It added more than two million acres of public land in California, Colorado, Idaho, Michigan, New Mexico, Oregon, Utah, Virginia, and West Virginia to the National Wilderness Preservation System. California congress members Barbara Boxer and Jim Costa were behind the effort to name the wilderness for Krebs, the man whose legislation had forever protected Mineral King from development.

❁ ❁ ❁

Mineral King meant different things to different people. To the Sierra Club, it was an outdoor haven to be treasured, a spark that ignited the legal battle to preserve wild places. To Jean Koch and other cabin owners, it was a home to be preserved, a historic legacy to be protected. To Walt Disney, it was a majestic wonderland that should be seen by more people, a fresh canvas on which to paint yet another dream.

"When I first saw Mineral King five years ago, I thought it was one of the most beautiful spots I had ever seen, and we want to keep it that way,"

Walt said in 1965, when Disney was awarded the rights to develop the valley for skiing.

It may not have happened the way Walt intended, but more than half a century later, Mineral King is, in fact, largely the same. The road into the area is just as long and serpentine as it ever was. Creeks still run, glistening under bright mountain sunlight as they flow. Stands of regal evergreen trees still watch over the area, the only difference being they've grown taller. The arched concrete bridge that Walt crossed by motorcade when he arrived in the valley for his final press conference back in 1966 is still intact. There are no ski lodges, no mountaintop restaurants, no chairlifts, no Disney-run gift shops, no highway offering easy access to the valley.

It's up to each individual if that's for the best.

ACKNOWLEDGMENTS

Like most things, this book started as a small idea that only grew with time. After discovering an interesting piece of Disney trivia—that Walt Disney tried, unsuccessfully, to build a ski resort in California in the 1960s—we started looking into the story and obsessively researching it. What we initially assumed was a small fact encompassed so much more: Walt Disney's conservation history, his death, the environmental movement, the women's liberation movement, a nearly fifteen-year battle between Disney and environmentalists over the project, and more.

We hope you find this story as fascinating as we have.

Thank you to our incredible agent, Annie Bomke, who shared our excitement for telling this story. Your encouragement, kind words, and help over the years have been tremendous and so appreciated. Our sincere thanks as well to our publisher, Rowman & Littlefield, and our editor, Christen Karniski. Thanks to Alan Kaufman for legal advice and his encouraging words about the book.

We are very grateful to our many sources on both sides of the battle who helped us tell this story by agreeing to be interviewed (sometimes multiple times), answering questions by email, sharing resources and memories, and more. Some of them were there at the time, whereas other times we relied on interviews with sources' descendants, as well as other experts.

Thanks to Michael McCloskey, Jean Koch, Mike Shannon, Jimmy Schaeffler, Danny Krebs, Frank Allnutt, Frank Stanek, Tom Turner, Jill

Tovey, Jerrold Klatt, Leland Selna, Congressman Jim Costa, Otto Tschudi, Bob Allen, Christopher Tremblay, John Lundin, Cathy Lean, and others.

Thank you to the Mineral King Preservation Society, in particular Sandra Stryd and Lisa Monteiro, who helped supply us with important archival information and other resources that were essential to this research. You were always so kind answering every question and request. Thanks also to Caitlin Moneypenny-Johnston and Bri Bertolaccini at the Walt Disney Family Museum.

We are also grateful for other archives and special collections, including those at the University of Denver, the University of Southern California, the Denver Public Library, the University of California, Berkeley, and the University of Nevada–Las Vegas.

Our research relies in large part on many newspaper and magazine articles by countless journalists who told the Mineral King story as it was happening, and we are grateful for their reporting.

Thanks to Erika Krouse, Jill Smith, Jenny Shank, and Tamara Chapman for thoughtful guidance at the beginning of our writing journey.

We are also appreciative of several people and organizations who supplied photos that helped bring this story to life. They include David Antonucci, Bill Briner, Danny and Hanna Krebs, Simon Williams, Michael McCloskey, Jerrold Klatt, Jill Tovey, Jean Koch, Kelley Baskins, the U.S. Ski and Snowboard Hall of Fame, the National Park Service, the Supreme Court of the United States, the University of Central Florida, the University of Southern California, and the University of Nevada-Las Vegas. Thank you for helping with images to share in this work.

Thanks to friends and family for their support and help, including Charlie and Leora Mayer; Jody Glasgow; Kelley Baskins (especially the Vail insight and the great photo!); Sarah and Adam Passarelli (thanks for the tip!); Victoria and Chris Francis; Charlie and Jessica Mayer; the Pfeiffers; the Eckert family—Jeanine, Mark, Josh, Hannah, and Gabi; Andrea Daddato and family; Shannon Mihaly; Chris Callaway; Erin Mitzen; Brian Glasgow; and our DU crew. And, of course, to Audrey.

Finally, to Gloria Cacioppo, who always wanted to hear the story, and encouraged goodness and kindness and instilled a love of words. You're forever in our hearts.

NOTES

CHAPTER I

1. "Mineral King Press Conference" (video), courtesy of The Walt Disney Family Museum.

2. Jay Crawford, "Disney Hints MK Project Speedup," *Tulare Advance-Register*, September 20, 1966, Newspapers.com.

3. Ken Castle, "How Sweet It Is," *Ski*, December 1999, 146.

4. Jeffrey Pepper, "New Heights: Mount Disney and Sugar Bowl," The Walt Disney Family Museum, January 16, 2012, accessed November 11, 2020, https://www.waltdisney.org/blog/new-heights-mount-disney-and-sugar-bowl.

5. United Press International, "MK Work Starts Soon," *Tulare Advance-Register*, December 18, 1965, Newspapers.com.

6. Ron Taylor, "Quick Okay for Disney Resort Is Seen after EDA Grant Approval," *Fresno Bee*, September 20, 1966, Newspapers.com.

7. "Mineral King Moves Foreward [*sic*] with State, U.S. Highway Plans," *The Disney World*, November 1966, 7.

8. Neal Gabler, *Walt Disney: The Triumph of the American Imagination* (New York: Alfred A. Knopf, 2006), 818.

9. Richard Snow, *Disney's Land: Walt Disney and the Invention of the Amusement Park That Changed the World* (New York: Scribner, 2019), 45.

10. Gabler, *Walt Disney*, 791.

11. Snow, *Disney's Land*, 5.

12. Louise Krasniewicz, *Walt Disney: A Biography* (Santa Barbara: Greenwood Biographies, 2010), 10.

13. Kathy Merlock Jackson (reprinting "Snow White's Daddy," by George Kent, *Family Circle*, June 24, 1938), *Walt Disney: Conversations* (Jackson: University Press of Mississippi, 2006), 11.

14. Michael Sporn, "Rico LeBrun's Guides," Michael Sporn Animation, May 9, 2008, accessed June 2, 2021, http://www.michaelspornanimation.com/splog/?p=1463.

15. Buena Vista Pictures, *Bambi* press kit, 1988 release, CineFiles, accessed August 22, 2021, https://cinefiles.bampfa.berkeley.edu/catalog/41303.

16. Lily Rothman, "Read *Time*'s Original Review of 'Grade-A' Bambi from 1942," *Time*, August 8, 2017, accessed June 22, 2021, https://time.com/4882887/disney-bambi-movie-1942-review.

17. Robin Murray and Joseph Heumann, "How 'Bambi' Hoodwinked American Environmentalists," Zocalo Public Square, April 19, 2016, accessed July 17, 2022, https://www.zocalopublicsquare.org/2016/04/19/how-bambi-hoodwinked-american-environmentalists.

18. Daniel Gifford, "Walt Disney: Stealth Conservationist," The Ultimate History Project, accessed November 2, 2021, https://ultimatehistoryproject.com/walt-disney----the-stealth-conservationist.html.

19. Bob Thomas, *Walt Disney: An American Original* (New York: Disney Editions, 1994), 206.

20. "Disney Legends: Al and Elma Milotte," D23, accessed May 14, 2021, https://d23.com/walt-disney-legend/al-and-elma-milotte.

21. Jim Korkis, "Walt and the True-Life Adventures," The Walt Disney Family Museum, February 9, 2012, accessed September 4, 2022, https://www.waltdisney.org/blog/walt-and-true-life-adventures.

22. "True-Life Adventure *Seal Island* Wins an Oscar® for Short Subject/Two Reel," D23, accessed September 7, 2022, https://d23.com/this-day/true-life-adventure-seal-island-wins-an-oscar-for-short-subjecttwo-reel.

23. Korkis, "Walt and the True-Life Adventures," The Walt Disney Family Museum.

24. Jackson, *Walt Disney: Conversations*, 69 (reprinting interview by Dave Griffiths from Walt Disney archive).

25. Michael Barrier, *The Animated Man: A Life of Walt Disney* (Berkeley: University of California Press, 2007), 208–9.

26. Korkis, "Walt and the True-Life Adventures," The Walt Disney Family Museum.

27. Jackson, *Walt Disney: Conversations*, 54 (reprinting interview by Don Eddy from *The American Magazine,* August 1955).

28. Korkis, "Walt and the True-Life Adventures," The Walt Disney Family Museum.

29. Jim Korkis, *The Vault of Walt Volume 2: MORE Unofficial, Unauthorized, Uncensored Disney Stories Never Told* (Theme Park Press, 2013), 175.

30. Stacy Conradt, "15 Facts about Disney's Jungle Cruise," Mental Floss, May 9, 2018, accessed September 9, 2021, https://www.mentalfloss.com/article/66098/15 -facts-celebrate-jungle-cruises-60th-birthday.

31. Gifford, "Walt Disney – Stealth Conservationist."

32. Gifford, "Walt Disney – Stealth Conservationist."

33. Gifford, "Walt Disney – Stealth Conservationist."

34. Daniel P. Selmi, *Dawn at Mineral King Valley: The Sierra Club, the Disney Company, and the Rise of Environmental Law* (Chicago: University of Chicago Press, 2022), xiii.

35. National Wildlife Federation, "Vintage National Wildlife Week PSAs— Walt Disney," YouTube.com, accessed April 20, 2021, https://www.youtube.com /watch?v=in0ZPNR2JDo.

36. Robert Jackson, "Walt Disney Biography," memorandum to Marty Sklar, August 15, 1968, Robert B. Hicks Papers, Mineral King Preservation Society.

37. Jackson memorandum.

38. Jackson memorandum.

CHAPTER 2

1. Roger Rapoport, "Disney's War against the Wilderness," *Ramparts,* November 1971, 30.

2. Charlie Meyers, "Dynamic Willy Schaeffler a Giant in Skiing World," *Denver Post*, January 31, 1973, 86.

3. Robert Ajemian, "King of the Hill," *Sports Illustrated*, April 1, 1957, accessed September 10, 2020, https://vault.si.com/vault/1957/04/01/king-of-the-hill.

4. Peter Miller, "Willy Schaeffler: The Original Rebel," *Skiing History Magazine*, May 24, 2022, accessed August 11, 2022, https://www.skiinghistory.org/news /willy-schaeffler-original-rebel.

5. Willy Schaeffler, letter to Larry Jump, July 6, 1948, Laurence (Larry) Jump and Arapahoe Basin Records, Denver Public Library.

6. Jimmy Schaeffler, "The Legacy of Skiing Coach Willy Schaeffler," *University of Denver Magazine*, winter 2015, accessed September 10, 2020, https://maga zine-archive.du.edu/magazine/winter-2015/legacy-skiing-coach-willy-schaeffler; and authors' interview with former DU ski team member Otto Tschudi.

7. Willy Schaeffler, "The New Way to Ski," *Sports Illustrated*, November 25, 1957, accessed September 10, 2020, https://vault.si.com/vault/1957/11/25/the-new -way-to-ski.

8. Douglas Martin, "Alexander Cushing, Who Brought Winter Olympics to West Coast, Dies at 92," *New York Times*, August 21, 2006, accessed November 2, 2019, https://www.nytimes.com/2006/08/21/sports/22cushingcnd.html.

9. Martin, "Alexander Cushing, Who Brought Winter Olympics to West Coast, Dies at 92."

10. David C. Antonucci, *Snowball's Chance: The Story of the 1960 Olympic Winter Games, Squaw Valley & Lake Tahoe* (Booksurge, 2009), 15.

11. Michael Crawford, "New Heights: Walt and the Winter Olympics," The Walt Disney Family Museum, January 18, 2012, accessed December 7, 2019, https://www.waltdisney.org/blog/new-heights-walt-and-winter-olympics.

12. Crawford, "New Heights."

13. Crawford, "New Heights."

14. Antonucci, *Snowball's Chance*, 20.

15. Crawford, "New Heights."

16. Jim Korkis, "Walt Disney and the 1960 Winter Olympics," Mouseplanet, May 13, 2015, accessed April 11, 2020, https://www.mouseplanet.com/11012/Walt _Disney_and_the_1960_Winter_Olympics.

17. Korkis, "Walt Disney and the 1960 Winter Olympics."

18. Korkis, "Walt Disney and the 1960 Winter Olympics."

19. Korkis, "Walt Disney and the 1960 Winter Olympics."

20. Crawford, "New Heights."

21. Antonucci, *Snowball's Chance*, 60.

22. Scott Richter, "Charles Hirt: The Miracle at Squaw Valley," *Disney News*, Winter 1993, 28.

23. Crawford, "New Heights."

24. Crawford, "New Heights."

25. Crawford, "New Heights."

26. Crawford, "New Heights."

27. Guy Shipler Jr., "Backstage at the Winter Olympics," *Popular Science*, February 1960, 138.

28. Harrison "Buzz" Price, *Walt's Revolution! By the Numbers* (Orlando: Ripley Entertainment, 2004), 46.

29. Price, *Walt's Revolution!*, 49.

30. "History," Mineral King District Association, accessed January 4, 2020, https://www.mineralking.net/page/history.

31. Rapoport, "Disney's War against the Wilderness," 30.

32. Robert Hicks interview, February 6, 2014, Mineral King Preservation Society.

CHAPTER 3

1. John Harper, *Mineral King: Public Concern with Government Policy* (Arcata: Pacifica Publishing Company, 1982), 5.

2. Harper, *Mineral King*, 61.

3. Harper, *Mineral King*, 64.

4. Harper, *Mineral King*, 61.

5. Tom Turner, *David Brower: The Making of the Environmental Movement* (Oakland: University of California Press, 2015), 59.

6. David Brower and Richard Felter, "Surveying California's Ski Terrain," *Sierra Club Bulletin*, March 1948.

7. Turner, *David Brower*, 60.

8. Turner, *David Brower*, 49.

9. Turner, *David Brower*, 57.

10. Turner, *David Brower*, 58.

11. Turner, *David Brower*, 59.

12. Harper, *Mineral King*, 55.

13. Louise Jackson, *Beulah: A Biography of the Mineral King Valley of California* (Tucson: Westernlore Press, 1988), 145.

14. John Muir, *Our National Parks* (Boston: Houghton Mifflin, 1901), 19.

15. "Working Conditions in Factories," Encyclopedia.com, accessed July 17, 2022, https://www.encyclopedia.com/history/encyclopedias-almanacs-transcripts-and-maps/working-conditions-factories-issue.

16. Robert Righter, *The Battle over Hetch Hetchy: America's Most Controversial Dam and the Birth of Modern Environmentalism* (Oxford: Oxford University Press, 2006), 4.

17. Donald Worster, *A Passion for Nature: The Life of John Muir* (Oxford: Oxford University Press, 2008), 458.

18. Harper, *Mineral King*, 66.

19. Harper, *Mineral King*, 71.

20. Omer Crane, "Disney's $35 Million Bid Earns Him Favorite's Role," *Fresno Bee*, September 5, 1965, Newspapers.com.

21. Harper, *Mineral King*, 78.

22. Harper, *Mineral King*, 80.

23. Harper, *Mineral King*, 80–81.

CHAPTER 4

1. Sierra Club Board of Directors, *Minutes*, May 1–2, 1965, 13, at http://www.oac.cdlib.org/ark:/28722/bk0007b0j7k/?order=50&brand=oac4.

2. Sierra Club Board of Directors, *Minutes*, May 1–2, 1965, 13.

3. Rachel Carson, *Silent Spring* (Boston: Houghton Mifflin, 1962), 86.

4. Roddy Scheer and Doug Moss, EarthTalk, "How Important Was Rachel Carson's *Silent Spring* in the Recovery of Bald Eagles and Other Bird Species?," *Scientific American*, August 31, 2012, accessed September 3, 2022, https://www.scientificamerican.com/article/rachel-carson-silent-spring-1972-ddt-ban-birds-thrive.

5. Edgar Wayburn, interview by Susan Schrepfer, 1976, Sierra Club Oral History Project, 39, at https://digitalassets.lib.berkeley.edu/roho/ucb/text/wayburn_edgar.pdf.

6. Sierra Club Board of Directors, *Minutes,* May 1–2, 1965, 12.

7. Martin Litton, interview by Ann Lage, 1980, Sierra Club Oral History Project, 28, at https://archive.org/details/sierraclubleaders01lagerich/page/n7/mode/2up.

8. Martin Litton interview, 28.

9. David Brower, interview by Susan Schrepfer, 1976, Sierra Club Oral History Project, 177, at https://archive.org/details/environmentalact00browrich.

10. John Harper, *Mineral King; Public Concern with Government Policy* (Arcata: Pacifica Publishing Company, 1982), 86.

11. Fred Eissler, "Report on Mineral King," The Wilderness Society Records, Denver Public Library, 1.

12. Eissler, "Report on Mineral King," 2.

13. Harrison "Buzz" Price, *Walt's Revolution! By the Numbers* (Orlando: Ripley Entertainment, 2004), 17.

14. Price, *Walt's Revolution,* 19.

15. Economics Research Associates, *Economic Potentials of a Resort Development at Mineral King, California,* 1965, 1–1.

16. "Walt Disney May Develop Mineral King Area," *Tulare Advance-Register,* August 19, 1965, Newspapers.com.

CHAPTER 5

1. Frank Allnutt, unpublished memoir, 11–10.

2. Omer Crane, "Disney's $35 Million Bid Earns Him Favorite's Role," *Fresno Bee,* September 5, 1965, Newspapers.com.

3. Ron Taylor, "Mineral King Bids Overwhelm Officials," *Fresno Bee,* September 1, 1965, Newspapers.com.

4. Vernon Scott, "Disney Plans New Project," *Honolulu Star Bulletin,* September 26, 1965, Newspapers.com.

5. John Harper, *Mineral King; Public Concern with Government Policy* (Arcata: Pacifica Publishing Company, 1982), 87.

6. Harper, *Mineral King,* 94–95.

7. Jake S. Friedman, *The Disney Revolt: The Great Labor War of Animation's Golden Age* (Chicago: Chicago Review Press, 2022), 234.

8. Friedman, *The Disney Revolt,* 219.

9. Neal Gabler, *Walt Disney: The Triumph of the American Imagination* (New York: Alfred A. Knopf, 2006), 994.

10. Gabler, *Walt Disney,* 995.

11. Gabler, *Walt Disney,* 996.

12. "Obituary: Janet Leigh," Backstage, October 4, 2004, accessed July 30, 2021, https://www.backstage.com/magazine/article/obituaries-13-22578.

13. Ron Taylor, "More Delay Is Seen on Mineral King," *Fresno Bee,* October 21, 1965, Newspapers.com.

14. Charles Connaughton, interview by Elwood Maunder, 1976, Forest History Society, 112, at https://foresthistory.org/wp-content/uploads/2016/12/Connaughton _Charles_A.pdf.

15. Editorial, "Mineral King: Final Round," *Tulare Advance-Register*, November 1, 1965, Newspapers.com.

16. Harper, *Mineral King*, 93.

17. Robert Hicks, interview by Mineral King Preservation Society, February 6, 2014.

18. Associated Press, "$50 Million Sequoia Plan Given U.S.," *Pasadena Independent*, November 9, 1965.

19. Harper, *Mineral King*, 94.

20. Elvis Lane, "Disney's Secrets Revealed," *Orlando Evening Star*, November 16, 1965, Newspapers.com.

21. Elvis Lane, "Walt Disney on 'Safari' to 'Tomorrow-Yesterday,'" *Orlando Evening Star*, November 16, 1965, Newspapers.com.

22. Gabler, *Walt Disney*, 981.

23. Martin Comas, "Journalist Who Broke Disney Story Dies at 88," *Orlando Sentinel*, July 28, 2003, accessed September 14, 2022, https://www.orlandosentinel .com/news/os-xpm-2003-07-29-0307290048-story.html.

24. Douglas Doubleday, "$100-Million Development Is Outlined," *Tampa Bay Times*, November 16, 1965, Newspapers.com.

25. Associated Press, "Disney Bringing $6 Billion Boom to State," *Orlando Sentinel*, November 25, 1965, Newspapers.com.

26. Gabler, *Walt Disney*, 983.

27. McClatchy Newspapers Service, "Disney Is Awarded Mineral King Contract," *Fresno Bee*, December 17, 1965, Newspapers.com.

28. United Press International, "MK Work Starts Soon," *Tulare Advance-Register*, December 18, 1965, Newspapers.com.

CHAPTER 6

1. Economics Research Associates, *Economic Potentials of a Resort Development at Mineral King, California*, 1965, V-5.

2. Don Peri, *Working with Disney: Interviews with Animators, Producers, and Artists* (Jackson: University Press of Mississippi, 2011), 42.

3. Richard Snow, *Disney's Land: Walt Disney and the Invention of the Amusement Park That Changed the World* (New York: Scribner, 2019), 360.

4. "Marc Davis and His Early Days at WED," ImagineeringDisney.com, accessed December 4, 2019, http://www.imagineeringdisney.com/blog/2011/9/25/marc-davis -and-his-early-days-at-wed.html.

5. Dustin Fuhs, "Top 10 Jungle Cruise Puns," Steps to Magic, accessed June 12, 2022, https://stepstomagic.com/ten-best-jungle-cruise-jokes.

6. "The Birds, Beasts, and Beauty of Disney's Audio-Animatronics Characters," D23, accessed March 11, 2021, https://d23.com/audio-animatronics-disneyland-magic-kingdom-walt-disney-world.

7. "Welcome to the Fair! The 1939 and 1964 New York World's Fairs," New York State Library, accessed December 2, 2020, https://www.nysl.nysed.gov/collections/worldsfair.

8. Paul Goldberger, "Robert Moses, Master Builder, Is Dead at 92," *New York Times*, July 30, 1981, accessed June 7, 2022, https://www.nytimes.com/1981/07/30/obituaries/robert-moses-master-builder-is-dead-at-92.html.

9. Alyssa Carnaham, "Look Closer: 1964 New York World's Fair," The Walt Disney Family Museum, June 26, 2012, accessed January 6, 2021, https://www.waltdisney.org/blog/look-closer-1964-new-york-worlds-fair.

10. Jimmy Johnson, *Inside the Whimsy Works: My Life with Walt Disney Productions* (Jackson: University Press of Mississippi, 2014), 106.

11. Chuck Schmidt, "The Marty Sklar Interview: Part 1—Disney's Participation at the World's Fair Was a Defining Moment in the Company's History," April 7, 2010, accessed April 12, 2022, https://www.silive.com/sinotebook/2010/04/an_interview_with_marty_sklar.html.

12. Snow, *Disney's Land*, 328.

13. Ron Taylor, "Disney Survey Team Findings Will Guide Resort Development," *Fresno Bee*, February 4, 1966, Newspapers.com.

14. John Harper, *Mineral King; Public Concern with Government Policy* (Arcata: Pacifica Publishing Company, 1982), 108.

15. "Disney to Start Work on Sierra Ski Resort," *Los Angeles Times*, June 3, 1966, Newspapers.com.

16. Ron Taylor, "Walt Disney Aides Say Mineral King Highway Appears 'Go,' Mapping Near," *Fresno Bee*, June 2, 1966, Newspapers.com.

17. Michael Barrier, *The Animated Man: A Life of Walt Disney* (Berkeley: University of California Press, 2007), 273.

18. Bosley Crowther, "Screen: Sleeping Beauty," *New York Times*, February 18, 1959, accessed January 4, 2020, https://www.nytimes.com/1959/02/18/archives/screen-sleeping-beauty.html.

19. Bob Thomas, *Walt Disney: An American Original* (New York: Disney Editions, 1994), 295.

20. Thomas, *Walt Disney*, 295.

21. Keith Gluck, "Celebrating 50 Years of Mary Poppins," The Walt Disney Family Museum, August 27, 2014, accessed February 12, 2021, https://www.waltdisney.org/blog/celebrating-50-years-mary-poppins.

22. Bosley Crowther, "Screen: 'Mary Poppins': Julie Andrews Stars as Famous Nanny," *New York Times*, September 25, 1964, accessed May 7, 2021, www.nytimes.com/archives/screen-mary-poppinsjulie-andrews-stars-as-famous-nanny.html.

23. Philip Scheuer, "Disney Fantasy Film—Amazement and Delight, Even for Grownups, Squares," *Los Angeles Times*, August 16, 1964, Newspapers.com.

24. Walt Disney Productions, *1966 Annual Report to Shareholders and Employees*, 2.

25. Walt Disney Productions, *1966 Annual Report*, 15.

26. Laura Ruttum Senturia, "Celebrity Sports Center: Bowling, Video Games, and Your Very First Water Slide," Denver Public Library, Genealogy, African American and Western History Resources, January 25, 2020, accessed February 1, 2021, https://history.denverlibrary.org/news/celebrity-sports-center.

27. Thomas, *Walt Disney*, 350.

28. Thomas, *Walt Disney*, 350.

29. United Press International, "Walt Disney Back on Job Minus Lung," *Eureka Humboldt Standard*, November 23, 1966, Newspapers.com.

30. Thomas, *Walt Disney*, 351.

31. Peri, *Working with Disney*, 52.

CHAPTER 7

1. Bob Thomas, *Building a Company: Roy O. Disney and the Creation of an Entertainment Empire* (New York: Hyperion, 1998), 298.

2. Bob Thomas/Associated Press, "Disney's Studio Will Carry on His Policies," *Stockton Evening and Sunday Record*, January 9, 1967, Newspapers.com.

3. Thomas, *Building a Company*, 297.

4. "Walt Disney: Man and Monument," *Los Angeles Times*, December 16, 1966, Newspapers.com.

5. Bob Thomas, *Walt Disney: An American Original* (New York: Disney Editions, 1994), 354.

6. "Roy Disney's Statement," *Orlando Sentinel*, December 16, 1966, Newspapers.com.

7. Robert Hicks interview, June 17, 2013, Mineral King Preservation Society.

8. Marc Eades, "Remembering Roy O. Disney, Walt Disney's Brother, 45 Years after His Death," *Orange County Register,* December 22, 2016, accessed November 27, 2021, https://www.ocregister.com/2016/12/22/remembering-roy-o -disney-walt-disneys-brother-45-years-after-his-death.

9. Neal Gabler, *Walt Disney: The Triumph of the American Imagination* (New York: Alfred A. Knopf, 2006), 266.

10. Ken Pilcher, "50 years ago: Roy Disney made Walt's dream come true," October 27, 2021, ClickOrlando.com, accessed March 5, 2019, https://www.click orlando.com/theme-parks/2021/10/01/50-years-ago-roy-disney-made-walts-dream -come-true.

11. Jim Korkis, "The Forgotten Brother Who Built a Magic Kingdom," Mouse-Planet, March 16, 2011, accessed December 1, 2021, https://www.mouseplanet .com/9562/The_Forgotten_Brother_Who_Built_a_Magic_Kingdom.

12. Shauna Murray, "The History of Disneyland," A Day in LA Tours, September 1, 2020, accessed October 2, 2022. https://www.adayinlatours.com/blog/the -history-of-disneyland.

13. *White House Conference on Conservation: Official Proceedings* (Washington, DC: U.S. Government Printing Office, 1962), 100.

14. Adam Rome, "'Give Earth a Chance': The Environmental Movement and the Sixties," *Journal of American History*, September 2003, Vol. 90, No. 2, 533–34.

15. Don Irwin, "Udall Bids for Monorail Route to Mineral King," *Los Angeles Times*, March 12, 1967, Newspapers.com.

16. Stewart Udall, *The Quiet Crisis* (New York: Holt, Rinehart and Winston, 1963), viii.

17. Ron Taylor, "State Okays Mineral King Route Funds," *Fresno Bee*, April 21, 1967, Newspapers.com.

18. John Harper, *Mineral King; Public Concern with Government Policy* (Arcata: Pacifica Publishing Company, 1982), 133.

19. Ron Taylor, "Mineral King Deadline May Be Extended Because of Okay Delay," *Fresno Bee*, November 17, 1967, Newspapers.com.

20. *Quest for Quality: U.S. Department of the Interior Conservation Yearbook* (Washington, DC: U.S. Government Printing Office, 1965), 111.

21. Harper, *Mineral King*, 134.

22. Ron Taylor, "Udall's Okay Gives Green Light for Mineral King," *Fresno Bee*, December 27, 1967, Newspapers.com.

23. United Press International, "MK Project at Standstill over Road," *Tulare Advance-Register*, September 29, 1967, Newspapers.com.

24. "Mineral King Road Gets Federal Okay," *Tulare Advance-Register*, December 27, 1967, Newspapers.com.

25. Estheranne Billings, "Skiing with Estheranne Billings" (column), *Van Nuys News*, January 5, 1968, Newspapers.com.

CHAPTER 8

1. Jean Koch, letter to Edmund Brown, April 16, 1965, Mineral King Development Records, Special Collections, USC Libraries, University of Southern California.

2. Authors' email interview with Jean Koch, February 19, 2022.

3. Richard Koch, MD, obituary, Legacy.com, accessed April 4, 2022, https://www.legacy.com/us/obituaries/latimes/name/richard-koch-obituary?id=10145522.

4. National Wildlife Federation, letter to Jean Koch, March 31, 1967, Mineral King Development Records, Special Collections, USC Libraries, University of Southern California.

5. National Wildlife Federation, letter to Jean Koch, August 31, 1967, Mineral King Development Records, Special Collections, USC Libraries, University of Southern California.

6. Adam Rome, "'Give Earth a Chance': The Environmental Movement and the Sixties," *The Journal of American History*, Volume 90, Number 2, September 2003, 535.

7. Rome, "'Give Earth a Chance,'" 536.

8. Authors' interview with Jill Tovey, September 1, 2022.

9. "What Price Road?," editorial, *New York Times*, January 24, 1968.

10. Anthony Wayne Smith, "Mineral King," *National Parks Magazine*, July 1967, 2.

11. Bruton Peterson and James Rascoe, directors, *Mineral King*. University of Southern California School of Cinematic Arts, 1972, 9:40, https://www.amazon.com/Mineral-King-Bruton-Peterson/dp/B01BWNUPJO.

12. Peterson and Rascoe, *Mineral King*, 10:30.

13. "Disney's Dream Wonderland OK'd," *Hollywood Evening Citizen News*, January 28, 1969, Newspapers.com.

14. John Harper, *Mineral King; Public Concern with Government Policy* (Arcata: Pacifica Publishing Company, 1982), 148.

15. Associated Press, "Disney's Project in Sierra Is Approved," *Napa Register*, January 28, 1969.

16. Daniel P. Selmi, *Dawn at Mineral King Valley: The Sierra Club, the Disney Company, and the Rise of Environmental Law* (Chicago: University of Chicago Press, 2022), 154.

17. Harper, *Mineral King*, 155.

18. Selmi, *Dawn at Mineral King Valley*, 100.

19. Ron Taylor, "Rescuers Dig Body from Sierra Cabin," *Fresno Bee*, February 27, 1969, Newspapers.com.

20. Bob Edkin, "Fire Suffocates Avalanche Victim," *Tulare Advance-Register*, February 27, 1969, Newspapers.com.

21. Jean Koch, letter to editor of *Los Angeles Times*, May 21, 1969, Mineral King Development Records, Special Collections, USC Libraries, University of Southern California.

22. Harold Peterson, "Brower Power Awaits the Verdict," *Sports Illustrated*, April 14, 1969, accessed January 14, 2020, https://vault.si.com/vault/1969/04/14/brower-power-awaits-the-verdict.

CHAPTER 9

1. Michael McCloskey, *In the Thick of It: My Life in the Sierra Club* (Washington, DC: Island Press, 2005), 4.

2. Bill Duncan, "Mineral King: A Resort in Limbo," *Long Beach Independent*, December 14, 1969, Newspapers.com.

3. Walt Disney Productions, "The Disney Plans for Mineral King," brochure, 1966.

4. Associated Press, "Sierra Club Files Suit to Halt Disney Mineral King Resort," *Sacramento Bee*, June 6, 1969, Newspapers.com.

5. Henry MacArthur, "Sierra Club Action Draws Public, Federal Opposition," *Press-Tribune* (Roseville, CA), June 16, 1969, Newspapers.com.

6. Memorandum of Decision, *Sierra Club v. Hickel*, No. 51,464 (N.D. Cal. 1969).

7. Bestor Robinson interview by Susan Schrepfer, 1974, Sierra Club Oral History Project, Robinson, 41, at https://digitalassets.lib.berkeley.edu/roho/ucb/text/sc_reminiscences1.pdf.

8. McClatchy Newspapers Service, "Disney Sticks to Mineral King," *Sacramento Bee*, February 4, 1970, Newspapers.com.

9. Lee Fremstad, "Fate of Disney's Mineral King Resort Rests with U.S. Court of Appeals," *Sacramento Bee*, February 10, 1970, Newspapers.com.

10. United Press International, "Mineral King Gets New Court Attention," *Tulare Advance-Register*, January 12, 1970, Newspapers.com.

11. Karl Kidder, "Disney Aide Rebuts Mineral King Critic," *Fresno Bee*, March 16, 1970, Newspapers.com.

12. Ron Taylor, "Skiers Get Close Look at M-K Sierra Slopes," *Fresno Bee*, April 12, 1970, Newspapers.com.

13. Taylor, "Skiers Get Close Look at M-K Sierra Slopes."

14. McCloskey, *In the Thick of It*, 106.

15. "America's National Park System: The Critical Documents," National Park Service, accessed July 20, 2021, https://www.nps.gov/parkhistory/online_books/anps/anps_6l.htm.

16. McCloskey, *In the Thick of It*, 104.

17. John Harper, *Mineral King; Public Concern with Government Policy* (Arcata: Pacifica Publishing Company, 1982), 173.

18. *Sierra Club v. Hickel*, 433 F.2d 24 (9th Cir. 1970).

19. *Sierra Club v. Hickel*, 433 F.2d 24 (9th Cir. 1970).

20. *Sierra Club v. Hickel*, 433 F.2d 24 (9th Cir. 1970).

21. "Sierra Club in High Court," *San Francisco Examiner*, November 5, 1970, Newspapers.com.

22. "Mineral King Ruling Pleases Mathias, Shocks Sierra Club," *Tulare Advance-Register*, September 18, 1970, Newspapers.com.

23. Daniel P. Selmi, *Dawn at Mineral King Valley: The Sierra Club, the Disney Company, and the Rise of Environmental Law* (Chicago: University of Chicago Press, 2022), 166.

24. "Sierra Club in High Court," *San Francisco Examiner*, November 5, 1970, Newspapers.com.

CHAPTER 10

1. William O. Douglas, *The Court Years 1939–1975: The Autobiography of William O. Douglas* (New York: Random House, 1980), 391–92.

2. M. Margaret McKeown, "The Trees Are Still Standing: The Backstory of *Sierra Club v. Morton,*" *Journal of Supreme Court History*, Volume 44, Issue 2, July 2019, 197.

3. William O. Douglas, *Of Men and Mountains* (New York: Harper & Bro., 1950), 244.

4. Douglas, *Of Men and Mountains*, 13.

5. "William O. Douglas," Oyez.org, accessed September 13, 2022, https://www.oyez.org/justices/william_o_douglas.

6. McKeown, "The Trees Are Still Standing: The Backstory of *Sierra Club v. Morton,*" 192.

7. William O. Douglas, *A Wilderness Bill of Rights* (Boston: Little, Brown & Co., 1965), 86.

8. *Sierra Club v. Morton* transcript.

9. *Sierra Club v. Morton* transcript.

10. *Sierra Club v. Morton* transcript.

11. *Sierra Club v. Morton* transcript.

12. *Brief for the Wilderness Society, Izaak Walton League of America, and Friends of the Earth as Amici Curiae*, Sierra Club v. Morton.

13. McKeown, "The Trees Are Still Standing," 204.

14. Potter Stewart, Opinion, *Sierra Club v. Morton*.

15. "Club Sees Invitation by Court to Refile Its Plea," *Los Angeles Times*, April 20, 1972, Newspapers.com.

16. Harry Blackmun, Dissent, *Sierra Club v. Morton*.

17. William O. Douglas, Dissent, *Sierra Club v. Morton*.

18. Stewart, Opinion, *Sierra Club v. Morton*.

19. "Club Sees Invitation by Court to Refile Its Plea," *Los Angeles Times*.

20. "Sierra Club Files New Mineral King Suit," *Los Angeles Times*, June 7, 1972, Newspapers.com.

21. James Moorman, interview by Ted Hudson, 1984, Sierra Club Oral History Project, 82–83, at https://archive.org/details/attorneyenvironment00moorrich.

22. Dick Marlowe, "Thousands See Disney Dream Live," *Orlando Sentinel*, October 26, 1971, Newspapers.com.

23. Peggy Poor, "Mickey Mouse Is Tapped by the Conservation Team," *Florida Magazine/Orlando Sentinel*, August 2, 1970, pp. 46–47.

CHAPTER 11

1. Disney Legends: Card Walker, D23, accessed February 22, 2022, https://d23.com/walt-disney-legend/card-walker.

2. "All Aboard: A Celebration of Walt's Trains," The Walt Disney Family Museum, accessed February 7, 2022, https://www.waltdisney.org/exhibitions/all-aboard-celebration-walts-trains.

3. "All Aboard: A Celebration of Walt's Trains," The Walt Disney Family Museum.

4. Philip Fradkin, "Disney Firm Cuts Back on Mineral King Plans," *Los Angeles Times*, May 4, 1972, Newspapers.com.

5. James Foley, "Sierra Club Will Meet on Ski Resort," *Fresno Bee*, May 4, 1972, Newspapers.com.

6. Disney A to Z: "Walt Disney World Resort," D23.com, accessed November 17, 2021, https://d23.com/a-to-z/walt-disney-world-resort.

7. John Harper, *Mineral King; Public Concern with Government Policy* (Arcata: Pacifica Publishing Company, 1982), 187.

8. United Press International, "Reagan OK's Ban on Sierra Hwy.," *The Press Democrat*, August 20, 1972, Newspapers.com.

9. *The Optimist* newsletter, summer and fall 1973 edition, Mineral King Development Records, Special Collections, USC Libraries, University of Southern California.

10. Jerrold Klatt, "Save for All," letter to the editor, December 29, 1971, *Daily Times-Advocate* (Escondido, CA), Newspapers.com.

11. *The Optimist*, fall 1972, Mineral King Development Records, Special Collections, USC Libraries, University of Southern California.

12. Bruton Peterson and James Rascoe, directors, *Mineral King*. University of Southern California School of Cinematic Arts, 1972, 18:40, https://www.amazon.com/Mineral-King-Bruton-Peterson/dp/B01BWNUPJO.

13. Peterson and Rascoe, *Mineral King*, 22:30.

14. "Ski Area That Didn't Happen #1—Independence Lake," Tahoetopia.com, accessed February 22, 2019, https://tahoetopia.com/news/ski-area-didn-t-happen-1-independence-lake.

15. Philip Fradkin, "Disney Studying Lake Near Truckee for Sierra Resort," *Los Angeles Times*, September 3, 1974, Newspapers.com.

16. Authors' interview with Jimmy Schaeffler, July 10, 2022.

17. Fradkin, "Disney Studying Lake Near Truckee for Sierra Resort."

18. Douglas H. Strong, "Disney's Independence Lake Project: A Case Study of California's Environmental Review Process," *California History*, Volume 61, Number 2, Summer 1982, 102.

19. Doug McMillan, "Disney Plans for Sierra Resort Unveiled," *Reno Gazette-Journal*, July 17, 1975, Newspapers.com.

20. McMillan, "Disney Plans for Sierra Resort Unveiled."

21. Associated Press, "A Joint Effort on Wilderness," *Reno Gazette-Journal,* December 20, 1974, Newspapers.com.

22. Associated Press, "Disney Resort Hits Land Snag," *Merced Sun-Star,* November 14, 1975, Newspapers.com.

23. Robert Hicks, letter to John Leasure, March 28, 1975, reprinted in *Mineral King Recreation Development: Final Environmental Statement,* United States Department of Agriculture, February 29, 1976, 3.

24. Hicks, letter to John Leasure, 6.

25. Michael McCloskey, letter to Douglas Leisz, March 31, 1975, reprinted in *Mineral King Recreation Development: Final Environmental Statement,* United States Department of Agriculture, February 29, 1976, 3.

26. Associated Press "Divided Response on Resort," *Merced Sun-Star,* May 22, 1975, Newspapers.com.

27. Associated Press, "Forestry Has New Plan for Mineral King," *San Bernardino County Sun,* August 30, 1975, Newspapers.com.

28. Ron Taylor, "Revised Mineral King Plan Will Be Presented to Public," *Fresno Bee,* February 24, 1976, Newspapers.com.

CHAPTER 12

1. Gene Rose, "Solon against MK Development," *Fresno Bee,* May 30, 1976, Newspapers.com.

2. Eli Setencich, "Krebs: Long Journey from Nazi Terror to Public Office," *Fresno Bee,* March 15, 1970, Newspapers.com.

3. John Harper, *Mineral King; Public Concern with Government Policy* (Arcata: Pacifica Publishing Company, 1982), 204.

4. United Press International, "Solon from California Opposes Development," *Oroville Mercury Register,* March 15, 1976, Newspapers.com.

5. "Mineral King: Krebs Announces Opposition to Project," *Tulare Advance-Register,* March 15, 1976, Newspapers.com.

6. Paul Deauville, "Laud Krebs' Study" (letter to the editor), *Fresno Bee,* April 13, 1976, Newspapers.com.

7. Hearing Before the Subcommittee on Parks and Recreation of the Committee on Energy and Natural Resources, United States Senate, Ninety-Fifth Congress, Second Session, on S. 88, U.S. Government Printing Office, Washington, D.C., 1978, 18.

8. "13 Reasons Why Jimmy Carter Is America's Greenest President," More Than Just Parks, August 10, 2022, accessed August 20, 2022, https://morethanjustparks.com/jimmy-carter-americas-greenest-president.

9. *The Presidential Campaign 1976,* Volume 1, Part 2, U.S. Government Printing Office, 1978, 859.

10. Michael McCloskey, *In the Thick of It: My Life in the Sierra Club* (Washington, DC: Shearwater Books, 2005), 170.

11. Associated Press, "Mineral King Suit by Sierra Club Dismissed," *Independent* (Long Beach, CA), March 18, 1977, Newspapers.com.

12. "Disney Files in Sierra County," *Portola Reporter*, August 18, 1977, Newspapers.com.

13. Walt Disney Productions, *Annual Report 1977*, 20.

14. "Draft EIR on Disney Plan Slated for March," *Portola Reporter*, October 27, 1977.

15. "Disney Project Off to a Start," *Oakland Tribune*, August 14, 1977, Newspapers.com.

16. Associated Press, "A Protest in Living Color," *Contra Costa Times*, September 18, 1977, Newspapers.com.

17. Tom Eastham, "The Sequoia Tempest in a Ski Spot," *San Francisco Examiner*, October 28, 1977, Newspapers.com.

18. Kathy Batts, "Mineral King Appears Headed for Inclusion in Sequoia National Park," *Hanford Sentinel*, October 28, 1977, Newspapers.com.

19. Batts, "Mineral King Appears Headed for Inclusion in Sequoia National Park."

20. "Krebs' Mineral King Bill Debated," *Tulare Advance-Register*, October 28, 1977, Newspapers.com.

21. George Baker, "Divergent Groups Clash over Development of Mineral King," *Fresno Bee*, October 28, 1977, Newspapers.com.

22. Tom Eastham, "Carter Says No on Mineral King," *San Francisco Examiner*, January 26, 1978, Newspapers.com.

23. Card Walker, letter to Jimmy Carter, February 13, 1978, reprinted in *The Disneyland Line*, February 23, 1978, via WDW News Today, accessed April 2, 2022, https://wdwnt.com/2020/05/the-abominable-snowman-arrives-at-the-matterhorn-bobsleds-in-this-february-1978-edition-of-the-disneyland-line.

24. Daniel P. Selmi, *Dawn at Mineral King Valley: The Sierra Club, the Disney Company, and the Rise of Environmental Law* (Chicago: University of Chicago Press, 2022), 253.

25. Associated Press, "Bill Proposed for Park at San Antonio Missions," *Victoria Advocate* (Victoria, TX), October 25, 1978, Newspapers.com.

26. Jessica Boerner, "A History of the National Park Service through the Lens of Legislation," *DttP: Documents to the People*, Vol. 45, Number 4 (2017), accessed September 8, 2022, https://journals.ala.org/index.php/dttp/article/view/6566/8758.

27. "National Parks and Recreation Act of 1978 Statement on Signing S. 791 into Law," The American Presidency Project, UC Santa Barbara, accessed July 1, 2022, https://www.presidency.ucsb.edu/documents/national-parks-and-recreation-act-1978-statement-signing-s-791-into-law.

28. "History," Mineral King District Association, accessed January 4, 2022, https://www.mineralking.net/page/history.

29. Walt Disney Productions, *Annual Report 1978*, 3.

CHAPTER 13

1. Authors' interview with Mike Shannon, July 28, 2022.

2. Kathryn Walsh, "Tips for Skiing at Whistler," *USA Today*, March 15, 2018, accessed May 2, 2022, https://traveltips.usatoday.com/tips-skiing-whistler-2239 .html.

3. Andrew Gomes, "Mickey on Vacation," *Honolulu Star-Advertiser*, August 21, 2011, Newspapers.com.

4. Shannen Michaelsen, "Carousel of Progress 'Future' Finale Scene Updated at Magic Kingdom, Now References 'Food Rocks,' EPCOT, and More," WDW News Today, July 1, 2022, accessed July 29, 2022, https://wdwnt.com/2022/07/breaking -family-gets-new-outfit-in-final-carousel-of-progress-scene-at-magic-kingdom.

5. Oliver Houck, "Noah's Second Voyage: The Rights of Nature as Law," *Tulane Environmental Law Journal*, Vol. 31, No. 1 (Winter 2017), 25–26.

6. Daniel P. Selmi, *Dawn at Mineral King Valley: The Sierra Club, the Disney Company, and the Rise of Environmental Law* (Chicago: University of Chicago Press, 2022), 329.

7. Adam Sowards, "Should Nature Have Standing to Sue?," *High Country News*, January 19, 2015, accessed December 7, 2021, https://www.hcn.org/issues /47.1/should-nature-have-standing-to-sue.

BIBLIOGRAPHY

This list includes books cited, as well as books used for reference but not cited.

Ancinas, Eddy Starr. *Squaw Valley and Alpine Meadows: Tales from Two Valleys, 70th Anniversary Edition.* Mount Pleasant, SC: Arcadia Publishing, 2019.

Antonucci, David C. *Snowball's Chance: The Story of the 1960 Olympic Winter Games, Squaw Valley & Lake Tahoe.* N.p.: Booksurge, 2009.

Barrier, Michael. *The Animated Man: A Life of Walt Disney.* Berkeley: University of California Press, 2007.

Carson, Rachel. *Silent Spring.* Boston: Houghton Mifflin, 1962.

Douglas, William O. *The Court Years 1939–1975: The Autobiography of William O. Douglas.* New York: Random House, 1980.

———. *Of Men and Mountains.* New York: Harper & Bro., 1950.

———. *A Wilderness Bill of Rights.* Boston: Little, Brown & Co., 1965.

Dunlop, Beth. *Building a Dream: The Art of Disney Architecture.* New York: Disney Editions, 2011.

Friedman, Jake S. *The Disney Revolt: The Great Labor War of Animation's Golden Age.* Chicago: Chicago Review Press, 2022.

Fry, John. *The Story of Modern Skiing.* Lebanon, NH: University Press of New England, 2006.

Gabler, Neal. *Walt Disney: The Triumph of the American Imagination.* New York: Alfred A. Knopf, 2006.

Gennawey, Sam. *Disneyland Story: The Unofficial Guide to the Evolution of Walt Disney's Dream.* N.p.: Unofficial Guides, 2013.

Harper, John. *Mineral King; Public Concern with Government Policy*. Arcata, CA: Pacifica Publishing Company, 1982.

Jackson, Kathy Merlock, ed. *Walt Disney: Conversations*. Jackson, MS: University Press of Mississippi, 2006.

Jackson, Louise. *Beulah: A Biography of the Mineral King Valley of California*. Tucson, AZ: Westernlore Press, 1988.

Johnson, Jimmy. *Inside the Whimsy Works: My Life with Walt Disney Productions*. Jackson: University Press of Mississippi, 2014.

Korkis, Jim. *The Vault of Walt Volume 2: MORE Unofficial, Unauthorized, Uncensored Disney Stories Never Told*. N.p.: Theme Park Press, 2013.

Krasniewicz, Louise. *Walt Disney: A Biography*. Santa Barbara, CA: Greenwood Biographies, 2010.

McCloskey, Michael. *In the Thick of It: My Life in the Sierra Club*. Washington, DC: Island Press/Shearwater Books, 2005.

Muir, John. *Our National Parks*. Boston: Houghton Mifflin, 1901.

Nash, Roderick Frazier. *The Rights of Nature: A History of Environmental Ethics*. Madison: University of Wisconsin Press, 1989.

Peri, Don. *Working with Disney: Interviews with Animators, Producers, and Artists*. Jackson: University Press of Mississippi, 2011.

Price, Harrison "Buzz." *Walt's Revolution! By the Numbers*. Orlando: Ripley Entertainment, 2004.

Quinn, Rees. *Disney*. N.p.: CreateSpace, 2016.

Righter, Robert. *The Battle over Hetch Hetchy: America's Most Controversial Dam and the Birth of Modern Environmentalism*. Oxford: Oxford University Press, 2006.

Selmi, Daniel P. *Dawn at Mineral King Valley: The Sierra Club, the Disney Company, and the Rise of Environmental Law*. Chicago: University of Chicago Press, 2022.

Snow, Richard. *Disney's Land: Walt Disney and the Invention of the Amusement Park That Changed the World*. New York: Scribner, 2019.

Thomas, Bob. *Building a Company: Roy O. Disney and the Creation of an Entertainment Empire*. New York: Hyperion, 1998.

———. *Walt Disney: An American Original*. New York: Disney Editions, 1994.

Turner, Tom. *David Brower: The Making of the Environmental Movement*. Oakland: University of California Press, 2015.

———. *Wild by Law: The Sierra Club Legal Defense Fund and the Places It Has Saved*. San Francisco: Sierra Club Legal Defense Fund, 1990.

Udall, Stewart. *The Quiet Crisis*. New York: Holt, Rinehart and Winston, 1963.

Worster, Donald. *A Passion for Nature: The Life of John Muir*. Oxford: Oxford University Press, 2008.

Wyss, Robert. *The Man Who Built the Sierra Club: A Life of David Brower*. New York: Columbia University Press, 2016.

INDEX

Page references for images are italicized.

ABOUT THE AUTHORS

Greg Glasgow is a longtime writer and journalist for numerous magazines and newspapers in Colorado and elsewhere, including *The Denver Post*, *5280*, and the *Boulder Daily Camera*, where he worked for ten years as arts and entertainment reporter and editor. He lives in Colorado with his wife and coauthor, Kathryn Mayer, and their dog, Audrey. This is his first book.

Kathryn Mayer is a Denver-based writer and journalist whose work has appeared in numerous publications including *Health*, *Observer*, *Insider*, and *PopSugar*. She primarily writes about business, covering workplace health and benefits strategies, and she has appeared on radio, TV, and podcasts as an industry expert. This is her first book.